THE MAFIA AT WAR

I told 'em somethin' hadda be done with this guy Hitler. I said that if somebody could knock off this son of a bitch, the war would be over in five minutes.

Charles 'Lucky' Luciano

I'll talk to anybody, a priest, a bank manager, a gangster, the devil himself, if I can get the information I need. This is a war.

Lieutenant Commander Charles Haffenden,
US Naval Intelligence

The Mafia at War

Allied Collusion with the Mob

Tim Newark

Greenhill Books, London

The Mafia at War
Allied Collusion with the Mob

First published in 2007 by Greenhill Books, Lionel Leventhal Limited,
Park House, 1 Russell Gardens, London NW11 9NN
www.greenhillbooks.com

British Library Cataloguing-in Publication Data
Newark, Timothy
The Mafia at war
1. World War, 1939-1945 – Secret service 2. Mafia – History
3. War and crime
I. Title
940.5'486

ISBN: 978-1-85367-672-7

Library of Congress Cataloging-in Publication Data available

For more information on our books, please visit
www.greenhillbooks.com, email sales@greenhillbooks.com
or telephone us within the UK on 020 8458 6314.
You can also write to us at the above London address.

Typeset and edited by Donald Sommerville

Printed in the United States of America

Contents

Illustrations

Dedication

To Vicky Newark
For her enthusiasm and good company
on long train journeys

Acknowledgements

For their help in the research of this book, I would like to thank the following:

Peter Newark, for his extensive crime and photographic library; the staff of the National Archives, Kew, and the British Library; Eric van Slander and Timothy K. Nenninger at the National Archives and Records Administration, College Park, Maryland; Mary M. Huth of the Rush Rhees Library, University of Rochester, NY; Tamar Evangelestia-Dougherty of the Herbert H. Lehman Suite and Papers, Columbia University Rare Book and Manuscript Library, New York, NY; Richard L. Baker of the US Army Military History Institute, Carlisle PA; Maggie E. Bird of the Metropolitan Police Historical Collection; Susi Rogol of the London Police Pensioner Magazine; William Capp and Martin Gerrard, for police memories of Sicily; His Grace the Duke of Wellington; Michael E. Gonzales of the 45th Infantry Division Museum; Edward Dojutrek and Carl Q. Topie of the 3rd Infantry Division Society; Charles T. Pinck of the OSS Society; Malcolm Brown of the Imperial War Museum; Monica Tavazzani, Laura Kurz, John Whitworth, for lending me books; Lisa Donafee, for her translations; in Rome, Rohan MacCullum; in Palermo, Lucy Wildman, for her welcome spaghetti, Serena Gambarini, for her fearless driving, Giada Platania, Salvatore Cabasino, Maia Mancuso, and the staff of the Biblioteca Centrale della Regione Siciliana; Ray Moseley, Robert A. Rockaway, and Christopher Duggan for their advice; Richard Hammer, Andrew Roberts and Charles Messenger for their kind words.

At Greenhill Books, I would like to thank my publisher Michael Leventhal, for his inspiration and friendship, my editor, Kate Baker, and the staff of the Mango Rooms, our branch office in north London.

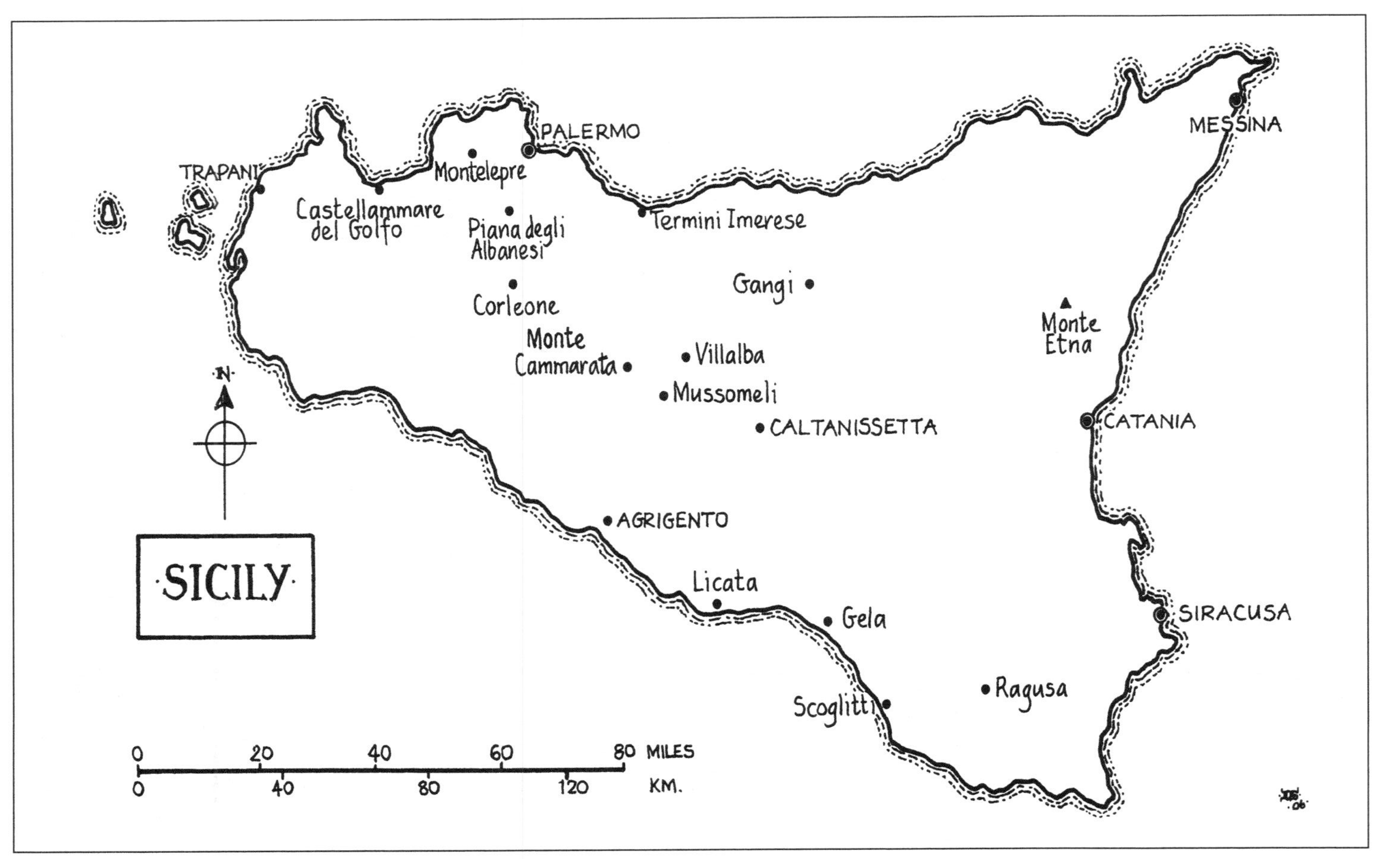

·SICILY·
N
TRAPANI
Castellammare del Golfo
Montelepre
PALERMO
Piana degli Albanesi
Corleone
Termini Imerese
Gangi
Monte Cammarata
Villalba
Mussomeli
CALTANISSETTA
AGRIGENTO
Licata
Gela
Scoglitti
Ragusa
Monte Etna
MESSINA
CATANIA
SIRACUSA
0 20 40 60 80 MILES
0 40 80 120 KM.

Introduction

The ghosts of past conflicts and crimes still haunt the streets of Palermo. Near the harbour, around Piazza Fonderia, you can see the bomb-shattered remains of buildings hit by the Allies in preparation for their invasion of the island in 1943. In the Giardino Garibaldi, with its ancient fig trees with drooping aerial roots, you can see a plaque dedicated to the memory of New York detective Joseph Petrosino, gunned down by a Mafia godfather in 1909. Along the elegant Via Roma, you can step into the foyer of the Grand Hotel Et Des Palmes, little changed in its marble and mirrored luxury since Lucky Luciano stayed there in 1946, making transatlantic deals with the local Mafiosi.

Talking to Sicilians in Palermo you soon get a clear picture of how they view their own history. They remember the delight of their parents on being liberated by the Allies from Fascist rule and German occupation. They recall the pleasure of being given sweets and food by American soldiers – and wearing American clothes sold in local markets for years afterwards. But when you talk to them about the Mafia and the Allies, they have one certain vision of what happened. 'They make the same mistake, they make all the time', says one Palermo resident, whose parents saw the bombs rain down on their city. 'They made a deal with the bad guys and then we got stuck with the Mafia back in control.' But is this true?

There are many anecdotes that support the notion that the US authorities did strike a deal with the Mafia to help in the conquest of Sicily. The most famous story is that Allied troops and tanks rolled into Sicily in 1943 carrying yellow flags emblazoned with the letter 'L', the 'L' representing the infamous mobster Lucky Luciano. From his Great Meadow prison cell in New York State, Luciano had struck a devil's deal with the US government to help secure New York's docks from

Nazi or Fascist sabotage. As an extension of this pact, it is said, not a single shot was fired by Italian troops at the invading Americans in Sicily.

Despite Mussolini's successful crusade against the Mafia, in the early 1940s the Mafia still commanded tremendous influence in Europe and America. As a result, it is claimed, the Allies needed the Mafia. Arguably, the US wartime government could not have controlled the vital New York docks without the assistance of the Mob. The Mafia even believed it could alter the course of the war by assassinating Hitler and his top henchmen.

To uncover the truth of these claims, I have explored archives in London, Washington and New York, analysing first-hand intelligence reports made by Allied agents dealing with the Mafia. Many of these reports have never been published or cited before. I have visited the sites of notorious Mafia crimes and report the testimony of people who were there at the time – including those recorded in the Herlands Report which remained secret for decades after the events described. These accounts bring to life one of the most important hitherto unexplored aspects of the war in Europe.

Some of the players in the game are known. Allied connections with the Mafia undeniably reached the highest level. Recommendations to work alongside mobsters were put before senior US generals and politicians – including supreme commander Dwight D. Eisenhower. Even war leaders Churchill and Roosevelt were keen to exploit Italian-American connections. Notorious gangsters Lucky Luciano, Meyer Lansky, Frank Costello, and Vito Genovese all played their part in the war on Hitler and Mussolini, mixing easily with senior military officials on both sides.

Some remarkable new characters also emerge: the implacable Lord Rennell who took on the Mafiosi in their own realm; the humble Sergeant Orange C. Dickey who defied everyone – including his own superiors – to arrest a top Mafioso. We see how Sicilian mobsters and bandits exploited the chaos of war to carve out an independent fiefdom for themselves in the Mediterranean.

Many of these tales have never been investigated or published before. Here, for the first time, is a complete account that definitively answers one of the greatest mysteries of World War II – did the Allies make a secret pact with the Mafia?

Tim Newark
2007

Chapter One

The Burning Ram

Giuseppe Bonanno was head of one of the five Mafia families in New York. When he looked back on his life, at the age of seventy-eight, he remembered the colours and tastes of his childhood in Sicily. He grew up near the ancient Greek temple at Segesta:

> The color of the temple would change with the progress of the sun, from a soft gold at noon to a bronze at sunset. Orange poppies grew on the hillside. You could hear the bleating of sheep and the lowing of cows. On rainy days, I would roam through the temple grounds foraging for snails, which my grandmother fried in garlic.

Bonanno was brought up in a Mafioso family. To him, it was a fine description, a word meaning spirited, brave, handsome, vibrant and alive.

His father, Salvatore, was a 'Man of Honour', the head of one of two rival clans in Castellammare del Golfo, a seaside town built around a castle on the north-western tip of Sicily. They owned land, some cattle and horses. Salvatore came to head his family when his older brother was shot dead in a stable. Two members of the rival clan later met their deaths.

Bonanno called the creed in which he was raised 'the Tradition'. He said it developed in reaction to centuries of foreign invaders who had come to Sicily – Greeks, Romans, Moors, Normans and Spanish. Prevented from participating in the rule of their own land, Sicilians depended on their own extended families for justice and assistance. Everyone inside the family was a friend, everyone outside it a possible enemy. Because they could not even understand the languages of their colonial rulers, Sicilians developed their own laws and business practices. If a crime was committed against you, then it was up to you and your family to organise punishment. You could depend on no one else.

When revolution came to Sicily in 1860, men of the Tradition joined with Giuseppe Garibaldi and his Red Shirt army to throw out the hated Bourbons. But whereas Garibaldi saw this as a step towards the creation of a unified Italian state, the men of Tradition saw it differently – an opportunity to win more independence for themselves, or so Bonanno claimed:

> The years between the unification of Italy and World War I have been described as the golden age of my Tradition. The new rulers were willing to tolerate or make accommodations with men of my Tradition in exchange for their political support.

The Mafiosi formed a shadow government existing alongside the official bureaucrats.

Salvatore Bonanno's career as a Mafioso and rancher came to an end in World War I. He was drafted into the Italian Army, was wounded in combat with the Austrians in 1915 and sent back home. There, he became seriously ill from an infection in his wound. He died while holding his only son in his arms. Giuseppe Bonanno was just ten years old. His family was now without a protector and that role fell to a close family friend, Stefano Magaddino.

It was Stefano who taught Giuseppe how to hold himself as a man. He instructed him on the rules of the Tradition and how to fight. 'If a man is in a fight, he would tell me, then he must fight to the end.'

In his memoirs, Bonanno described the Tradition as something worthy and vital, a weapon to defend himself and his family against outside oppression. But his family were winners in this struggle in which cattle-owning clans battled with each other. Bonanno even claimed that members of the Mafia elite were taller than other natives of the island because they ate more meat. Many, many more Sicilians suffered from a way of life in which the strongest constantly preyed on the weakest. Bonanno failed to portray the full horror of the situation.

One of the strictest rules of the Tradition was silence or *omerta*. If you suffered at the hands of someone, then you should not go to the state authorities for justice, you should instead go to your local Mafioso or, better, deal with the crime yourself. *Omerta* has been translated as meaning 'manliness' and you are a real man if you sort out your own problems. Anyone who broke *omerta* was called *infame* and faced terrible punishment.

On one occasion, a shepherd was searching for some sheep and a ram that had been stolen from him. He knew very well the rule about not dealing with the police, but when he heard that they had seized some animals from two bandits, he recognised them as his and had to claim them. The police offered to escort him back to his village, but when he got close to his home he felt nervous about being seen in their company and told them to leave him to carry on alone. A short time later, four masked men holding guns emerged from beneath a bridge over a stream and confronted the shepherd. Neither the shepherd nor the armed men said a word to each other. The shepherd knew exactly what this was about. He had broken *omerta*.

Two of the armed men held him, while the other two grabbed the ram from the herd of sheep. They then poured a can of paraffin over the animal and set it alight. The ram screamed and bucked, trying to escape from the pain, but the flaming animal soon keeled over. 'You see what we did to your ram?' said one of the armed men to the shepherd. 'Now we're going to do the same to you.' They poured paraffin over his hair and clothes and flicked a flaming light at him. The shepherd died in agony as the men stood by. Then they took his sheep. That was justice in Sicily according to the Mafiosi.

This murder was recounted by Cesare Mori, a policeman born in Pavia in northern Italy and posted to Sicily in 1904. Mori spent twelve years on the island winning a reputation as a fearless man of the law. During this period, he made a detailed study of the criminals he fought against. Like Bonanno, Mori sought to explain the rise of the Mafia in Sicily. He too saw it originating in a legend of chivalric independence applied to bandit heroes who fought against foreign government. But, he said:

> This process, in the course of time, ended in a special form of oppressive tyranny, tinged with boasting and veiled in deceit; it fixed itself parasitically on the country and gathered to itself all the criminals of the island, constraining them to adopt a point of view calculated, above all, to monopolise and exploit all criminal initiative and activity.

The result was that the Mafia substituted itself for the state power in all relations between criminal forces and the people.

According to Mori, the Mafia in Sicily at the beginning of the twentieth century was not a formally organised association or group:

> There are no marks of recognition. They are unnecessary. The Mafiosi know one another partly by their jargon, but mostly by instinct. There are no statutes. The law of *omerta* and tradition are enough. There is no election of chiefs, for the chiefs arise of their own accord and impose themselves.

The logic of the Mafia was strange but understood in its community:

> Starting from the almost mystical conception that crime exists and must exist since it was created, not only does [the Mafia] deny all effectiveness to the legal provisions for combating it, but considers the struggle against crime . . . an error, a useless waste of energy, and an act against nature . . .

The role of the Mafia was to intervene between the criminal and the victim so as to reduce the damage caused. Their aim was not to punish the criminal but settle the situation. A favourite Mafia phrase was 'Le picciotti hanno a vivere!' Bandits have a right to live too!

With that philosophy in mind, a Mafioso would deal with a crime in the following manner. If cattle were stolen, he would seek out the bandit responsible. He would then offer to return the cattle to the victim if he paid up a third of their value. If the victim agreed, he would get his cattle back, the Mafioso would take a commission, and the bandit would receive a portion of money. As part of his fee, the Mafioso would then assure the victim that his cattle would not be stolen again. It was, of course, a protection racket. Frequently, it would be the Mafioso himself who had organised the cattle theft.

This then was the golden age of the Tradition recalled by Giuseppe Bonanno. His father was accused of being one of these cattle-rustling Mafiosi and Giuseppe would probably have stepped up and joined the family business if the situation in Sicily had not changed radically during and after World War I. With the reduction of export markets in war-torn Europe, Sicily's farming economy collapsed. Even its sun-rich wine, which could have been sold to the army, was deemed to be too high in alcohol for the military. Wheat and meat were requisitioned for the war, which meant there was little left to sell at market. When men were conscripted into the army it meant the end of profitable small-holdings. Wages dropped as food prices kept on rising.

The crisis worsened in 1918, when tens of thousands of soldiers came back from the war. While these young men had been risking their lives in battle, older members of the Mafia had been lining their pockets. With land rent so low, a Mafioso would sub-let a piece of farming land, raise crops and animals to sell at inflated prices, and generate ten times what the landowner was making from rent. The result of this was that many Mafiosi ending up buying land from the old aristocracy, further increasing their influence.

Young war veterans could see little in this for them. They joined gangs of bandits, stole cattle and threatened the lives of settled Sicilians. The older Mafiosi were overwhelmed by the sudden explosion in crime – the *picciotti* had no respect for them. Cesare Mori, who had been absent from Sicily during the war, was now called back in 1919 to help deal with the crime wave.

With his detailed knowledge of Sicilian crime and criminals, Mori would soon take a firm grip on the situation. But he was not there merely to protect the old order – including the Mafiosi – from the ravages of angry young men. Within a few years, he would take on the Mafia itself

World War I changed a lot of things in Italy. It was a turning point not only for the Mafiosi in Sicily, but also for a dynamic young man living in the north of Italy who had fallen foul of the state police. He had a police file that described him as 'a member of the Dovia Socialist faction: height, 1.67 metres [5 feet 5½ inches]; build, robust; hair, light chestnut brown; face, pallid; forehead, high; eyes, dark; nose, aquiline; beard, dark chestnut brown; mouth, large . . .' The outlaw was Benito Mussolini.

His crimes were not ones of material gain, but of political agitation. At the age of eighteen, he had passed his exams with distinction and gained his first job as a school-teacher. He then followed his father into revolutionary politics, making speeches at Socialist meetings, and travelling to Switzerland where he mixed with fellow socialists and anarchists. Looking every inch the bohemian rebel, he was eager to incite revolution, but when he called on the workers of Berne to start a general strike, he was arrested and deported. It was the beginning of his police record.

When World War I came, Mussolini was thirty-one years old. He faced a major dilemma. Italian Socialists wanted nothing to do with the war. Mussolini was a devout Socialist, but he also wanted to do the right thing by his nation. 'Above all there was my own Country', he recalled in his autobiography. 'I saw that Internationalism was crumbling. The unit of loyalty was too large.'

Mussolini began to argue the case for war against Austria and Germany. It was a fateful decision. For this, he was sacked from his job as editor of the Socialist *Avanti* and expelled from the party he loved. A short time afterwards, he created the Fascisti – a group of young men committed to taking direct action on the streets of Italy. Outside the Socialist Party, Mussolini 'felt lighter, fresher. I was free! I was better prepared to fight my battles than when I was bound by the dogmas of any political organisation.'

When Italy finally entered the war in 1915, Mussolini responded to jibes of cowardice by volunteering to join the elite Bersaglieri. He also founded a newspaper, *Popolo d'Italia*, and continued to write articles for it from front-line trenches in the Alps. Like Bonanno's father, Mussolini was wounded in the fighting against the Austrians, although in his case it was an accident:

> One of our own grenades burst in our trench. There were about twenty of us soldiers. We were covered with dirt, smoke, and torn by metal. Four died . . . My wounds were serious. The patience and the ability of the physicians succeeded in taking out of my body forty-four pieces of the grenade.

When Mussolini eventually returned home from the front line, he and his comrades in northern Italy faced social turmoil every bit as bad as that endured by the Sicilians. One day in Milan, Mussolini recalled with disgust:

> I saw a Socialist procession – with an endless number of red flags, with thirty bands, with ensigns cursing the War . . . They had numerous meetings. They clamoured amnesty for the deserters. They demanded the division of the land!

Ex-servicemen were sickened by the attitudes of the Socialists. The last thing they wanted to hear was that their sacrifices had been in vain. They formed armed groups, called *arditi* and *squadristi*, and they fought the Socialists in the cities and the countryside, burning their headquarters, torching their newspaper offices, and beating their supporters. Many of these street fighters joined the black-shirted ranks of Mussolini's Fascists.

The Socialists responded by calling out workers on strikes that paralysed industry and the transport system. Workers who refused to join strikes were assaulted and sometimes killed. In the countryside, Socialists called for the great estates to be broken up and handed over to the peasants. The middle classes and wealthy owners of factories and farms were running scared. They turned to anyone who could help them.

In 1919, Mussolini and the famous conductor Arturo Toscanini stood as Fascist parliamentary candidates in Milan. They pledged to end the disorder and political crisis provoked by the Socialists. But few people believed they could deliver on their promises and they were soundly defeated by the Socialists, who became by far the largest party in the Chamber of Deputies – Italy's parliament – in Rome. The Fascists failed to win any seats at all.

It was an humiliating failure for Mussolini, but he would not give up his campaign. He took up fencing so as to be able to duel with any politicians he insulted in the pages of *Il Popolo d'Italia*, and his followers stored grenades in his newspaper offices ready for street battles. The *arditi* swelled his ranks of supporters, providing the same edge of steel as ex-stormtroopers did for anti-Socialist forces in Weimar Germany. Mussolini boasted:

> They were our troops of assault, of the first rush. They threw themselves into the battle with bombs in hands, with daggers in the teeth, with a supreme contempt for death, singing their magnificent war-hymns. There was in them not only the sense of heroism, but an indomitable will.

Fighting between Socialists and Fascists and other factions grew in ferocity. Gangs of motorcycle-mounted Black Shirts led raids into the countryside, attacking and sometimes killing Socialists. The Socialists would strike back, beating to death any Fascists they caught. The police tended to side with the Fascists in these conflicts, sharing their hatred of Bolsheviks. Even the Italian Army ended up battling striking workers armed with rifles and machine guns in city streets in central Italy. Mussolini revelled in this:

> In some contingencies violence had a deep moral significance. It was necessary to make our way by violence, by sacrifice, by

> blood; it was necessary to establish an order and a discipline wanted by the masses, but impossible to obtain through milk-and-water propaganda and by words, words and more words, and parliamentary and journalistic sham battles.

The parliamentary victory of the Socialists had failed to bring political stability and, as the unrest continued into 1920, more and more people turned to Mussolini's Black Shirts in the hope that they would bring discipline back to their lives. In 1921, the Socialists lost a third of their seats in the Chamber of Deputies while the Fascists won thirty-eight seats. Among the new deputies was Mussolini himself.

The street fighting continued and in Bologna the Fascists turned on the prefect there. A prefect was the regional representative of central government and in Bologna the post had just been given to an implacable policeman with a reputation for taking on tough challenges – Cesare Mori.

The year before, Mori had cut short his battle against crime in Sicily. The reason he now returned to the mainland was because he had proved himself a fierce defender of civil order against both Socialists and Nationalists. As Questore (chief of police) of Rome, he had broken a protest by killing some students and faced prosecution as a result. He was the sort of man of action the Fascists liked, but his strength was a double-edged sword. Politically, Mori had no time for the Socialists, but his job was to uphold the law and that meant treating Socialists and Fascists equally. He insisted that local employment should not be conditional on which party you belonged to. The Fascists hated this and Mori became their enemy.

In May 1922, some 20,000 Fascists invaded Bologna. It was a massive show of strength and they surrounded the city hall. They demanded that Mori resign, but he refused and barricaded his offices against them. The Fascists refrained from storming the building, but instead showed their disdain for him by urinating against the walls of the city hall. As a result of this clash of wills, Mori was removed from his post in Bologna and appointed prefect of Bari in the south of Italy where the Fascists were not so dominant.

The Socialists responded to the increased violence by calling general strikes throughout major cities in northern Italy. The Fascists brutally broke the strikes. With the support of tens of thousands of armed Black Shirts, Mussolini now felt confident enough for an even greater display than the occupation of Bologna or Milan or Ferrara. He would aim for the centre of government in Italy – Rome.

Before that, through the pages of his newspaper, he reassured the army and the king of his loyalty to the crown. In October 1922, the Fascists took control of towns and government buildings throughout northern Italy. The army readied itself for confrontation but generally took a friendly approach towards the Fascists.

Some 26,000 Fascists were ready to march into Rome. On 28 October, King Victor Emmanuel was asked to declare a state of siege but he refused, fearing disorder. His decision paved the way for Mussolini's final rise to power. The king invited the Fascist leader to become prime minister and form a government.

In Sicily, the Mafiosi read the newspapers with interest but had little real enthusiasm for their new Fascist prime minister and his government. They had their own problems with Socialist agitators, but not to the extent of the general strikes and mass violence in the north. In Sicily, resistance to the Socialists took a different form. Factory owners and grand farmers would have a quiet word with their local Mafiosi. A little later, the troublesome strike leaders would be found murdered.

Sometimes an ambitious local Mafioso might ally himself with a Socialist land grab. It would gain him great popularity with the local peasantry. A compromise would then be reached with the terrified owners and part of the land handed back. It was just another version of the Mafia protection racket, this time operated under a red flag.

Giuseppe Bonanno was seventeen years old when Mussolini took power, but he was not impressed by him:

> Mussolini was a cowardly man pretending to be a tough guy and I think I have a measure of expertise on the subject . . . A true tough guy, whether you agree with him or not, knows he is superior to most men. The phony tough guy lacks this sense of security . . . Mussolini was a bully – a phony tough guy.

Cesare Mori did not welcome the news either. He was fifty years old and probably considered his public career at an end. With the Fascists in power, he could not see himself gaining any advancement under them. So, in November 1922, he resigned his office in Bari and went into early retirement in Florence.

Mori spent the next eighteen months writing his first book about the Mafia in Sicily, *Tra le zagare oltre la foschi* – 'Through the orange blossoms and beyond the mist' – a typically flowery title from a man who liked to write poetry. He even considered calling his later account of the battle against the Mafia, published in 1933, 'Lictorial dawn over the flowering orange blossoms'.

When Mussolini took power in 1922, he wanted to reassure the country that he was no tyrant. In his first administration, there were fifteen Fascist ministers and under-secretaries of state serving alongside fifteen ministers from other parties. But he would not compromise on his pledge to bring an end to the instability and violence that had haunted Italy since the end of World War I.

In a speech to the Chamber of Deputies on 16 November 1922, he said: 'I could have made of this dull and grey hall a bivouac of corpses. I could have nailed up the doors of Parliament and have established an exclusively Fascist government. I could have done these things . . .' But for the time being he would not. Instead, he addressed those problems that needed immediate resolution. 'We intend to give the Nation discipline', he declared. 'We will give it. Let none of our enemies of yesterday, of today, of tomorrow, have illusions in regard to our permanence in power.'

Mussolini wished to bring a new vigour to the solving of national problems. The army and the various police forces, including the paramilitary Carabinieri, fully supported him. His Black Shirt street fighters, the veterans of World War I, were transformed into a voluntary militia for national security and defence. They were now a reserve strength that could be called out whenever Mussolini needed to enforce his political manifesto.

'With Fascism at the wheel', he proclaimed, 'everything illegal and disorderly had to disappear.' At first, this meant the Socialists and Communists his Black Shirts had battled against. But this would come to embrace other enemies of the nation, and that included the Mafia, as he said in a later speech to the Chamber of Deputies:

> Gentlemen, it is time that I showed the Mafia up to you. But first of all I want to divest this association of brigands of any kind of fascination or poetry, to which it has not the least claim. Let nobody speak of the nobility or chivalry of the Mafia, unless he really wishes to insult the whole of Sicily.

Here, Mussolini was attacking the very root appeal of the Mafia. Like Giuseppe Bonanno, he knew it justified itself as an opposition to outside oppression but, like Cesare Mori, he knew it had degenerated into a ruthless criminal organisation.

Fascism was a phenomenon of northern Italy where the fight against the Socialists had been at its most heated. Mussolini had very little knowledge or interest in the problems of the south. But, as Prime Minister of the whole country, he had a duty to raise support for his cause everywhere.

In May 1924, Mussolini went to Sicily on an official visit. He was shown around the island by the local Fascist leader, Alfredo Cucco. In a speech at Agrigento on 11 May, Mussolini stood on the balcony of the municipal palace and addressed a local audience:

> I understand that you all need certain things. You've spoken to me about the streets, about water and about reclaimed land, but you've also said that you need me to guarantee the safety and property of the people who work in this city.
>
> So, I tell you now that I will take every measure necessary in order to protect people from crime. It is intolerable that a few hundred criminals should be allowed to undermine, impoverish and demean people as magnificent as you are.

The speech was received with rapturous applause.

That Mussolini's battle with the Mafia would go beyond mere rhetoric was demonstrated by a widely reported story of an incident during his tour of Sicily. An hour's drive from Palermo is the town of Piana degli Albanesi. It was known then for its colourful immigrant community of Albanians. Cucco had little time for these people, considering them anti-fascist, but Mussolini was keen to visit the town. A strong police escort was arranged for Il Duce but his security was also discussed with the local mayor, a Mafioso called Don Ciccio Cuccia, who was allowed to drive in the same car as Mussolini.

After the visit, Mussolini wished to return to Palermo. Obviously feeling inflated by his association with Il Duce, Don Ciccio pointed at the accompanying police escort and told the dictator he had no need of such protection. Instead, he indicated his own henchmen. 'Your excellency has nothing to fear when you are by my side', said Don Ciccio in a loud voice, so everyone could hear his proclamation. 'Let no man dare touch a hair of Mussolini's head. He is my friend and the best man in the world.' Mussolini was outraged and humiliated. His Fascists were supposed to be the power in the island, not Don Ciccio. It reinforced his determination to crush the Mafia.

A month before Mussolini's visit to their island, Sicilians had expressed their approval of the new regime by giving the Fascist candidates sixty-eight per cent of the vote. Most of the votes, it is claimed, were raised by traditional conservative landowners, probably including some Mafiosi, who could see some virtue in allying themselves with the new strong man in town. This flirtation with Fascism quickly evaporated in June with the scandal caused by the murder of the left-wing political leader Giacomo Matteotti. Five Black Shirts had bundled him into a car outside his block of flats and then beaten him to death, quickly burying his body in wasteland outside Rome.

Suddenly the dark side of Mussolini's regime was exposed. This, combined with the fact that Sicilians still felt ignored by central government, with a rural crime wave running out of control in western Sicily – the territory of the Mafia – meant that many Sicilians questioned the efficiency of the Fascists.

In the run-up to local elections in August 1925, former Prime Minister Vittorio Emmanuele Orlando gave an electrifying speech in Palermo – a rallying cry to all those who still believed in the value of the Tradition. He was the Sicilian-born leader who had seen Italy through the Great War and sat with the Big Four during the Paris Peace Conference. His words counted for much:

> People of Palermo, if by 'Mafia' we mean an exaggerated sense of honour, a passionate refusal to succumb to the overbearing and arrogant, a nobility of spirit that stands up to the strong and indulges the weak, a loyalty to friends that is more steadfast and enduring even than death – if these characteristics, albeit with their excesses, are what we mean by 'Mafia', we are dealing with ineradicable traits of the Sicilian character, and I declare myself to be Mafioso, and I am happy to be such.

Alfredo Cucco was worried by this speech and so was Mussolini when they spoke on the phone. Their reaction was to put Black Shirts in trucks riding round the streets of Palermo on polling day singing patriotic songs. Later that day, Fascists clashed with local police armed with new steel truncheons for the purpose. The Fascists won the local elections but the opposition polled a good many votes too. The Mafia were rumoured to have delivered many of these anti-government votes.

Mussolini's big claim, to bring an end to indiscipline in Italian life, was clearly running into trouble in Sicily. Cucco was summoned to Rome and he reminded Mussolini of his vow to end lawlessness in Sicily. Mussolini followed this meeting with a conversation with the Minister of the Interior, Luigi Federzoni. Cucco and Federzoni met for a meal at the restaurant Ulpia, overlooking the ancient Roman remains of Trajan's market. There, they discussed launching a campaign against the Mafia in Sicily. It was a risky project. It might be popular with the ordinary people – outside the Mafia circle – but it might further alienate the Sicilian establishment who had already demonstrated their opposition in the local elections.

For Mussolini, however, the situation was intolerable. The Mafia had to be brought to heel. It was, he said later, the beginning of a broader crusade against organised crime: 'an inexorable fight against the Mafia in Sicily, the bandits in Sardinia, and against some other less known forms of crime, which had humiliated entire regions.'

Over their meal, Cucco and Federzoni discussed who might lead the war on the Mafiosi. Cucco suggested a former prefect of Palermo, but he was unavailable. Then the name of Cesare Mori came up. Federzoni was not too keen.

The year before, Mori had been called away from his writing desk in Florence to deal with a crime wave in the province of Trapani, in western Sicily. Unsurprisingly, he came into conflict with the local Fascists. They, in turn, protested to Federzoni, who seemed ready to pension him off for good. But Cucco insisted that someone with a strong police background would be the right man for the job. Thus, reluctantly perhaps, it was decided to transfer Mori from Trapani to Palermo.

Mussolini would take on the Mafia and Cesare Mori would be his commander in the field. Under their breath, Cucco and Federzoni no doubt mumbled, God help the Fascists if we get this wrong. Mori, naturally, was more confident. 'The struggle with the Mafia', he later recalled, 'was fought to a finish for the first time under the Fascist regime . . .'

It had to be. As Giuseppe Bonanno's 'Uncle' Stefano had told him, 'If a man is in a fight, then he must fight to the end.'

Chapter Two

Humiliation in Gangi

'The hour of liberation had come', declared Cesare Mori. 'In the name and by the will of the Duce action was at last going to be taken. Thus it was that, called to the honour of taking part in it, I returned to Sicily for the third time.'

Mori was itching to take on the Mafia. He had spent the best part of two decades studying their ways and now he was ready to deliver to Mussolini their heads on a plate. He knew it would not be easy:

> The country, forced into silence, remained shut into itself. The authorities said that it was impossible to act against crime because not only did the people refuse to help them, but the very sufferers favoured the evildoers instead of co-operating with justice.

They did this because they feared the retribution and punishment of the Mafiosi more than the state.

But Il Duce presented Mori with a useful weapon – a new sense of determination unhindered by the niceties of constitutional government.'Under the Fascist conception of the State', said Mori, 'the government was specifically concerned in rendering the existence of the Mafia – an-anti-state – impossible.' It helped, he argued, that the Fascists abolished the electoral system from which the Mafia gained much of their local influence. The bitterly fought Palermo election of 1925 was the last one in the island until a national plebiscite in 1929. No more would ex-prime ministers declare themselves to be Mafiosi.

Several attempts on Mussolini's life in 1925 and 1926 sharpened his intolerance towards opposition forces. In April 1926, an English woman pulled a pistol near his car and fired a close-range shot that grazed his nose. A centimetre difference and the shot might have been fatal. A few months later, a young anarchist fired a shot at him as he sat in his car at an official function. 'The shot burned my coat', Mussolini remembered, 'but again I was quite safe. The crowd in the meanwhile, seized by an impulse of exasperated fury, could not be restrained. It gave summary justice to the man.'

Mussolini's response was immediate. He instructed the Ministry of Internal Affairs to introduce a series of laws for the defence of the regime. Among these was the abolition of the independent press.

Step by step, the attributes of democracy, which had been perverted by the Mafia to their own profit, were being removed by the Fascist state. Mori was not disappointed by this turn of events. It was for him a simple question of will in which reluctance to undertake responsibility, sentimentality and legal formalism needed to be overcome. If the Mafiosi had abused the legal system in Sicily by manipulating and intimidating it to their own ends, then Mori would not be held back by the strict word of the law in his own battle against them:

> For my own part, though in these matters I respect the sanctity of law, I am, and have always been, for granting free initiative, naturally within the limits of the law, but regarding the law as a guiding principle, not an obstacle to action.

Mori would deploy the law to the greater purpose. The ends would definitely justify the means and neither clever lawyers nor corrupt judges would get in his way.

You could not challenge Mori's integrity or his adherence to the principle of fairness before the law. He was incorruptible. He had proved that against the Fascists in Bologna and to the cost of his own career. But clearly he admired Mussolini's dynamism and that included putting aside aspects of democracy and legality in order to win a battle against evildoers.

By doing this, Mori felt he had a good chance of winning a war against the Mafia.

Mori's campaign strategy involved two main points of attack. One was to launch a major assault against the strongest and most significant of the positions held by the Mafia. This would be a highly visible demonstration of state power. The second was to win the hearts and minds of the ordinary people of Sicily – a classic doctrine of anti-insurgency warfare. He wished to:

> . . . involve the Sicilian people in the action, by executing it in their name . . . to give the timid, the disappointed and the discouraged confidence in themselves . . . and to give the Mafia, not only a severe blow from without, but a feeling that its environment was against it.

It helped that Mori was an impressive man in his own right. He had a strong, solid frame, had a healthy, ruddy complexion, could stand before an audience and give a rousing speech, was intelligent and observant, and could ride well. He was a natural leader of men and was physically and mentally fearless.

Mori was born in Pavia in northern Italy in 1872. The first seven years of his life were spent in an orphanage before his natural parents finally acknowledged him as their own. He was maybe in pursuit of some emotional security when he sacrificed a military career in order to marry his wife, Angelina Salvi. Her father could not afford to pay the dowry expected of a military officer, but Mori went ahead with the marriage anyway, preferring to give up the army. He remained devoted to her for the rest of his life.

At the age of twenty-three, Mori won a medal for valour by disarming a gunman who had just wounded a soldier in a fight in a brothel. This incident pointed him towards a career in law enforcement and he came first out of 107 in a national public security competition. His first major posting as a policeman was in Ravenna, but an embarrassing incident in which he frisked a knife-carrying politician led to his placement in Sicily.

It was in Sicily that Mori won his spurs. In his early years there, his most celebrated encounter was with the cop-killing bandit Paolo Grisafi. The outlaw had such a notorious reputation for being untouchable that locals believed he was *maato* or bewitched. With a small group of policemen, Mori hunted down the bandit and his gang.

When Mori rode out with his men, he dressed elegantly, befitting a man of his status. He wore a necktie around a stiff collar, a smart jacket with a white handkerchief, neatly pressed, protruding from the breast pocket. He wore trousers tucked into riding boots, a wide-brimmed hat, and carried his favourite Winchester repeating rifle.

Mori and his team eventually cornered the outlaws in a little white-washed house in Sciacca. At 2.30 one morning, a fierce fire-fight broke out in which the police riddled the cottage with bullets. The bandits placed mattresses on a balcony so they could fire more accurately at the surrounding police. The shooting continued until dawn when it started to attract an audience of local people. After more volleys poured into the cottage, Mori could hear the bandits shout out their surrender. At first, Mori would not accept it, then the cries became desperate. When the police eventually entered the cottage, they found a small armoury loaded with Mauser rifles, revolvers and a large store of ammunition. So why did Grisafi give himself up?

> He looked at me and made no answer [said Mori]. And at that moment, in the eyes of the man who had shed so much blood and caused so much terror for the last twelve years, I saw the frightened look of a bull that is being led to slaughter.

With such high-profile arrests behind him, Mori brought with him to Palermo in 1925 a useful reputation. It amused him that Sicilians called him 'a man whose heart is covered with hair'. Others called him simply 'the beast'.

Mori set about the first part of his campaign – a major assault against a high-profile target – by raising an inter-provincial police service. These policemen were drawn from all parts of the island. They were to be independent of provincial concerns and to be highly mobile, able to swoop on criminals without the need of bringing in local police. Their first task was to gather accurate information on major gangs. Their second task was to bring overpowering firepower to secure their surrender. In order to move easily among the Sicilian population, Mori instructed his men to behave well and respect local customs. To slow the passage of criminals around the island, Mori insisted that photographs appeared on all passports and identity documents.

For his curtain-raising battle, Mori settled on the Mafia based in the Madonie, a range of mountains situated between Palermo and Messina along the northern edge of the island. For three decades, the Mafia and bandits associated with them had dominated the region, creating a state within the state. They dominated the local government, farming, and virtually every aspect of daily life. Armed gangs rode around the countryside extorting heavy *taglie* or taxes from the land-owners. All criminals in Sicily regarded the Mafia of the Madonie as the most successful and powerful. If Mori could break them, it would open up the rest of the island.

Mori's intelligence gathering told him there were about 130 Mafia 'soldiers' in the area and that they belonged to three gangs led by Nicolo Andaloro, the Ferrarello brothers, Giuseppe and Nicolo, and the Dino brothers, Giovanni and Carmelo. These men were wealthy, owning their own houses and farms. The centre of their operations was the hillside village of Gangi with its buildings hewn out of the rock. Each of the leading gangsters had a house there with special hiding places and secret exits burrowed into the side of the hill. No detailed plans were available for the layout of the village and Mori anticipated it would be a hard nut to crack.

Mori chose the winter of 1925–6 as the best time to approach Gangi. His men rode into the area of the Madonie, their intention being not to make contact with the gangsters but merely to alert them to their presence. That way, they confined them to the region. Mori's small army included Carabinieri and militia volunteers from Palermo alongside his inter-provincial police servicemen.

After a few days, Mori drew the net a little tighter, encircling the area around Gangi. At first, the bandits made no response to this, considering it yet another show of force intended to reassure civilians, but make no real effort to catch them. They sat comfortably in their houses, enjoying the food they had pillaged from their neighbours. Then Mori sent his police force into the farms and estates of the friends of the Mafia, taking over the buildings and setting up his own men to guard the roads and paths out of Gangi.

By now, the gangsters knew it was something more than just a routine action, but it was too late for them to escape. They retired to their hiding places within the village, beneath the floors and in the walls of their houses. It was what Mori expected. 'While waiting on events', he recalled, 'they all disappeared into the bowels of the village, as though sucked up by a colossal sponge.' There was one policeman who had the thankless task of patrolling the village and he informed Mori that the gang leaders had gone to ground.

In early January, Mori pounced and sent his men into Gangi so they completely surrounded the village buildings. The scene was set for a major shoot-out, but Mori did not want to create martyrs out of the Mafia leaders. He wanted to humiliate them. He sent a telegram to the mayor of Gangi saying: 'I summon the *latitanti* [renegades] who are in your territory to give themselves up within twelve hours, on the lapse of which I shall proceed to extreme measures.' A town crier walked among the deserted streets of the village, pounding his drum, and proclaiming the ultimatum.

Mori then sent his men into the houses of the bandits, tramping around above their hiding-places but not hauling them out. Mori had one final insult for them. He took their cattle and slaughtered them in the streets, selling the pieces of meat to the oppressed villagers at bargain prices. It was not looking good for the gangsters. Men who had proudly walked the streets of the village were holed up like rats. Where were their guns now? Mori relished their discomfort:

> People began to laugh at these terrible bandits who, though laden with arms and ammunition and distinguished by a past of bloodshed and conflicts with the police, stayed like rabbits in their burrows without the courage even to put their noses out to resist the havoc that was being played with their property.

It has been claimed that it was not only their cattle that Mori's men took. They also took their women and children as hostages. Mori makes no mention of this at Gangi, but he does admit, during other sieges, to loading families of gangsters – men, women and children – on to lorries and taking them away until the Mafiosi gave up.

Knowing that they had blown their opportunity for an heroic armed resistance, the subterranean bandits felt they had little choice but to give themselves up – and one by one, they emerged out of their trap-doors. One pretended to be ill and escaped through a secret passage into the countryside, but the now emboldened villagers volunteered to hunt him down and he gave himself up. The humiliation hung heavily on the bandits and one of their leaders, Giuseppe Ferrarello, hanged himself as soon as he got to prison.

Mori's tremendous victory over the Mafia of the Madonie had its effect. Other bandits from around the island gave themselves up to the prefect. Mussolini was delighted and sent a congratulatory telegram to Mori on 6 January 1926:

> Fascism, which has healed Italy of so many wounds will, if necessary, cauterise with fire and hot iron the wound of crime in Sicily. Five million hard-working and patriotic Sicilians must no longer be oppressed, held to ransom, robbed or dishonoured by a few hundred criminals.

With this seal of approval from Mussolini, the local Fascists now rallied to Mori's triumph and paraded before him at the Teatro Massimo in Palermo. In his speech Mori told them:

> The offensive which has now been fully launched will be pushed inexorably to the finish without regard for anybody. To those who stand on the other side I say these few but solemn words. It is useless to be under the illusion that this is merely a puff of wind. It will be a regular cyclone which will carry away everything, root and branch . . .
>
> There is, therefore, nothing left for you, unhappy men on the other side, but the inexorable dilemma which I put to you now for the last time either to redeem yourselves loyally through honest labour or to die.

One of these unhappy men on the other side was Giuseppe Bonanno, future head of a New York Mafia family. He now felt himself caught up in the Fascist cyclone.

With his father and mother dead and 'Uncle' Stefano busy protecting his clan, Giuseppe Bonanno had to decide his own future. Living on the coast at Castellammare del Golfo, he looked to the sea for his career. He decided to become a sea captain and enrolled in a nautical school at Trapani. For his second year of studies, he transferred to Palermo. He loved the freedom of living in a big city and enjoyed chasing women, parading around town in the brilliant white uniform of a naval cadet. In 1924, he was nineteen and entering his third year of naval studies when he collided with the Fascists.

Images of Mussolini were everywhere in Palermo and Bonanno witnessed how a totalitarian regime penetrated every aspect of daily life. At his college, students were expected to sing a Fascist song each morning. They were told they should demonstrate their patriotism by joining the Fascist party and wearing black shirts rather than their usual white. Bonanno hated this.

Bonanno rallied other students around him and they protested. The college authorities were furious when they turned up still wearing white shirts. They threatened to expel any students who refused to wear a black shirt. Only seven students refused – including Bonanno and his cousin Peter Magaddino, nephew of Uncle Stefano. He could not blame the others for choosing their careers first. Bonanno and his cousin were suspended for three months and returned to Castellammare. There, they realised that if their naval career was denied to them they had little choice but to embrace the Mafia lifestyle of their family, but the Fascists were closing that down too. Bonanno recalled:

> The special prefect for Sicily was Cesar [*sic*] Mori. He claimed that the island's 'mafioso' tradition was keeping its people mired in a feudal society. Mori spoke like a contemporary sociologist; but when it came to hunting down men, he did his job as well as any medieval grand inquisitor.

In the local newspapers, Bonanno read of hundreds of Mafiosi rounded up and imprisoned. 'They were tried and sentenced with utter disregard for their civil liberties', he observed, without any trace of irony. Bonanno could see no future for himself in Sicily and his cousin agreed. They decided to start a new life in America and would travel there via Tunisia and France. Neither of them had a visa to enter the USA and so they ended up sailing from La Havre to Havana, Cuba. From there a little fishing boat took them to Tampa, Florida.

Intent on making it all the way to New York, they caught a train to Jacksonville. By then, their luck had run out and they were picked up by immigration officers and slammed in a detention centre. Bonanno had one telephone call and he phoned the brother of his mother who lived in Brooklyn. He phoned another cousin, Stefano Magaddino in Buffalo, nephew of Uncle Stefano, also from Castellammare. Three days later, $1,000 was paid for each of the young illegal aliens to get them out of the detention centre.

Waiting for them outside were two men. One of them was Willie Moretti, an associate of Joe the Boss – the most powerful figure in the New York underworld in the mid-1920s. Moretti would later join Lucky Luciano's family. Bonanno had landed on his feet. To celebrate their first day of freedom in America, Moretti fixed up the newcomers with a couple of broads in a hotel. It was just as Uncle Stefano told him – it was important for a man to have friends.

Giuseppe Bonanno had become Joe Bonanno.

Mori followed up his victory at Gangi with more round-ups – *retate* – of bandits and Mafiosi. With such a visible challenge to the Sicilian Tradition, the practice of *omerta* was loosened and peasants came to Mori and his men with tales of 'deaths unavenged, sorrows without a name, obscure tragedies, formidable losses, impositions, vexations, injustices and terrible obsessions'. All were logged and saved for the trials.

Over 150 people were arrested in the Madonie region for crimes including murder, blackmail, robbery and cattle-stealing. It was not only the little criminals that were swept up, but the Mafia bosses too. The head of the Mafia in the district of Mistretta was taken away, along with ninety letters implicating his whole crime network. The letters revealed how the Mafia had set themselves up as a tribunal, passing sentences on trouble-making criminals who refused to pay them a tribute.

In this process of multiple arrests, Mori was happy to pick up merely suspicious characters, whom he knew full well might not be convicted for want of evidence, since this served his purpose of stamping out all criminal activity in an area, even if it was only temporary. Sometimes this would be a major operation – involving the arrest of over 300 people in five villages or more. It would come at the time of harvest when peasants were especially vulnerable to Mafia stealing wagon-loads of grain and rustling hundreds of animals.

Some have alleged that torture was used to extract confessions from suspects. Knowing the violent nature of the Fascists, this is not surprising, though there is little direct evidence. Mori is said to have re-introduced the *cassetta*, a wooden box to which a prisoner was secured while he was flogged:

> His dangling hands and feet were fastened with wires to the side of the case [claimed Socialist journalist Michele Pantaleone]. The wretched man was then drenched with brine and whipped with an ox-thong. In this way the lashes were the more painful but left no mark. Then his hair and his nails were torn out and the soles of his feet burnt. He was given electric shocks, his genitals were forcibly squeezed, and every now and then a funnel was stuck into his mouth, his nostrils were pinched, and he was made to swallow salt water till his stomach swelled.

But Mori did not even need confessions. He formulated an offence of association for criminal purposes to get round the difficulty of linking particular crimes with specific evidence. It was enough to have a bad reputation to get you arrested. His purpose was to revive the power and prestige of the state and he did not care how many people he swept up in his net. Many of the convicted felons were banished to penal islands off the Sicilian coast.

Mori's reward was to win the respect of the people of the countryside who called him *prefetto contadino* – the Peasant Prefect. To tighten this relationship, Mori instituted the awarding of medals for valour to civilians who had taken direct action against criminals. Many Sicilians paid with their lives for giving information to Mori and the police.

On one occasion, Mori visited the small town of Misilmeri, not far from Palermo. There, a young man called Mariano Da Caro had recently stood up to the local Mafia but been killed for being so bold. A few students dared to tell the tale of his death, but the rest of the townspeople kept quiet, not wanting to bring the wrath of the Mafia on themselves.

Mori wanted to commemorate the death of Mariano Da Caro with a memorial stone and to celebrate its unveiling he arranged a concert in the middle of the town square. At first, the townspeople were reluctant to approach the stage, but, as the sun set, when the pianist started to play so the crowd relaxed. When he finished, the once silent crowd gave him a rousing round of applause.

Some townspeople feared that the memorial stone would be immediately mutilated by local criminals, but when they looked closely at the inscription it said – *a memoria – ad onore – a monito.*

'What does *monito* ('a warning') mean?' said one.

'It means "*Ca cu tocca ca ci sata a testa*"', said another. 'Anyone who touches it will get his head cut off.'

Mori was delighted to hear this – it meant they feared him more than the Mafia.

On the economic front, Mori struck two further blows at the Mafia. He instituted a new system of branding and marking in which owners received official documents recognising their ownership of their animals. This greatly reduced the incidents of cattle-rustling but annoyed insurance companies who had made a good deal of money out of insuring against frequent theft.

Mori also attacked the widespread racket in which the Mafia rented land from the great property owners at a pittance of its true value. It was, in effect, forced land redistribution, in which the Mafiosi sublet the land to peasants at a huge profit to themselves. Mori brought in the police and Commission of Agriculture to ensure that the rental value for a piece of land reflected its true yield. A grateful landowner told

Mori that an estate worth only 4,000 lire a year over the previous three decades was now bringing in 60,000 lire. This enriched everyone in the rural community but denied the Mafia a significant source of income. The Bank of Sicily noticed the difference – its agricultural loans went up from 61 million lire in 1924 to 154 million in 1928.

To cut away further at the power of the Mafia, Mori raised a 1,300-strong irregular unit of armed, mounted volunteer agents who could ride to the assistance of the police. He recruited them from the armed field guards of landowners – known as *campieri*. Their typical outfit was jacket and breeches, a cap (*coppola*) and riding boots. On a field near Roccapalumba, he gathered them together for a swearing-in ceremony. With a roar, all the volunteers swore to serve the King and the state – and not the Mafia.

When they distinguished themselves in defence of their farming comrades, Mori would reward a *campiere* with a small brass buttonhole badge in the shape of an ear of corn between two crossed muskets. At an award ceremony, Mori asked a recipient if he minded wearing the badge. 'You would have to wear it all the time and what if someone called you *sbirro* [a derogatory word for a policeman]?' he said.

The man shrugged. 'Then I would have to shoot him', said the *campiere*.

'Bravo!' said Mori.

It seemed he was winning their hearts and minds.

To check if Mori's triumph was true it is useful to hear the voice of an independent eye-witness. Charlotte Gower was an American anthropology student who came to Sicily in 1928 to research a study of a typical peasant community. Her trip coincided with the final phase of Mori's crusade.

The journey to Milocca, a village in western Sicily, was a difficult one. No railroad or highway led to it directly and you had to pick your way by foot or mule along rough paths. It had no electricity. For this reason, it had avoided much of the modern world and that suited Charlotte Gower just fine. She had spent the previous year at the Illinois Institute for Juvenile Research in Chicago, learning the Sicilian dialect spoken in the region. She knew the place would give her the most authentic view of the old Sicilian ways.

It was a hot topic, for in the first decade of the century thousands of Sicilians had left their island for a better life in America – half of all

Chicago's Italian immigrants were Sicilian – and it was important that the US government understood the culture they were coming from. As Gower observed:

> The lure of America is strong, especially to the younger peasants [of Milocca] who dream of riches gained by labor lighter than that which they know, riches with which they could return, buy land, and settle down as respected proprietors.

No other part of the world held the same promise for these Sicilians and their narrow view of life outside their village was reflected in the name they gave to all non-Catholics, regardless of their nationality or faith – Turks.

Arriving in Palermo, Gower first received a letter of introduction from Prefect Cesare Mori. He did not have much good to say about the little community, but the letter ensured that the mayor of Milocca set up the student with lodgings in the home of the village midwife. She stayed for eighteen months.

The surrounding countryside was harsh. 'In the late summer', she wrote, 'the broken landscape is burned to a yellowish white, with here and there giant outcrops of gypsum . . . It is no garden land but stark and, as seen from the train, apparently uninhabited.'

A large sulphur mine was located near Milocca, but none of the locals worked there. Instead, they scraped a living from the tough land, growing wheat, broad beans, olives, grapes and almonds. They ate pasta with basic tomato sauce, sometimes enlivened by a slaughtered goat.

Immediately after World War I, Milocca had suffered from Socialist unrest like elsewhere in Italy. In 1920, several hundred peasants took over the estates of absentee landlords. Local communities fought with these men to regain the estates and the conflict was only settled when the Milocchese were allowed to rent some of the land they had taken. The Socialist rebels were led by Don Toto Angilella, a wealthy merchant at odds with the local aristocracy.

A lawyer associate of Angilella went even further and declared Milocca an independent Socialist state with the red flag flying over the town hall. The little republic lasted only twelve hours, by which time the Carabinieri arrived and banished the lawyer. Come the Fascists, Don Angilella ingratiated himself with the Black Shirts and was eventually rewarded with the post of local commissar in 1927. He used the position to ensure that a leading member of a rival faction in the village was imprisoned on suspicion of being a Mafioso.

Bowing to Prefect Mori was not enough. Because of its isolated position, Milocca was a favourite refuge for bandits and Gower was clear that the Mafia presence was strong in the village. Among the ordinary people, she observed a powerful sense of menace:

> Those were days when a woman saw her husband go off to the fields and did not know whether he would return alive, or whether he would be killed with his own mattock by the men who stole his mules . . .
>
> Men who had to ride long distances went in groups, or took a police guard, and even that was not secure, for one traveller was murdered despite the presence of an armed guard. Law-abiding citizens did not dare incur the disfavor of the mafiosi, and almost anyone who had extensive property in the country was obliged to protect himself by extending favors to them.

At the beginning of his war, Mori had concentrated on the major Mafia strongholds in Sicily but by early 1928 he was sweeping lesser crime zones. He had already expressed his dislike for the village when Gower approached him for a letter of introduction. Now he was to act on the information he received. It came from the mother of a bandit killed in a dispute between gangsters. In her grief, she pointed the finger at Milocca. Gower witnessed the crackdown:

> The police descended in force, by night and proceeded to make their arrests. Some of their victims escaped, in spite of the suddenness of the attack, but the members of their families were taken and held in their stead. If this did not produce the desired persons, all their livestock was confiscated . . .
>
> No one felt safe. A bride who set out to make her nuptial calls was ordered back to her home, for this was no time to be abroad. Pity was mixed with fear, pity for the unhappy animals, the bereft families, the arrested men, and even for the police, who had come without adequate provisions and had to beg bread from the terrified townspeople.

About 100 Milocchese were imprisoned. Gower, because of her letter from Mori, was believed to have some influence with the prefect and was treated well in the hope she might be able to help the release of the prisoners. The entire village went into mourning. Feast days were not celebrated with their usual enthusiasm. Many of the wives of the imprisoned Mafiosi suffered real hardship and were given free food by the community. But, Gower, had to admit, crime itself had come almost to a full stop. Paradoxically, although the local people mourned the loss of so many of their menfolk, the action of the government in making arrests and destroying crime was always praised.

It must be considered, however, that Gower had the whiff of Mori about her and no one would be foolish enough to denounce the prefect in front of her. A truer view perhaps was expressed in 1929 when the Fascists held a plebiscite throughout Italy to demonstrate popular support for their regime. On this occasion, Gower overheard a local man say 'We will vote as they tell us, but God knows what is in our hearts.'

The Mafia may have been brought to heel by Mori, but he now faced the even greater challenge of putting them on trial – and not even Mori could guarantee that Sicilians would look beyond centuries of mistrust of outside justice.

Chapter Three

Confined in Cages

The process of bringing all the hundreds of Mafia suspects to trial was a long one. At one point, it was thought better to try them outside Sicily, so as to avoid the inevitable intimidation of juries. But Prefect Cesare Mori held out for trials before native juries, arguing that it would be a greater triumph for Sicilians if they could be seen to convict these criminals without fear. The liberal procurator-general in Palermo was replaced by the tougher and more outspoken Luigi Giampietro. He set the tone for the following trials by saying 'Kindness is regarded as weakness, and makes criminals cocky.'

The first prisoners to be put on trial were the bandits of the Madonie, housed behind 50 metres of steel bars alongside one wall of the courtroom.

> The accused persons were confined in four cages [said a report in the London *Times*]. They were of all ages, and of both sexes. Some of them were old with a terrible past of crime, others were mere juveniles and carried themselves impudently. They were dressed in various styles, but all wore caps, which the Mafia appear to prefer to hats. Several, like the doctor of Villadoro, were men of considerable means, while others bore every sign of poverty.

An old church had been converted to house the trial at Termini Imerese, a port half way along the coast between the Madonie and Palermo. It took place almost two years after the original round-up and two of the leading bandits had died in prison, including Giuseppe

Ferrarello, who committed suicide. But there were enough outlaw characters to keep the world's press interested. One of them was Giuseppa Salvo, mother of the Andaloro gangsters. The London *Times* dubbed her Queen of Gangi, while the *New York Times* called her:

> This mother of a ferocious brood . . . Sixty-two years old, with snow white hair, she stills stands perfectly upright, is quick in her movements, strong-framed and not devoid of a certain dignity of bearing. Yet her sinister look and the evil leer permanently distorting her features make one's blood run cold.

She had spent her whole life among outlaws. Her father, then her husband, and, finally, her eldest son had been chief of the Gangi gang. When she rode out with them, she wore man's clothes. She was not slow to order sentences of death and frequently set the price of ransoms for kidnapped victims. 'She forced girls to marry members of her band', added the London *Times*, 'intervened in disputes between peasants, and issued decisions against which there was no appeal.'

Another gangster to catch public attention was Pietro Albanese, thanks in part to a photograph of him, which was passed round the court. It showed him sitting proudly on a horse, dressed as a bandit with bandolier and gun. Albanese denied the obvious truth of the picture, saying it had been taken at a party at a farmhouse where he was working. He claimed he had to borrow the horse and gun for the photograph. It was merely fancy dress.

The accused faced a variety of charges from murder, theft and cattle-raiding to extortion and blackmail. Most of them denied the charge of criminal association – Mori's useful catch-all for Mafiosi. A few admitted to crimes, but in true Tradition style, claimed they were righting a wrong against them. Some of the methods by which the Mafia dominated the countryside were revealed. One criminal practice was to foist a Mafia member on a landlord as an agent overseeing his estate, but at an inflated salary of 15,000 lire a year. A typical threatening letter was read out in court:

> We bandits have the right to live on the landlords. If you do not do your duty we will punish you. It is useless to tell you to whom you should address yourself if you care to save yourself from ruin. You will find persons trusted by us, or you will address yourself to someone of this district.

If a landowner resisted such a demand, he could be murdered.

The trial was a massive undertaking, with over 300 prosecution witnesses giving evidence. But Mori and Mussolini did not want the trial to last forever. Fascist justice was swift justice, they said, and should proceed at a more Fascist rhythm. After just three months, the jury was ready to give its verdict.

Virtually all the 147 accused were found guilty of criminal association. Seven of the leaders received life sentences with hard labour; a further eight were given 30 years; Giuseppa Salvo was sentenced to 25 years, along with one of her daughters. Most of the rest received sentences of between 5 and 10 years. Only eight were acquitted. It was an excellent result for Mori. Fascist justice had been seen to be done and the newspapers joined in the celebration.

Mussolini's own journal, *Il Popolo d'Italia*, proclaimed the Mafia had received a death blow. The London *Times* said 'Mussolini has dared to threaten the monster in its native haunts, and has throttled it with success.' The *New York Times* declared 'Breaking the backbone of the Mafia is one of Premier Mussolini's great achievements . . . The magnitude of Premier Mussolini's victory is evidenced by the fact that it was possible to hold the trial in Sicily at all.'

Mori's gamble on the people of Sicily being able to judge the Mafia had come off and the *New York Times* praised him for it:

> Prefect Mori of Palermo, who has broken the back of the Mafia in Sicily . . . will go down in history as a deliverer and superman . . . Mori had to take the lead, to put himself in constant danger, to be a shining mark for the assassin's knife or bomb. His method, showing the spirit and resolution of the man, was to strike at the top.

Journalist Arnaldo Cortesi went further. Mori had become a legendary figure, he wrote, a man against whom it was useless to struggle. It was said that a gang of Mafiosi had fortified a house and resisted all efforts to carry it by storm. Mori boldly walked up to the house, rapped on the door and called in a loud voice to those within to surrender.

'Who is that?' the bandits asked. 'Mori', he replied. Without a further word they surrendered, believing it was useless to fight if Mori was there.

In Sicily, epic poems began to appear, praising Mussolini and his war on the Mafia. Most were anonymous, but one was signed by Salvatore Romano. A couple of verses demonstrate the heroic language:

Blessed the fascio thou hast formed.
And blessed be thou that made it.
Thou hast removed all delinquency,
Thieves, evil doers, and gangsters.
As is just thou gavest the command
To put in order all the capitalists.
Thou hast tamed the thieves who stole
Who go no more through the countryside.

We Italians all speak well
Of the just things done by Mussolini.
True that he holds all under lock and key
But it is with reason, o citizens!
It is proper that we should be bound
And do just things for a good end
While Mussolini sustains us.
It is duty to stay in order, Italians.

The line mentioning that he holds all under lock and key seems almost satirical now. Prefect Mori makes an appearance in another anonymous poem:

The law is so finely systematised
According to the ordinance of the Prefect . . .
Everyone carries his own pictures
On an identification card issued by the Prefect
So that the suspect can be recognised.
Even mice have to walk in a straight line
Or they will feel the claws of the cat.

From 1927 to 1929, fifteen more major trials of the Mafia followed, condemning hundreds of Mafiosi and associated outlaws to imprisonment. When the evidence proved too flimsy for even a Fascist court, or witnesses retracted their statements, then Mori stepped in with a punishment of *confino* or banishment, sending the suspects to a wilderness island off the coast of Sicily.

At the end of his account of his war against the Mafia, Cesare Mori proudly presented the figures. In the province of Palermo, he declared there were 223 murders in 1922; in 1928, just five. In 1922, there were 246 robberies; in 1928, just 14. In 1922, there were 51 major cattle-rustling raids; in 1928, just six. Kidnapping had disappeared. As far as he was concerned, the war against crime in Sicily had been won.

Il Duce had proved that the Fascist state was stronger than even the Mafia.

While Mori had been fighting the Mafia in Sicily, the local Fascists had been fighting Mori. Alfredo Cucco was the head of the Black Shirts on the island and he claimed to have pushed for the appointment of Mori as prefect of Palermo. But with Mori came an extension of his powers, by government decree, giving him full control over the island's police force and the authority to issue ordinances. This severely reduced the influence of Cucco who had hoped to exert some control over Mori and maintain his own status among the island's elite.

At first, Cucco sought to praise Mori and his campaign in his local newspapers, but when, during the round-up at Madonie, local families appealed to him for help against Mori, he began to lobby for his removal. His timing could not have been worse. Madonie was a real success for the Fascists in Rome and Minister of the Interior Luigi Federzoni told Cucco the government had no intention whatsoever of removing the prefect. Cucco persisted as a voice of doubt, saying in *La Fiamma* in January 1926:

> One thing worries us, namely that when the war is over, the guerrilla action could persist; that after the criminal armies have been destroyed, their general staffs might not be fully eliminated, and could continue, with their oblique and underhand manoeuvres, to infect the moral and material life of Sicily.

Such comments were unhelpful to Mori and the relationship between the two men deteriorated through 1926. Political allies of Cucco were denounced as associates of Mafiosi. In retaliation, Cucco had gangs of Black Shirts demonstrate in the street outside the prefect's office – it was an unsavoury echo of events in Bologna. Mori was furious, but for the time being the two maintained a façade of unity, touring the island together, even exchanging official photographs of each other.

Behind the scenes, however, it appears that Mori received a tip-off that Cucco was sending newspaper articles to a contact in New York, highlighting Mori's brutal methods in his war against the Mafia. This was too much for Mori and in early 1927, the Palermo Fascist party was dissolved and Cucco expelled. The official accusation against Cucco was one of corruption in that he allegedly helped a friend avoid military service. Cucco tried to fight back, but Mussolini was too impressed by Mori's victories to overturn the result of the political vendetta. Cucco was out, Mori remained.

Mussolini underlined his support for Mori in a speech to the Chamber of Deputies on 20 May 1927:

> From time to time, there come to my ears doubting voices that wish to suggest that to-day we are going too far in Sicily, that an entire region is being harshly treated and that a slur is being cast over an island of the noblest traditions. I reject with utter contempt these suggestions which can only originate from persons of evil reputation.

This was a damning reference to Cucco and his supporters.

Mori enjoyed Mussolini's whole-hearted support for two more years after the fall of Cucco, but it could not last forever. Enemies were gathering and they also had the ear of Il Duce.

Antonino Di Giorgio was a hero of World War I, winning medals and leading armies at a time when Mussolini and Giuseppe Bonanno's father were both lowly soldiers on the Italian front line. After the war, he entered politics and became minister of war before falling out with the Fascist government and returning to his native Sicily in 1926, where he became commander of its military forces.

Di Giorgio supported Mori's campaign against the Mafia and told Mussolini he was right to get rid of Cucco. But, by early 1928, his opinion had changed and he told Il Duce he thought the prefect had lost all sense of proportion. Official figures quoted 11,000 arrests and even Mussolini thought this was too much. The general put his complaints in writing, saying that the 'victims [of the Mafia] were rounded up with the criminals at the time of the so-called *retate*, for no other reason than they had had contact with them.' This put intolerable pressure on the judiciary and led to many wrongful convictions. With innocent men being punished alongside the guilty, he said, there was widespread disillusion with the law, contrary to Mori's claims. After several years of tough action, the state was in danger of losing the respect it had gained:

> The long lines of handcuffed people you see on lorries, trains and stations, the disconsolate crowds of women and children who wait in the rain outside the prisons and courts, all lend themselves perfectly to damaging remarks and the propaganda of hatred.

Mussolini took this report very seriously. He was a master at understanding the media and popular feeling and it seems likely he could see little more to be gained from continuing Mori's campaign and possibly a good deal to be lost. He had all the headlines he wanted, especially around the world, showing him as tougher than the Mafia. Now, perhaps, was the time to bring an end to this particular Fascist show.

Mori was aware of Di Giorgio's views and received reports of discontent among the Carabinieri but rather then negotiate, he felt confident enough to attack Di Giorgio, by revealing his association with the Mafia of Mistretta. Di Giorgio's brother had married into a Mafioso family. Mussolini was presented with the evidence and felt betrayed. He asked the general to accept a posting outside Sicily. Di Giorgio refused and resigned. He was said to have confronted Mori in Palermo and slapped him across the face. Amazingly, the prefect had survived the most serious threat to his position, but his days were numbered.

Realising that Mussolini had tired of his campaign against the Mafia, Mori accepted that his work was coming to an end. Having inflicted a major defeat on the Mafia, the Fascist government now wanted to maintain its popularity by concentrating on the economy of the island. It wanted to shift money away from the police budget and invest it in public works, building roads, draining swamps, and promoting farming and tourism. Mori added his own support to this shift in emphasis by visiting provincial towns and handing out awards to their most successful farmers. Before an official visit, he would frequently ditch his car and mount a horse to ride into town. He liked being the Peasant Prefect.

Internationally, Mussolini continued to receive praise for his victory over the Mafia. Richard Washburn Child was a former American ambassador to Italy and he was a particularly keen advocate. In fact, it was his idea to get the dictator to tell his life story to an English-speaking audience in 1928. Child had read numerous biographies of the Fascist leader, but nothing, he said to Il Duce, could take the place of a book which he would write himself.

Mussolini leant on his desk and looked at the diplomat with astonishment. 'Write myself?' he said. He did not exactly have much spare time. But Child persisted, showing him a series of possible chapter headings on pieces of paper.

'All right', said Mussolini in English. 'I will.'

The Fascist leader dictated the memories of his life and the pages of the typed manuscript were shown to Child. 'What editing may I do?' asked the American diplomat.

'Any that you like' said Mussolini. 'You know Italy, you understand Fascism, you see me, as clearly as anyone.' And so Child presented Mussolini to the English-speaking world:

> I knew him before the world at large, outside of Italy, had ever heard of him. I knew him before and after the moment he leaped into the saddle, and in the days when he, almost single-handed, was clearing away chaos' own junk pile from Italy . . . He takes responsibility for everything – for discipline, for censorship, for measures which, were less rigor required, would appear repressive and cruel . . .
>
> He is a Spartan. Perhaps we need Spartans in the world to-day; especially that type whose first interest is the development of the power and the happiness of a race.

For many, in other parts of the world, Fascism seemed a strict but benign tyranny that might well be the answer to problems of political instability, organised crime, and the rise of socialism. The Fascist movement was far from becoming the international villain it was in the mid-1930s and later.

In late 1928, Mussolini signified his pleasure at Mori's contribution to his own reputation by making the prefect a member of the Italian Senate. But Mori had one more duty to perform for his Fascist patron. In March 1929, a national plebiscite was held to show the rest of the world that, despite doing away with democracy, the majority of Italians were happy with their Fascist regime. Mori did his best to encourage as many people to turn out as possible for the election. He made it clear that any 'no' vote was to be regarded as an act of treachery and he would be looking at electoral lists to see who had wavered in their duty. The reality of this plebiscite in Milocca was observed by Charlotte Gower:

> Fascists paraded to simulate general interest. On the election day, men were collected in groups and marched to the polling places escorted by the band. Voting was set forth as a patriotic duty for every Milocchese, so that the village might make a good showing and demonstrate its gratitude for the benefits it received under Fascism.

At the end of the count, Mori and Mussolini got exactly what they wanted. In Palermo, 92 per cent of the population voted in favour of the Fascist regime and in rural areas the vote was even higher, up to 96 per cent. Mori had succeeded in swapping one terror for another.

On 23 June 1929, Mori received a short telegram from Rome. It told him his career as Prefect of Palermo was over. A second, more fulsome telegram was distributed to the newspapers. In it, Mussolini declared:

> I wish to express to you once again my sincere praise and most fervent congratulations for what you have achieved in Palermo and in Sicily in the last four years. These years will remain sculpted in the history of the moral, political and social regeneration of the noblest of islands.

Mori was fifty-seven years old. He was disappointed to be removed so abruptly from his position of power, but he cannot have been surprised. The Fascist machine was moving on to other battles. When Mori published his memoirs in 1932, he wrote without bitterness. He had only praise for Il Duce and his role in launching his campaign against the Mafia. The book was written in his usual flowery manner and received bad reviews in Italy but, when an English translation by Orlo Williams appeared in 1933, it was written in a more direct and exciting style, and was far more successful.

Mori was sent out of the way to Istria on the Adriatic coast where he spent the rest of the 1930s, overseeing the construction of roads and canals and the draining of marshes. In his spare time, he wrote poetry. He had no children but continued to be happily married, calling his wife the companion of his stormy existence. He always had a photograph of her on his desk.

Mori's successor as Prefect of Palermo was 33-year-old Umberto Albini. He had a reputation as a playboy and set the tone for his reign by arriving in Sicily by glamorous seaplane. Albini turned away from the deployment of *retate*, but expanded Mori's more discreet use of *confino*, sending a hit-list of Mafia suspects to penal islands off the Sicilian coast. This remained the main weapon against the Mafiosi throughout the 1930s, sending hundreds away for periods of up to five years.

There were two more mass trials in 1931 and one in 1932, this last being held at Agrigento and sentencing 244 men and women to a total of 1,200 years in prison. That Mori's methods of *retate* were still considered effective by mainland Italian police was proved in June 1934 when 400 gangsters were rounded up in Calabria. They had terrorised the area for years, extorting money and cattle in return for protection. They were thought to be renegades from Mori's purges. 'The police believe that many members of the gang formerly belonged to the Mafia in Sicily', said a newspaper report, 'and fled from the island after Prefect Cesare Mori of Palermo had stamped out banditry on the island.'

Despite the headlines, crime in Sicily remained and Mori received letters asking him to come back and sort out the situation. But it seems to have been low-level crime. The Fascists appear to have successfully replaced one regime of fear with another and, although corruption and criminal patronage persisted, the open display of Mafia rule, characteristic of a previous era, does seem to have been crushed. The biggest beneficiaries were the great landowners who were more secure in their position, no longer being forced to give up their land to Mafia intermediaries.

That the people themselves might merely be paying lip-service to the Fascists was recorded by Charlotte Gower. In Milocca in the late 1920s, she noted a continuing lack of identification with the Italian mainland. The islanders were Sicilian first, not Italians:

> The only direct representatives of the State that the rural Sicilian meets are the military police. The average Sicilian distrusts them, and he associates them with unpleasant events. When a retired policeman became mayor of Milocca, his praiseworthy attempts to put down brigandage in the region won him no sympathy from his fellow-townsmen, and finally resulted in his assassination.

Despite Mussolini's grand plans to reinvigorate the Sicilian economy, poverty and unemployment continued to afflict the island. Peasants were badly hit by the Great Depression, with reduced export markets for their olives, grapes and lemons. They responded by flocking to the big towns, such as Palermo, and setting up shanty-house slums.

The effective Fascist censorship of the local press ensured that the word Mafia was no longer even used to describe crime in Sicily in the 1930s, but this did not mean it had disappeared. Far from it, when key figures returned from *confino* they maintained their Mafiosi networks, but such activity was conducted discreetly. The Mafia in Sicily had become an underground organisation and that was the way it would stay while the Fascists were in power.

This was in stark contrast to the criminal activities of Sicilian immigrants in the USA. There, Mafia gangsters were the new anti-heroes, featuring in newspaper stories and pulp fiction, a notoriety that was just about to be ramped up by open warfare on the streets of New York.

Chapter Four

Fascists in New York

It was a summer morning in 1925 and New Yorker Lino Balatie, 24 years old, and Lapolto Petilo, 34 years old, from Newark, New Jersey, were looking forward to attending an Italian-American meeting in Laurel Gardens, Springfield Avenue, Newark. They were members of the Fascist League of North America.

That morning, they would be seeing their new 32-year-old leader, Count Ignazio Thaon di Revel, a dynamic young man with excellent contacts back in Fascist Italy but now working as a bond dealer on Wall Street. The last meeting they had gone to had been a big success. There had been some anti-Fascists there, but the Fascists had good speakers and convinced many undecided Italian-Americans to join them. They hoped for a similar result this time round. But when forty of them walked into the hall, the mood was different. Anti-Fascists had come armed and were ready to ambush them, as the *New York Herald Tribune* reported:

> There were yells of 'Here they come!' and as the Fascisti reached the center of the hall a half hundred Socialists closed in behind them, some flourishing guns. Every man in the hall rose and started for the center of the room.

Vicious fighting broke out between the two factions with both sides wielding stiletto knives, razors, sticks, and guns.

> The yells of the combatants, punctuated by occasional pistol shots, could be heard for blocks . . . The count escaped without a scratch. His men formed a circle about him as they fought.

By the time the police arrived in six patrol wagons, most of the audience had fled the scene, leaving only the wounded and piles of abandoned weapons. The police arrested those left behind. Most of them claimed to be members of the Fascist League who had been ambushed as they entered the building. Balatie and Petilo were among six seriously injured and taken to hospital. Both had stab wounds.

Emotions ran high in the Italian-American East Coast community when it came to Benito Mussolini. Even a civilised debate about Fascism between senior commentators could descend into violence.

On the evening of 11 March 1928, Fascists and anti-Fascists gathered at the Selwyn Theatre on West 42nd Street in Manhattan to listen to two distinguished speakers discuss the merits of Benito Mussolini. Dr Vincenzo Nitti, son of a former Italian premier, began the debate by condemning Il Duce for abolishing all political liberty in Italy. 'The warlike speeches of Mussolini', said Nitti, 'are having the same effect on the peace of Europe as the utterances of the Kaiser had before the World War.'

The Fascists, the larger proportion of the audience, sat high in the gallery and hissed at Nitti as he sat down. It was then the turn of American publisher Samuel S. McClure to argue the case for the Italian dictator. He had just returned from an eighteen-month trip to Italy and was highly impressed by the Fascist state. Mussolini had 'solved the problem of democracy' said McClure. He should be praised for 'suppressing the Mafia' and for having 'developed the most miraculous method in 100 years for making real democracy workable.'

Strangely, for a magazine publisher, he extolled Il Duce for turning the press into a 'house organ . . . maybe the most miraculous of his achievements'. Coining the most famous cliché about Mussolini, McClure noted 'he had never known a train to arrive behind schedule', which indicated 'the railway employees were contented and that they were no exception'.

The working man felt safe and happy in Italy, concluded McClure. This assertion got a barrage of loud laughs from the anti-Fascists sitting in the orchestra stalls. That made the Fascists furious and they yelled 'Patria!' at them.

When Dr Nitti rose to rebut McClure's claims, the Fascists booed. They called him a liar and asked him how much he had been paid to talk that night. A fist-fight broke out in the gallery and one man was about to fling himself at his opponents across the aisle when he was held back by his friends and carried out of the theatre.

McClure got more support by far among the audience and when the debate ended, he was hoisted on the shoulders of excited Fascists who carried him out on to 42nd Street as supporters sang Black Shirt songs around him. McClure waved his hat at surprised theatre-goers.

Mussolini was proving highly popular on the East Coast. He ensured he grabbed the headlines by teasing US democracy when he gave an interview to the *New York Times*:

> Democracy is a regime of luxury compatible with countries possessing great present and future resources. In the United States democracy, which in certain respects is more apparent than real, functions well because the immense riches of the country render possible compensation for the dispersion of energy, which it appears to me is inherent in a democratic regime.

In contrast, said Mussolini, Italy was a poor country and could not afford to disperse its energies:

> Life in a poor country is a continual struggle, for which it must be organised in a most efficacious manner, like militia, unable to permit itself to lose any battle, and over which the government must have complete authority and supreme command.

He made no apology for the hundreds of thousands of Italians who emigrated from his country. Once his grand public schemes had been completed, he expected many more to travel to America.

The Fascists capitalised on US interest in Mussolini by establishing a Fascist League of North America. As early as May 1921, there had been enthusiastic supporters of Mussolini in New York intent on organising their own Fascist groups in America. Many of their earliest members were Italian war veterans working in the USA. Top Fascists frequently referred to these centres of support as their colonies in America.

Mussolini's first ambassador to the United States, Gelasio Caetani, took a dim view of these early efforts. He knew that Il Duce wanted to maintain good relations with the US government in order to secure loans and moderate restrictive immigration legislation – and he did not want American Fascists giving the wrong impression of their movement.

> Unfortunately [Caetani reported to Mussolini], the less worthy elements of our colonies are often those which are the most active and who expose themselves publicly when it is a question of taking credit for promoting noble initiatives.

Caetani wanted American Fascist groups to limit themselves to charitable activities and not become involved in political events that might appear to threaten the US. To this end, with the blessing of Mussolini, he organised an official Fascist movement in New York called Fascio Centrale. It was run by Umberto Menicucci, a tailor from Pisa who now lived in Philadelphia and who had fought as an Arditi storm-trooper in World War I, and Dino Bigongiari, an assistant professor at Columbia University. Menicucci could control the war veterans while Bigongiari presented the right cultural face to the Anglo-Saxon establishment. With headquarters at 220 East 14th Street, the Fascio Centrale had up to 800 members. Elsewhere, there were some thirty branches throughout the US, including in the cities of Chicago and Detroit.

By bringing some discipline to Fascists in America, Caetani had hoped to reassure the US government of their peaceful intent. However, the American media continued to carry lurid stories highlighting the menacing side of the Black Shirt phenomenon. Brawls like those at Laurel Gardens were not good news. And it was not just street fights that worried Americans, it was the more profound influence of Fascist ideology.

William Green, President of the American Federation of Labor, spoke out strongly against Mussolini, calling his movement as dangerous as Communism. He framed his concerns in a letter sent out to all five million working members:

> Not satisfied with the powers of a dictator in Italy, he has extended the tentacles of Fascismo into other countries. His dictum that 'once an Italian always an Italian to the seventh generation', prohibits Italian immigrants to the United States becoming naturalized. They must remain Italian citizens to Fascismo. If they enter any organization having for its purpose opposition to Fascismo their property in Italy will be confiscated.
>
> Organizations have been formed in this country to discourage the naturalization of Italian immigrants . . . Fascismo and communism have the same fangs and the same

> poison which it is intended to inject into the political life of our nation.

With the appearance of numerous critical newspaper features, such as one in the *New York Herald Tribune* yelling 'Fascisti Invade United States in World Expansion', Caetani could see that he was failing to win the war of words. His advice to Mussolini was to shut down the Fascio Centrale. He received support from US Ambassador in Rome, Richard Washburn Child. Although a fervent admirer of Mussolini, even Child could see that the presence of foreign political organisations on American soil might not be purely benign.

This lack of official support for their movement made many Fascists furious with Caetani. Ignoring his attempts at diplomacy, Menicucci and Bigongiari declared their intention to fight radicals – that is, Socialist opponents – on the streets of New York. Among these, the most vociferous was Carlo Tresca.

Tresca was a Socialist activist who had already made a reputation for himself by supporting numerous strikes in Pennsylvania, Massachusetts, and New York state. In Minnesota, while inflaming striking miners, he narrowly escaped a lynching. He eventually settled in Greenwich Village in New York City where he was considered a leading character.

'Tresca has the distinction of having been 37 times in jail in this country for his ideals', enthused a sympathetic local newspaper, the *Greenwich Villager*. 'Carlo Tresca loves America. He finds her young, daring, beautiful, royal, with a "don't care" grandeur that is bewitching.'

'This is the fighting ground for me', said Tresca. 'I love it, and I hate it. I fight to make everybody happy.'

He did not make Caetani happy.

Tresca's newspaper *Il Martello* ('The Hammer') constantly criticised the Fascists and called Mussolini the arch-traitor of Italy. Caetani considered Tresca the principal enemy of Fascism in America and worked with the US Department of Justice to get his newspaper shut down. In 1925 they succeeded in getting him jailed for a year for obscenity, but the public outcry meant he was out after four months. In 1926, the Fascists failed to kill him with a bomb at an anti-Fascist rally. Tresca remained a thorn in the side of the Fascists for years to come until the Mafia finally intervened in the vendetta between Tresca and Mussolini – but that is a later story.

New York State Senator Salvatore Cotillo tried to ease the tension between American Fascists and anti-Fascists by steering a course between the two factions, as he said in March 1923:

> The American citizen of Italian extraction is actually earnestly engaged not in Fascismo but in Americanization. The Order of the Sons of Italy, 200,000 strong, with a membership of 40,000 in the state of New York, has assumed this great task . . . The Italian Ambassador, Prince Caetani, in his address to Italians, has urged them to become American citizens and he has also reiterated that they must not mix up Italian with American politics. This ought to be sufficient for the Fascisti of the United States to understand that America has no use for them . . .

To take his case further, Cotillo went with Caetani to Rome later that year to meet Mussolini. Like many others, he was impressed by the dictator and ended up calling Mussolini a 'commanding element of the highest order . . . as soon as I return in America, I will do everything I can to make Fascism known not as mere brigandage . . . but as a lawful and strong government, full of patriotic ardour . . .'

When he returned to America, Cotillo was interviewed by Carlo Tresca who quoted out of context his reference to Fascism as 'brigandage'. Mussolini was incensed and withdrew the decoration – the Cross of St Maurizio – he was about to bestow upon Cotillo. Cotillo responded by saying Tresca had misquoted him and that he retained the 'highest admiration' for Fascism in Italy, but, 'there is no place for it or any similar organization or association in America.'

Cotillo's fate was to remain caught in the crossfire of a savage battle between Fascists and anti-Fascists. Even when he was elected to the Supreme Court of New York State, he could not avoid controversy. When Harvard Professor Edward East called Italian immigrants 'the dregs' of Italy's population, Cotillo struck back. 'Such remarks', he said, 'as that Italy would be "well rid of" of southern Italians as of a "cancerous tumor" and that southern Italians are "incompetent and lacking in intelligence" . . . [indicate] rash and antagonistic thought.' He countered, saying that it was Italian immigrant workmen that helped build the New York subway and its skyscrapers.

However, Cotillo could not win. Emotions were running too high. Only the month before, the head of the New York branch of the Order of the Sons of America had condemned Cotillo for 'obeying the dictates of Communists in attacking its alleged Fascist policies'.

Caetani could not win either. Under a storm of criticism from American Fascists, resenting his muzzling of them, he gave up the struggle in October 1924 and resigned his post as ambassador. In July

1925, the Fascist organisation in the US was given a new name – the Fascist League of North America (FLNA). Numbers of supporters continued to grow with seventy branches throughout the USA and some 7,000 members.

Ignazio Thaon di Revel was put in charge of the FLNA as its president. He was a glamorous figure, an aristocratic young man who had worked in the movie business but now wanted to gain experience of American capitalism in the bond department of a brokerage company. He seemed a responsible figure to quieten the reputation of New York's Black Shirts. But almost immediately he lost control of the organisation and several violent incidents followed. It was Di Revel who led the forty Fascists in the Laurel Gardens brawl and he claimed to have been stabbed in the back during the fighting.

Just a month earlier, on Independence Day, a mob of Fascists clashed with anti-Fascists at the Garibaldi memorial at Rosebank, Staten Island. Carlo Tresca had given a speech to his Socialist supporters when it was the turn of the Sons of Italy to hold their own ceremony. The police allowed 350 Fascists to march in front of the memorial but not stop. A woman in a red dress then ran up to the Fascists and started to shout at them. The band of the Fascists struck up a marching song and a crowd of anti-Fascists jeered. The *New York Times* reported what followed:

> Bottles and stones were hurled in a great shower and the police sent out a fresh call for reserves. For twenty minutes the police had a stiff fight on their hands. They made vigorous use of their night sticks, and marched the Fascisti to the train at Tompkinsville that took them to the ferry for Manhattan.

Seven Fascists were arrested and two of them were said to have been armed with clubs wrapped in newspapers. Some policemen claimed they had been lashed by a weapon a prisoner called a riding crop, which he said was carried by all Black Shirts on parade. One policeman described this as being more like an extended blackjack.

The *New York Herald Tribune* pointed the finger at the red-shirted radicals for starting the trouble:

> The moral courage displayed by a small group of black shirted Fascisti, who remained peaceful in spite of a manifest desire to fight, was the final factor in winning the day for law and order. As fifty of these war veterans faced several hundred frenzied radicals they never once faltered, although a barrage of rocks and bottles rained among them.

It was the radicals who were arrested said the *Herald Tribune*, one carrying a police baton and another armed with what the police termed a 'dangerous oak club'.

Later that day, Fascists attacked an elderly red-shirted veteran of Garibaldi's liberation army. He was making his way to the office of Carlo Tresca's *Il Martello* when he was assaulted – the Black Shirts grabbed at the medals on his red shirt. He managed to escape up the stairs to the magazine, but a riot broke out behind him.

> The band of Fascisti were blocked [said a newspaper report]. They turned toward the street. A crowd was now surrounding them, and in it were numerous red-shirted enemies. The blacks started a harangue. A blow was struck. Then a free-for-all fight ensued. Women and children joined, either trying to extricate their men or taking revenge for injuries.

Police with night sticks restored order.

While black and red-shirted Italians brought their battles from the Old World to the New, other immigrant Italians kept their heads down and concentrated on getting richer. 'Prohibition provided a splendid and accelerated opportunity for immigrants to make money', recalled Joseph Bonanno.

In 1925, Bonanno was twenty years old and staying with an uncle in Brooklyn. The uncle offered to teach him how to make a living as a barber, but Bonanno was not interested. Since 1920, there had been a ban on the selling of alcohol in the US and the Sicilian could see that there was a gold-mine to be had in providing illicit liquor. In his extended Castellammarese family, he met other like-minded young men and they set up a bootlegging operation. They started with their own basement distillery making contraband whiskey. It was little different, he thought, from the centuries-old tradition of Sicilians making their own wine. Local Irish cops were easily paid off and soon Bonanno and his friends were living the high life, buying cars, wearing sharp suits and spending large amounts of money in nightclubs and dance halls.

It was the same story throughout the Italian immigrant community in New York. Bonanno was not the only Mafioso to have fled Sicily in the wake of the Fascist crack-down. Don Vito Cascio Ferro, the Palermo Mafia chieftain, is said to have organised an escape route by which some 500 young gangsters sailed from Sicily to Marseilles and on to America, or from Tunis to Cuba and then to Florida. Not only were they avoiding Mussolini's round-ups, they were also attracted by the huge sums of money to be made during Prohibition.

Don Vito had lived in New York City briefly around the turn of the century and been impressed by the criminal opportunities there. Back in Sicily, he liked to keep up links with New York in the hope, one day, of setting up a major criminal organisation there. In 1909, a New York policeman called Joseph Petrosino came to Sicily to investigate these links but one night, while wandering in the Piazza Marina near the harbour in Palermo, he was shot in the back several times by local Mafiosi. Legend has it that Don Vito interrupted his dinner with a senior politician to fire the finishing shot.

The death of Petrosino caused a sensation in New York. He had been sent out secretly to Palermo to gather the criminal records of Mafiosi and the police continued to refuse to discuss the purpose of his journey. More than 250,000 New Yorkers turned out in Little Italy to watch a funeral procession 7,000 strong. The great opera singer Enrico Caruso had been a friend of Petrosino ever since the detective trapped the writer of a Black Hand letter who was trying to extort money from the star.

Don Vito later became one of Mori's greatest scalps. He was arrested in 1929 on a charge of smuggling. During the trial, Don Vito remained aloof from the process, ignoring the court's authority. When finally convicted, he declared 'Gentlemen, as you have been unable to obtain proof of any of my numerous crimes, you have been reduced to condemning me for the only one I have never committed.' He died in prison in 1932.

One of the leading gangsters coming to America in the 1920s was Salvatore Maranzano. He was said to be a key associate of Don Vito and arrived in 1927 in New York with a strong reputation as a man of respect. Like Bonanno, he came from Castellammare del Golfo. It was the home town of many leading US Mafiosi, including Stefano Magaddino, Gaspar Milazzo and Joe Aiello. 'The Castellammarese tended to stick together', said Bonanno. 'We had our own distinct neighborhoods, not only in Brooklyn and Manhattan, but also in Detroit, Buffalo and Endicott, New York. Not only did we all know each other, but we were often related to one another.' They spoke Sicilian to each other, hardly ever used English, and asked for no favours from outsiders.

Bonanno knew Maranzano from Castellammare where he had been an effective 'soldier' for his Uncle Stefano. As a student in Palermo, Bonanno had had lunch with Maranzano several times. He liked his style. When Maranzano came to America, he dressed like a businessman in 'soft pinstripes on the blues' and wore no showy jewellery, only his watch and wedding ring. He was in his forties and powerfully built. Bonanno considered him a natural leader and immediately allied himself with him. Bonanno became one of his enforcers. They shared a hatred for the Fascist regime that had forced them into exile.

Maranzano quickly took to the bootlegging business, made money, and came to dominate the Castellammarese clan in Brooklyn and Manhattan. By 1928, Maranzano and his mob were attracting the attention of Giuseppe Masseria, known as Joe the Boss. Masseria was a squat, fat Sicilian who had made his reputation in street shoots-outs in the early 1920s. He too made a fortune out of bootlegging and attracted many of the toughest gangsters of New York. One of them was Charlie 'Lucky' Luciano. They concluded a gang alliance over a table groaning with Italian food.

> There was enough on that table for a banquet [recalled Luciano] and I kept figurin' that any minute half of Masseria's mob was gonna show up and sweep down on that table. But nobody showed. I think Masseria ate half of all that food himself, most of it with his fingers – and if he didn't look like a pig on two legs, I never saw one.

Luciano was thirty years old, lean, with a long knife scar on his right cheek that added to his mean look. He had been born in Sicily but left as a little boy and really grew up on the Lower East Side, a melting pot for all kinds of immigrants. Luciano started his career of crime early by threatening the kids around him. He found that some of the toughest kids were Jews and he made good friends among them – some would later become major gangster allies, including Meyer Lansky and Bugsy Siegel. Luciano's was a very New York approach to crime. He would work with whoever got things done. He did not mind where they came from.

This was different to Maranzano and Masseria, who brought Old World prejudices with them. Both of them had an inbred Catholic dislike for Jews and both preferred to work with Sicilians. Luciano disliked Masseria but he loathed Maranzano. The very aloof quality that Bonanno found attractive and sophisticated in Maranzano, Luciano found snobby and irritating. 'He was always tryin' to prove that he was superior, that nobody could be his equal', Luciano said of Maranzano. 'I didn't wanna put myself in a position where I hadda kiss his ring at nine o'clock every morning.'

By the late 1920s, Masseria had a firm grip on the New York underworld, dominating at least three of the five main crime clans, and he had more 'soldiers' on the streets than the Castellammarese. But Maranzano was a persuasive figure and he played on the Sicilian Tradition for support. A fourth Mafia family in Brooklyn was run by Joe Profaci who came from the same region of Sicily in 1921. Maranzano managed to persuade Profaci to stay out of the upcoming feud.

Tensions rose when Masseria encouraged Al Capone to move from Brooklyn to Chicago and compete with Castellammarese gangster Joe Aiello, who was already making his way in that city. Masseria then tried to split Aiello from his fellow Castellammarese ally in Detroit, Gaspar Milazzo. These Sicilians were all from the streets of Bonanno's home town. They told Masseria to back off.

Fighting first started in Chicago with Capone getting the best of Aiello and his gangsters. Then, in 1930, Milazzo was shot down in a Detroit fish market. It was not looking good for the Castellammarese and they held a war council in Brooklyn. Maranzano dominated the meeting and said that the killing of Milazzo was a declaration of war. Others wanted to quieten the situation so they could carry on with their businesses, but Maranzano persisted in arguing for the need for action and with the blessing of Stefano Magaddino in Buffalo, he became the wartime leader of the Castellammarese.

'We carried pistols, shotguns, machine guns and enough ammunition to fight the Battle of Bull Run all over again', recalled Bonanno. Maranzano and his closest associates travelled in two armoured Cadillacs fitted with steel plates on the sides and bullet-proof windows. 'Maranzano would sit in the back seat of his car with a machine gun mounted on a swivel between his legs. He also packed a Luger and a Colt, as well as his omnipresent dagger behind his back.' When Tom Reina of the Bronx was shot dead for expressing his admiration for Maranzano, the Castellammarese struck back by killing Masseria's right-hand man, Peter Morello, in his Harlem office, plus two of his men.

Luciano told a different story to Bonanno. He claimed that it was he who ordered Morello's death and Albert Anastasia carried it out.

Masseria blamed the Castellammarese and had Al Capone hit men kill Joe Aiello in Chicago.

A failed attempt to kill Masseria prompted Luciano and his Jewish associates to consider ending the war themselves. A meeting between Maranzano and Luciano settled this.

The final shoot-out occurred at a Coney Island restaurant, Nuovo Villa Tammaro, on 15 April 1931. Masseria drove his steel-armoured sedan to a lunch meeting with Lucky Luciano. Masseria ate a big meal of spaghetti with red clam sauce and lobster, all washed down with Chianti. Luciano ate sparingly and sipped a little red wine. After they finished eating, they played a card game, then Luciano excused himself to go the men's room. The *New York Times* took up the story:

> At 2 o'clock the quiet of the little street near the bay was broken by the roar of gunfire and two or three men walked out of the restaurant to an automobile parked at the curb and drove away. When the police got there they found Mrs Tammaro [the owner] bending over the body of Joe the Boss. He lay on his back. In his left hand was clutched a brand new ace of diamonds.

Albert Anastasia, Bugsy Siegel, Vito Genovese and Joe Adonis were the Luciano hit men who killed Masseria. Luciano emerged from the toilet and called the police. He said he saw nothing because he was having a 'long leak'. Maranzano and the Castellammarese were delighted – and so should have been Masseria. 'He died on a full stomach', said Bonanno, 'and that leads me to believe he died happy.'

Maranzano celebrated his victory by calling a meeting of all the American Mafiosi to confirm the new gangster hierarchy of five crime families with himself at the top, 'boss of bosses' – *Capo di Tutti Capi*. Maranzano outlined to them his concept of a more organised Mafia with strict rankings of bosses, under-bosses, lieutenants and soldiers.

Joseph Valachi was one of the lower-ranking gangsters at the gathering and noted the antique character of Maranzano's rules:

> I didn't know until later that he was a nut about Julius Caesar and even had a room in his house full of nothing but books about him. That's where he got the idea for the new organization.

Before going to a meeting with Al Capone in Chicago, Lucky Luciano asked Maranzano if he could take along his right-hand man,

Meyer Lansky. 'But Lansky was a Jew', recalled Bonanno, 'and could not take part in our Tradition.' Maranzano said Lansky could travel with Luciano but could not be in the same room when they had their meeting with Capone. 'A Sicilian of the old school would not even have thought about taking a Jewish friend along', said Bonanno.

Maranzano and Luciano continued to regard each other with disdain and suspicion. Maranzano constantly underestimated the power of New York's Jewish mobsters and so Luciano decided to take advantage of his Old World blindness by creating a hit squad of exclusively Jewish gangsters, headed by Samuel 'Red' Levine. From Toledo, Ohio, Levine was strictly religious and yet found no conflict with his job as a hired killer. If he had an assassination to attend to on the Sabbath, he wore a yarmulke under his hat.

Lansky oversaw their training in the Bronx, but in the meantime Maranzano was organising his own hit on Luciano. For that, he too went outside the Sicilian Tradition and hired an Irishman – Vincent 'Mad Dog' Coll – to kill Lucky and all his top associates. It was to be a bloodbath and both sides raced towards it. When Luciano heard that he and Vito Genovese were to attend a meeting at Maranzano's office, he got suspicious and activated his own assassination plan.

Four men dressed as Internal Revenue Service tax-inspectors burst into Maranzano's office. 'When I arrived at the Park Avenue office', said one witness, 'I found Maranzano and others lined up with their faces against the wall. I was told to face the wall.' What happened next no one saw – except the killers.

Maranzano, who at this stage still believed his visitors were genuine government agents – his lawyers had warned him of such just such a surprise visit – went in to his office to talk to two of the agents. With the door of the office closed behind them, the two agents pulled out knives to kill him quietly, but Maranzano fought back strongly. The two Jewish hit men had to use their guns to shoot him four times – in addition to inflicting six stab wounds and cutting his throat.

Coincidentally, Vincent 'Mad Dog' Coll was on his way up the stairs to see Maranzano in his office when Maranzano's bodyguards rushed down and told him their boss was dead. Coll shrugged and kept the $25,000 advance for his contract on Luciano.

Just five months after winning the Castellammarese war, Maranzano was dead. Luciano justified it by saying it would stop all the other killing. Luciano was now Boss of Bosses and ran his criminal empire with less attention to the Tradition and more on brutal efficiency.

Bonanno was saddened to hear of Maranzano's death but not surprised. Even he – a passionate advocate of the Tradition – had to admit that Maranzano represented 'a style that often clashed with that of the Americanized men who surrounded him'. Bonanno's main concern was survival. He met with Luciano who explained his killing of Maranzano by saying Maranzano had set Mad Dog Coll on him. Luciano now said he wanted peace and was happy to work with the Castellammarese clan. Bonanno had little choice but to accept. It meant he now headed his own crime family – the youngest man to do so.

Bonanno celebrated the end of the Castellammarese war and his own elevation to Padre of his people by getting married. Shortly after, his wife Fay gave birth to a boy they called Salvatore, after Bonanno's father. A lot had happened since Bonanno had taken himself away from the Black Shirts in Sicily.

As Italian gangsters died on the streets of New York, so did Fascists. On 30 May 1927 – Memorial Day – a group of fifteen Black Shirts gathered near the stairs of a station on the elevated railway in the Bronx. One of them, 39-year-old Joseph Carisi, a tailor and war veteran, stopped to buy an Italian newspaper. A reporter described what happened next:

> Suddenly two men, wearing flaring red neckties, stepped from a post near the entrance at Turin's restaurant, at 4,423 Third Avenue . . . One of the strangers looked in the direction of Carisi and started running towards him, at the same time pulling a knife from his sleeve.
>
> Carisi had heard the pattering of footsteps and turned just as the long knife blade came into sight. He shouted for help, and as he looked upward to where his companions were approaching the top of the flight of stairs the stranger stabbed him six times. The blows were delivered with lightning speed and were all within a space of inches and around the collarbone.

The other Fascists ran down the stairs to chase the murderer but lost him. Then they heard a shot. Nicholas Amorroso, aged twenty-two, a printer, was a block away when he saw a second stranger run towards him. Before Amorroso could move, the man produced a knife and stabbed him in the chest, just above his heart, but it was not a killing blow. The assassin realised this, pulled a revolver from his hip pocket, and shot Amorroso through the heart. Both Carisi and Amorroso were dead at the scene, as was reported by another newspaper:

> The dual killing may have been a case of mistaken identity. The opposing Italian groups had been bitter for some time. Police believe the plot was engineered to do away with Giacomo Caldora, president of the Fascist organization in the Bronx . . . He was following closely after Amorroso but was untouched by any of the four bullets.

Later that afternoon, more violence erupted in West 45th Street. *The World* reported that one Black Shirt was set upon as he smoked a cigarette outside the Fascist League's headquarters. He called for help and 200 Fascists pounded down the steps of the office to pursue the three red-tie-wearing Socialists across town. 'Across the broad plaza they ran', said the newspaper, 'toward the Hotel Astor, while astonished pedestrians fled for cover before the onrush of whip-waving, yelling Italians. Traffic officers blew their whistles. Motorists clamped brakes.'

Ignazio Thaon di Revel, leader of the Fascist League of North America, responded to the front-page news by saying that the killing of Carisi and Amorroso was not part of a Fascist/anti-Fascist war but was 'simple murder'. His cool reaction was not what Fascists in Italy wanted to hear. They were outraged and even Mussolini telegrammed his US ambassador demanding that measures be taken to control the anti-Fascists. But what should have been a propaganda coup for the Fascists in America turned into a disaster during the following trial. Two anarchists were charged with the murders but Carlo Tresca organised their defence and very effective it was too. One witness stood up and declared: 'I abandoned the Fascist League of North America because it is a nest of criminals, foremost among them being its Presidente Count Ignazio Thaon di Revel.' It was even suggested that the two deaths might have stemmed from in-fighting within the Black Shirts. The anarchists were acquitted.

As a result of the murderous incident, parades of Black Shirts – along with the Ku Klux Klan – were banned by the New York police. Further negative newspaper stories revealed the torn allegiances of American Fascists. Thaon di Revel exacerbated the crisis by claiming that 90 per cent of Italian-Americans were pro-Fascist.

Mussolini was getting angry now. Just as Luciano and Bonanno wanted to step back into the shadows to conduct their criminal business, so Mussolini wanted an end to bad publicity in America. The axe finally fell in December 1929, two days before Christmas. The Fascist League of North America was dissolved. Di Revel went back to Wall Street.

At a time when New Yorkers might be finally breathing a sigh of relief that Fascism no longer seemed a threat to their city – and the Sicilian gangsters seemed to have shot themselves to pieces – then a new menace loomed. It came from northern Europe and was headed by another disaffected war veteran. The Nazis were coming to Manhattan . . .

Chapter Five

Nazis in Manhattan

When the Nazis came to Manhattan, Meyer Lansky was waiting for them. 'My friends and I saw some good action against the Brown Shirts around New York', said the mobster. 'I got my buddies like Bugsy Siegel – before he went to California – and some other young guys. We taught them how to use their fists and handle themselves in fights, and we didn't behave like gents.'

Lansky was a bad enemy to have. Physically unimpressive, just 5 feet 4 inches tall, with a slight build, brown hair and eyes, he had a mean temper and was completely fearless. As a kid on the Lower East Side, he had been picked on by a gang of older Irish boys as he carried a plate of food home for his family. The Irish boys told him to drop his pants to show if he was circumcised. Lansky rammed the plate at the bigger boy and nearly killed him with the jagged edge of broken china. By the time the fight was broken up, the Jewish boy was covered in blood but unbeaten.

Lucky Luciano lived in the same part of town as Lansky and remembered trying to shake down the little Jew for protection money:

> I was about a head taller than this midget, but he looked up at me without blinkin' an eye, with nothin' but guts showin' in his face, and he said, 'Fuck you.' Well, I started to laugh. I patted him on the shoulder and said, 'Okay, you got protection for free.' He just pulled away and yelled, 'Shove your protection up your ass, I don't need it!' Believe me, I found out he didn't need it. Next to Benny Siegel, Meyer Lansky was the toughest guy, pound for pound, I ever knew in my whole life . . .

It was the beginning of a profitable relationship. By the time he was thirty, Lansky had established a stolen car ring supplying trucks to criminals, graduated to leading his own gang of enforcers, been charged with murder several times, set up a major bootleg organisation smuggling in liquor from Canada, and brought together the first national gangster gathering at Atlantic City. Respected for his intelligence as much as his guts, Lansky was a key member of Luciano's underworld empire.

Since coming out on top at the end of the Castellammarese War in 1931, Lucky Luciano and his associates had entered a boom time of crime. They dominated prostitution, narcotics, loan-sharking, gambling and labour rackets throughout New York. Even when Prohibition came to an end in 1933, they moved from bootlegging into controlling the legitimate import of whiskey.

Luciano's preference was to drop the whole Mafia infrastructure as designed by Maranzano. He preferred a much looser, less pretentious association of independent outfits, but Lansky persuaded him to keep it going as it provided an ethnic power base to fight off other ethnically-based gangs. The reality was that Jewish gangsters probably outnumbered the Italian Mafia at the time.

Lansky brought together many Jewish gangs at a meeting at the Franconia Hotel in Manhattan in November 1931. Aside from his crime partner, Bugsy Siegel, they included Louis Lepke, Joseph 'Doc' Stacher, Harry 'Big Greenie' Greenberg, Hyman 'Curly' Holtz, Harry Teitelbaum, and Lewis 'Shadows' Kravitz, all them major players in the underworld. All these gangsters agreed to respect each other's territories and form a national crime syndicate along with the Italians. Or, as Bugsy Siegel reputedly put it: 'The yids and the dagos would no longer fight each other.'

Lansky managed to keep a low profile throughout the 1930s, but Luciano was more flamboyant and became the face of organised crime in New York. This attracted the attention of an ambitious young lawyer called Thomas E. Dewey. Aged just twenty-eight in 1931, Dewey took up the post of Chief Assistant United States Attorney. He was the youngest man to hold the post. His baby-face did not help and he grew a moustache to give himself some maturity. He now headed a Federal Government office of sixty lawyers. With such an effective machine to call on, he switched from prosecuting Wall Street criminals to gangsters.

Dewey's first target was Dutch Schultz, a hot-headed hoodlum who ran the numbers game in Harlem. Dutch Schultz had Mad Dog Coll gunned down – the man who was going to kill Luciano for Maranzano. When Dewey went after Schultz, closing down his operations, Schultz swore to put a hit on the prosecutor. Luciano and Lansky considered this the last thing they needed – the heat would be too much for their criminal enterprises. Instead, they decided to hit Schultz and he was shot down in the toilet of the New Jersey Palace Chop House. Dewey would know nothing about his narrow escape from assassination – all thanks to Luciano's intervention. Instead, Dewey made his intentions clear:

> Today crime is syndicated and organized. A new type of criminal exists who leaves to his hirelings and front-men the actual offences and rarely commits an overt act himself. The only way in which the major criminal can be punished is by connecting to him those various layers of subordinates and the related but separate crimes on their behalf.

This was his justification for the introduction of the so-called Dewey Law, which allowed the connecting of similar offences in one single indictment with a significantly heavier sentence. When Dewey went after Luciano in 1936, he nailed him for prostitution along with eight other gang members. Straight after the trial, the Special Prosecutor revealed his true agenda to the *New York Times*:

> This, of course, was not a vice trial. It was a racket prosecution. The control of all organized prostitution in New York by the convicted defendants was one of their lesser rackets. The four bookers of women who pleaded guilty were underlings. The prostitution racket was merely the vehicle by which these men were convicted.
>
> It is my understanding that certain of the top-ranking defendants in this case, together with the other criminals under [Luciano], have gradually absorbed control of the narcotic, policy, loan shark and Italian lottery syndicates, the receipt of stolen goods and certain industrial rackets.

Luciano was sentenced to an unprecedented 30–50 years behind bars. It was a tremendous blow to organised crime in New York and turned Dewey into a crime-busting celebrity. With this major triumph under his belt, he soon graduated to a political career. Dewey became Governor of New York in 1943 and stood as Republican candidate for President in 1944 and 1948.

Amazingly, Lansky had managed to avoid Dewey's assault and it was left to him and Frank Costello, originally from Calabria in south-west Italy, to run Luciano's underworld business on the outside during the late 1930s and early 1940s. They would visit him in jail on a regular basis and take back his orders to the rest of their organisation.

For the first few weeks, life was grim in Clinton State Prison at Dannemora in upstate New York, near the Canadian border – 'Little Siberia'. Luciano initial work placement was in the laundry room, but then he started to use his influence. 'After a few weeks I found where to spread the dough around', he recalled. 'Pretty soon I was up in the library, where it was clean, quiet and I could so some real thinkin' and plannin'.'

It was Lansky who later claimed to have set up the secret alliance between Luciano and US Naval Intelligence. He knew that Italian-American Fascist sympathies in the docks could prove a weak point for America when war came to Europe. He was speaking for Luciano as well when he said:

> We both knew that when Mussolini went into the war some of the Italians in America were proud. They were second-class citizens in America – to be poor you're automatically second class. It was very important for them that Mussolini was winning. It gave them pride. Even if he was a friend of Hitler they did not care. This was a small minority of the Italian-Americans, you understand, but they did exist – and a few others were terrorized by Fascist agents.

For Lansky it was all part of the same war:

> The reason why I cooperated [with the US government] was because of strong personal convictions. I wanted the Nazis beaten. I made this my number one priority even before the United States got into the war. I was a Jew and I felt for those Jews in Europe who were suffering. They were my brothers.

Lansky's family knew all about Old World anti-Semitism. They had fled from it in 1911 when they left Grodno (now in Belarus but then part of the Russian Empire), to escape pogroms inflicted on their people. There, he had been born Maier Suchowljansky. His name was later Americanised at school in Manhattan.

When the Nazis came to New York in the 1930s, Lansky was not going to run before them.

Whereas Italian-American Fascist organisations had been most active in the 1920s, it was not until 1933, when Adolf Hitler finally became Chancellor of Germany, that a major Nazi presence was established in America. In July 1933, the German-American Bund was created out of the remnants of previous German-American societies. It had three main branches or 'Gau': one in Milwaukee, one in Los Angeles, and a third in New York City under the command of Fritz Kuhn, a former employee of the Ford Motor Company in Detroit.

Henry Ford himself was a prominent anti-Semite and Adolf Hitler took inspiration from him in the 1920s, even referring to him in *Mein Kampf*: 'Every year makes them [American Jews] more and more the controlling masters of the producers in a nation of one hundred and twenty millions; only a single great man, Ford, to their fury, still maintains full independence.' The support of establishment people like Ford really worried Lansky. 'Important WASPs', he said, 'as we would call them now, openly made anti-Semitic statements and some magazines and papers backed them.' In July 1938, Henry Ford was awarded the Grand Cross of the German Eagle by the German Vice-Consul in Detroit. It was the highest honour Hitler could bestow on a foreigner.

The dictator regretted the departure of so many Germans to America and was happy to fund Nazi organisations on American soil. Over dinner on 6 August 1942, Hitler proclaimed: 'Our country today is overpopulated, and yet the numbers who emigrated to America are incredible. How I wish we had the German-Americans with us still! In so far as there are any decent people in America, they are all of German origin.'

The Gaue of the German-American Bund were divided into ninety-three local organisations called 'Ortsgruppen'. The US Department of Justice estimated that there were 8,000 German-American members of the Bund, but this may have risen to 100,000, while another source claims the Nazis had a mailing list of 250,000 German-Americans with relatives in the Third Reich. The Bund published four weekly German-language newspapers, ran German language schools, and even raised several divisions of Hitler Youth who paraded at their twenty-two camps. At Camp Hindenburg, near Buffalo, a Bund parade was reviewed by the German Ambassador Hans Dieckhoff in August 1937.

A typical recruiting ground for the Bund was recalled by Arlene Stein, who was a child in the 1930s:

> Ridgewood was primarily a German neighborhood and some customs from the Old Country were still practiced. A ritual of cleaning took place every Saturday morning. Homeowners or janitors would clean the halls and stairs, scrub the front stoop and sweep the sidewalk to the curb . . . These were hard-working, law-abiding people with virtues of cleanliness, discipline, thriftiness and honesty.

But then the mood changed, as Stein remembered:

> There was a house on St Nicholas Avenue that people spoke of in whispers. The shades were almost always pulled down. On a few occasions the shades were up and on the far wall was a well-lit picture of Adolf Hitler. This was the late 1930s. Our country was not at war yet, but it was evident that the problems of Europe would eventually effect the USA.
>
> It was to the dismay of most German-Americans that Nazi Bund meetings were taking place right in our neighborhood. Bund members were mostly young men and women in their teens and twenties who dressed in uniform, white blouses and shirts/black skirts and trousers, with a black hat with a red symbol.

By March 1936, Fritz Kuhn had taken over leadership of the Bund. His movement had grown in ambition and he campaigned on behalf of Alfred Landon, the Republican candidate for President. He spoke on the radio alongside Dr Ignatz Griebl, leader of the Friends of New Germany and a Nazi spy. The Bund also campaigned for a senator and a member of Congress. In October 1937, a massive rally was held at Madison Square Garden when 1,150 uniformed Bund stormtroopers marched to the sound of the Nazi beat.

Such activities greatly worried the Jewish community in New York and Meyer Lansky was contacted by two of its prominent members. Rabbi Stephen Wise asked him to do something about the dangerous trend. Even an upholder of the law, New York state judge Nathan Perlman, turned to Lansky for help in 1935. He said to Lansky:

> Nazism is flourishing in the United States. The Bund members are not ashamed to have their meetings in the most public places. We Jews should be more militant. Meyer, we

> want to take action against these Nazi sympathizers. We'll put money and legal assistance at your disposal, whatever you need. Can you organise the militant part for us?

So even here, at this early stage, there was the offer of a secret alliance between a part of the US establishment and the underworld. 'I'll fight these Nazis with my own resources', replied Lansky. 'I don't need your cash. But I will ask you one thing, that after we go into action you'll try to make sure the Jewish press don't criticize me.'

In return for breaking up Bund rallies, but not actually killing Bund members – a disappointing constraint for the gangster – Lansky received from Perlman the names of leading Bund activists and the locations of their meetings. Even Walter Winchell, the legendary reporter and broadcaster (and early critic of Hitler), got in on the act, telephoning an address of a Bund meeting to Lansky.

On one night, Lansky went to Yorkville, the heart of the German community in Manhattan, with Siegel and other Jewish gangsters at his side:

> We got there that evening and found several hundred people dressed in their brown shirts. The stage was decorated with a swastika and pictures of Hitler. The speakers started ranting. There were only about fifteen of us, but we went into action.
>
> We attacked them in the hall and threw some of them out the windows. There were fist fights all over the place. Most of the Nazis panicked and ran out. We chased them and beat them up, and some of them were out of action for months. Yes, it was violence. We wanted to teach them a lesson. We wanted to show them that Jews would not always sit back and accept insults.

Judge Perlman, Rabbi Wise, and Winchell were all delighted with the results. But it was just the start of Lansky's personal campaign against East Coast Nazis. He led raids on them throughout New York and New Jersey. Even his Italian mobster friends wanted to get in on the action, said Lansky:

> The Italians I knew offered to help, but as a matter of pride I wouldn't accept. I neglected my business many times to travel around and organize our counterattacks. I must say I enjoyed beating up those Nazis. There were times when we treated a Bund leader or other big anti-Semite in a very special way, but

> the main point was just to teach them that Jews couldn't be kicked around.

New York newspapers reported one such battle in Yorkville Casino in April 1938. The Bund was celebrating Hitler's forty-ninth birthday at 210 East 86th Street when trouble broke out inside the casino. Several Bund speakers were lined up for the evening, including the wife of Fritz Kuhn, but it was an Otto Wegener who ignited the action. He congratulated Hitler on his seizure of Austria and demanded that President Roosevelt accept the *Anschluss*. At that point a man rose in the audience and shouted: 'Is this an American or a German meeting?' The man was 39-year-old war veteran Jean Mathias.

'At that moment,' reported the *New York Herald Tribune*, 'someone slugged him from behind. He turned on his assailant and began to grapple as American war veterans swarmed to his assistance.' Uniformed 'Storm Troopers' surged forward and whipped Mathias with Sam Browne belts pulled from their uniforms. In retaliation, a hundred Jewish war veterans stood up and donned the blue overseas caps of American Legionnaires before joining the fight. Bund chairman Gustave Elmer tried to calm the audience by ordering the band to play, but this only provided a weird soundtrack to the events. Witnesses spoke of 'gray-shirted arms rising and falling, wielding blackjacks . . . The Storm Troopers [then] took off their belts, equipped with heavy buckles, and swung these as weapons . . .' As Mathias fought his way to the exit, he was hit with a chair and had multiple contusions on the face.

The Jewish protesters were eventually thrown out of the casino by Storm Troopers. Outside, they faced a large group of pickets made up of members of the German-American Workers Club and Young Patriots of the USA. Opposite them, on the north sidewalk, was a crowd of anti-Nazi protestors getting angrier by the minute. When they saw the bloodied faces of the Jewish war veterans, they pushed forward, wanting to get into the hall. A detail of twenty-four policemen had to hold them back, but fighting broke out on the street. When Bund members later tried to leave the hall, the angry crowd charged at them too. The police captain had to call up an extra fifty policemen to clear the street.

Among the four people arrested was Otto Geisler, of 302 East 91st Street, a seventeen-year-old German-American wearing a Nazi uniform, charged with carrying a dagger on his belt, and Jack Caback, 42, a Jewish war veteran, of 334 East 86th Street, charged with disorderly conduct in connection with fighting outside the casino.

Max Hinkes was an associate of New Jersey mobster 'Longy' Zwillman and he joined a Newark Jewish resistance group called the 'Minutemen'. They attacked a Bund meeting at Schwabben Hall on Springfield Avenue in a German neighbourhood of Newark. Hinkes recalled:

> The Nazi scumbags were meeting one night on the second floor. Nat Arno and I went upstairs and threw stink bombs into the room where the creeps were. As they came out of the room, running from the horrible odor of the stink bombs and running down the steps in to the street to escape, our boys were waiting with bats and iron bars. It was like running a gauntlet.
>
> Our boys were lined up on both sides and we started hitting, aiming for their heads or any other part of their bodies, with our bats and irons. The Nazis were screaming blue murder. This was one of the most happy moments of my life.

Even the Jewish-Italian-American Mayor of New York, Fiorello La Guardia, waded into the action. At a lunch for the American Jewish Congress, Mayor La Guardia told the audience he would like to see a 'chamber of horrors' at the forthcoming New York World's Fair with a 'figure of that brown-shirted fanatic who is now menacing the peace of the world'. The German Embassy protested most strongly at this insult to their Führer and a German newspaper *Angriff* inflamed the situation by calling La Guardia a 'Jewish ruffian' and 'New York gangster-in-chief' who is 'a protector of New York gangsters and everything vile and detestable . . .'

Although secretly pleased to see the Bund being given a tough time by Lansky and his gangsters, the Jewish establishment did not deliver on their promise to let up on their criticism of him in the press. Even the biggest Yiddish newspaper, the *Morgen Journal*, condemned him as a Jewish gangster, while other Jewish papers referred to the mob of Lansky and Bugsy Siegel. This was a shock for Lansky as he had never been publicly labelled a gangster. When this was picked up by the wider press and radio, Lansky argued with the journalists, but they said if it was good enough for Jewish reporters to use that term then it was good enough for them.

Lansky was getting uncomfortable with all the publicity and so was the Jewish establishment. 'One day we got a message from Rabbi Wise to stop our activity – people were saying it was morally wrong to use the same violence the Nazis were using.' So Lansky stopped, but the damage to him had already been done. 'I really think our action against the Bund created an atmosphere in which my name was easily connected with gangsterism and the Mafia.'

Lansky still believed in the righteousness of his cause, but he would pursue his campaign against Nazis and Fascists in a more discreet way. When war broke out, he was ready to broker a deal between Luciano and US Naval Intelligence.

Lansky's reluctant ceasefire with the Nazis of New York coincided with the decline of the Bund. The German government had already withdrawn its funding from the Bund following its Madison Square rally in October 1937. The event was embarrassing and they wished to pursue more subtle ways of manipulating American support for Hitler.

Undeterred, Fritz Kuhn pressed on with another impressive mass rally at Madison Square Garden on February 1939 to celebrate Washington's Birthday. It was attended by some 22,000 supporters. By the end of the year, however, he had been jailed for larceny, having siphoned off large amounts of money from the Bund to his own personal accounts. The following year pro-Fascist leader Edward James Smythe was trying to fix up an alliance between the Bund and the Ku Klux Klan, but this came to nothing, and Smythe was eventually charged with sedition before fleeing to Canada.

While Meyer Lansky had been told to cool it on the streets of Manhattan, Dr Hans Thomsen, German Chargé d'Affaires in Washington DC, had been trying to calm Nazi activities in America. Mass Nazi-style rallies only embarrassed Germany and when these were accompanied by street riots it alienated American supporters. Financial support had already been withdrawn from the Bund and Thomsen sought far more sophisticated methods of influence.

By the summer of 1940, with Europe at war, Thomsen could see that the pro-isolationist camp in America was losing ground. The German diplomat recommended that a 'well-camouflaged lightning propaganda campaign might well prove useful, for which there are the following possibilities where German influence would in no case be visible to the outside.'

These included a well-known Republican congressman gathering the support of fifty isolationist fellow Republican congressmen. They formed a committee to take out a full-page advert in all leading US newspapers saying 'Keep America out of War'. For this, Thomsen recommended Nazi Germany provide $43,000 of funding to the isolationist Republicans involved.

On a similar tack, Thomsen made contact with top American literary agency William C. Lengel to commission five books drawing public attention in America to the 'dangers of intervention'. The five authors included left-wing writer Theodore Dreiser and best-selling novelist and pacifist Kathleen Norris. 'None of the authors knows', said Thomsen, 'who is behind the publisher's offer'. For this project, he needed $20,000 of Nazi funding.

Above all, Thomsen did not want to see any crude attempts at sabotage on US territory:

> Please inform the Brigadeführer [he told the German Foreign Ministry in Berlin] that in the interest of keeping the USA out of the war it is absolutely necessary that no activity should develop here. Otherwise, owing to the incalculable mentality of the American people, irreparable damage can be caused to the German conduct of war. It is proposed that confidential agents in so far as they are not engaged purely in collecting information, be withdrawn. The Wehrmacht has been similarly informed.

In a later telegram, Thomsen was annoyed to note that the Wehrmacht had ignored his warning and had an agent active in the United States:

> The agent von Hausberger who has been trained in Germany in the use of all kinds of explosives is again receiving orders via Portugal from Major Osten instructing him to establish contact with American citizens of German descent, whose names have been given to him, and to train them successfully as saboteurs.

Thomsen feared that the circle of people this agent was contacting was becoming wider and:

> Thus the danger of being unmasked is constantly increasing . . . I cannot warn too urgently against this method. The example of 1917 shows that American public opinion was incited to war far less by German submarine warfare than by alleged and actual cases of sabotage.

The example referred to by Thomsen was the assault on American economic targets sanctioned by Franz von Papen, German military attaché in Washington during World War I. Because American industry was producing arms and munitions for the British and French during World War I, it was regarded as a legitimate target by German embassy officials long before the US actually entered the war. In April 1915, Berlin sent a naval reserve officer, Franz von Rintelen, with specific instructions to disrupt the Allied war effort. He identified the New York docks as the weak link in the supply chain, and soon recruited longshoremen to plant explosives on Allied ships. These caused mysterious fires and sinkings once the ships were at sea.

The plot was revealed when von Rintelen returned to Germany disguised as a Swiss businessman. His ship anchored at Falmouth, England, and von Rintelen was detained by British counter-intelligence. Von Papen and other German embassy officials were expelled from the US in December 1915, but acts of sabotage continued. The most spectacular came in July 1916, when ammunition freight cars and barges exploded at the Black Tom Island terminal in New York harbour, causing $14 million worth of damage – a staggering amount at the time. It was a devastating demonstration of what German spies could achieve on the American mainland. It was a threat not to be forgotten by US defence authorities.

Hans Thomsen was not the only person to fear a repeat of German sabotage on American soil. While the German Chargé d'Affaires sent his cautionary telegrams to the German Foreign Ministry, the Federal Bureau of Investigation was already on the look out for Nazi agents of destruction on the East Coast. With J. Edgar Hoover at its head, the FBI had been secretly authorised by President Roosevelt to gather information on German supporters within the United States. Its agents had infiltrated the activities of the German-American Bund and other pro-Nazi associations.

In the summer of 1940, the FBI got its first major break. It involved William G. Sebold. Born in Germany, he had fought in World War I in the German Army, but he left the country in 1921 to work in aircraft manufacturing plants in the USA and South America. On 10 February 1936, Sebold became a naturalised citizen of the United States. He then returned to Germany in February 1939 to visit his mother. While in Hamburg, he was approached by a Gestapo agent, who knew about a previous police record he had in Germany. This was followed up by a meeting with a Dr Gassner, a member of the German armed forces secret service – the Abwehr – in Mülheim in September 1939. He wanted to know everything that Sebold knew about US military planes and equipment. Gassner then asked the German-American to spy for the Third Reich in the United States.

Because Sebold feared that his family might be punished if he did not co-operate, he told the Abwehr that he would become an agent for them. But first he had to replace his US passport. When he went to the American Consulate in Cologne, he secretly told them about his predicament and said he wished to cooperate with the FBI on his return to America. They advised him to carry on with his training as a Nazi agent.

When Sebold's German secret service handlers thought he was ready, they gave him five sheets of microfilm containing instructions on how to send coded messages from the US back to Germany. He was meant to pass on three of the microfilms to other agents active in the United States. Finally, given the false name of 'Harry Sawyer', he sailed for New York in February 1940.

Informed of Sebold's arrival, the Federal Bureau of Investigation wasted no time in setting up 'Sawyer' with a business cover as a consultant diesel engineer. They gave him an office on Broadway and 42nd Street which was monitored by concealed cameras so they could see exactly who was coming and going as he established contact with several German agents. A key figure was Frederick J. Duquesne, a Boer from South Africa who hated the British and whose espionage career stretched back to World War I.

Duquesne operated a business known as the Air Terminals Company and he established contact with Sebold in New York City. In their first meeting, Duquesne was wary of FBI surveillance and they ended talking in an automat. Feeling more confident, Duquesne then provided Sebold with information about US national defence and technology, including photographs and specifications of a new type of bomb. Duquesne claimed some of this information came from secretly entering the DuPont plant in Wilmington, Delaware, but other data was gained by innocently pretending to be a student wanting to know more about a particular industrial process. Duquesne was also interested in industrial sabotage and discussed starting fires in factories. He even suggested turning candy-coated gum into miniature bombs. Much of this seditious talk was captured on film by the FBI.

The switch from information-gathering to sabotage alarmed the FBI and in June 1941 they swooped on Duquesne and thirty-two other

Nazi spies. In the subsequent high-profile trial in the Federal District Court, Brooklyn, New York, September–December 1941, the hours of FBI film shot in Sebold's fake office proved decisive evidence. J. Edgar Hoover himself provided the soundtrack:

> That's Heinrich Clausing, a cook on the liner *Argentina*. Clausing's work was to act as courier, carrying military information. The important-looking man is Hartwig Kleiss, who worked for the United States line as a cook. The money Kleiss is giving to Sawyer [Sebold] is for the purchase of a Leica camera to be used in his activities as a spy. In these pictures Kleiss has brought to Sawyer the blueprints of the steam ship *America*, showing the plans of her secret gun emplacements. There's Duquesne again, the leader of the ring and the most cautious of them all.

The thirty-three defendants were sentenced to a total of more than 300 years in prison. Duquesne was sentenced to eighteen years for espionage, plus a two-year concurrent sentence and $2,000 fine for violation of the Registration Act.

The convictions ended the activity of the largest single spy ring in US history, but it also sent a chill through the heart of the US defence establishment: twenty-five of the thirty-three convicted spies were naturalised American citizens. If German-Americans could be involved in this, what about Italian-Americans still loyal to Mussolini?

That many New Yorkers still supported the Fascist dictator had been underlined by a Columbus Day meeting on 13 October 1938. There, 35,000 New Yorkers booed Mayor La Guardia and cheered Mussolini.

> The gathering was definitely sympathetic toward the Fascist regime in Italy [said a newspaper report], shouting 'Viva Mussolini!' when a speaker praised the Italian dictator for his recent intervention for world peace.

The sensational trial of the Duquesne spy ring was what Hans Thomsen feared most. The American public now clearly knew their enemy was Nazi Germany, but it was too late anyway for Thomsen and his strategy of support for American isolationism.

Before the Duquesne trial had even come to an end, America was at war with the Third Reich. Four days after the Japanese attack on Pearl Harbor on 7 December 1941, Hitler declared war on America. It was up to Thomsen to deliver the news.

At 8.00 a.m. on 11 December, the German diplomat walked out of his red-bricked embassy in Washington DC carrying Germany's declaration to Secretary of State Cordell Hull. When Thomsen arrived, he was told that Hull was 'engaged' and he had glumly to hand the note to the Chief of the European Division. All Thomsen's efforts to keep America out of the war had come to nothing.

Later that day, Benito Mussolini joined his Axis comrade and also declared war on the USA.

With America officially at war with Germany, Italy and Japan, there was now a desperate race to prevent any further pre-emptive attacks. This time, on the Eastern seaboard.

Intriguingly, one of the foreign agents associated with the Duquesne spy ring and caught on film was Lieutenant-Commander Takeo Ezima of the Japanese Navy. A *New York Times* report later claimed that a 'Japanese agent was linked with the Nazi spy ring broken up in June, 1941, but that he escaped.' Acting under the cover of an engineer inspector called Satoz, he had agreed to ship samples of American war material to Germany on a more secure route via Japan. 'Ezima's program', said the report, 'outlined to the spies, was for a four-day run to the West Coast, where the materiel would be picked up every two weeks by boats sailing for Japan.' But as the FBI was arresting the spies, Ezima quietly left New York for the West Coast, boarded the Japanese freighter *Kamakura-Maru* and went home.

Such stories heightened a sense of imminent crisis faced by the US government as it looked to defending its homeland from a combined foreign assault. It did not help matters when several mysterious fires broke out along the waterfront in New York. The worst occurred on the morning of 9 January 1942, destroying Municipal Pier 83 and two buildings at 43rd Street and the Hudson River. The cause of the fire was later said to be an accident, but it was a worrying development and US defence agencies were keen to deal with anyone of influence who could help.

Lieutenant Commander Charles Radcliffe Haffenden was put in charge of the Third Naval District's investigations section, based at 50 Church Street in downtown Manhattan. Haffenden told a naval aide:

> I'll talk to anybody, a priest, a bank manager, a gangster, the devil himself, if I can get the information I need. This is a war. American lives are at stake. It's not a college game where we have to look up the rule book every minute, and we're not

> running a headquarters office where regulations must be followed to the letter. I have a job to do.

The initial attempts of Naval Intelligence to get a grip on the security situation on the New York docks were unimpressive, however. 'Everybody in New York', recalled mobster Meyer Lansky, 'was laughing at the way those naïve Navy agents were going around the docks. They went up to men working in the area and talked out of the corner of their mouths like they had seen in the movies, asking about spies.' Lucky Luciano was even less impressed. 'As far as Haffenden was concerned', he said, 'he didn't know nothin' that was goin' on except that he was sittin' there with his mouth open, prayin' I would say yes and help his whole department . . .'

It would take a spectacular disaster to get both sides talking seriously about protecting America's East Coast. That happened on the afternoon of 9 February 1942 when the *Normandie*, a luxury ocean liner turned troopship, burst into flames. Some 1,500 sailors and civilian workers fled the burning vessel. By the next day it was a smoking hulk. It was a bitter blow to the American war effort – but it pushed Lucky Luciano, Meyer Lansky, and the defense agencies together. A secret alliance between the New York underworld and the US government was about to be forged.

Chapter Six

Death of the *Normandie*

At 2.30 p.m. on 9 February 1942, fire broke out on the *Normandie*, anchored at Pier 88 in New York Harbor. Emergency vehicles rushed to the pier at the end of West 48th Street. As more and more assembled to help extinguish the fire, it soon became the biggest gathering of emergency services on American soil since the war had begun. There was a lot at stake.

The *Normandie* had just been converted to a troop carrier and was ready to take 10,000 American troops at a time across the Atlantic to wartime Britain. This would be a major contribution to the war effort and there were many – especially the Nazis – who would like to see the ship destroyed.

The *Normandie* had been launched ten years earlier at St Nazaire in France as a luxury ocean liner. She was the first great ocean liner to exceed 1,000 feet in length and Pier 88 had been especially constructed to make room for her. Her remarkable dimensions were matched by the elegance and luxury of her Art Deco interior. The wealthy and famous chose to travel with her, including movie stars Mary Pickford and Bob Hope.

Not only was she beautiful, she was also fast. The *Normandie* won the Blue Riband for crossing the Atlantic in just four days and three hours. Her speed and capacity made the ship a useful maritime asset and when the war came her luxury voyages came to a halt. Her French-owners feared for her safety as German U-boats began to prowl the Atlantic and she was 'mothballed' at New York's Pier 88. For over a year, the ship's owners maintained a skeleton crew to look after her. But, following the fall of France in June 1940, as the new Vichy French government collaborated with Germany, President Roosevelt acted decisively. The *Normandie* was a key French asset in his hands. He ordered the US Coastguard to board the liner in May 1941 and placed her under protective custody.

Just seven months later, Japan launched the pre-emptive strike at Pearl Harbor. Four days after that, Hitler declared war on the United States, along with Italian dictator Benito Mussolini. Hitler stood up in the Reichstag and vowed: 'We will always strike first! We will always deal the first blow!' Hitler immediately began to select potential targets for attack along the East Coast. The *Normandie* was at the top of the list. If the Japanese could strike at Pearl Harbor, then Nazi Germany would hit New York.

With America at war, the US Navy took over the *Normandie* and renamed her the *Lafayette*, after the French hero who helped the Americans during the Revolutionary War. She was repainted naval grey and a small army of dockworkers was put to work converting her into a troopship. Completion was set for 28 February 1942, when she would set sail for Boston to pick up her first cargo of troops to take to Britain.

It was a tight deadline and naval workers worked around the clock to meet it – until fire broke out on board the ship on the 9th. Some 1,500 sailors and civilians were on board when the fire started but most were quickly evacuated. A least 128 were injured, many suffering from smoke inhalation, and one died from his injuries – 38-year-old Frank Trentacosta of Brooklyn. Many escaped thanks to a precarious 85-foot firemen's extension ladder stretching from the West Side Express highway to the bow of the liner.

Thousands of New Yorkers came down to the dockside to watch the events unfold. A massive pall of smoke blew over Manhattan, leaving a smoke haze as far away as Times Square. Mayor La Guardia came down to the pier, stepping over the tangle of hoses, and said: 'The chief's got his fire out and now the naval people will watch the ship. It's very tender – see how she has listed – and now the job is to pump the water out and that's what we're doing.'

By 8.00 p.m. that evening, it was believed the emergency services had brought the fire under control. The fire had been restricted to the upper three decks and had caused only slight damage to the whole vessel. But fighting the flames had involved fireships pouring streams of water into the liner and this had caused her to list to one side. At first, it was not considered a problem, but by midnight, Rear Admiral Adolphus R. Andrews ordered the complete evacuation of the ship.

'Admiral Andrews has ordered all hands to leave the ship', blared loudspeakers on Pier 88. He then quickly issued a statement, lessening the dramatic impact of this order. 'The Admiral has ordered all hands off the ship as a safety precaution', it said. 'It does not mean that the ship has been abandoned or hope given up but no one can be certain what the reaction of the ship will be to the flood tide.'

Two small gangways crashed into the water as the liner slowly tilted further. Sailors stood by with ropes to make any last-minute rescues. Observers could hear objects sliding inside the ship, clattering down the decks towards the rails.

> The general scene was one of a war catastrophe [said the *New York Herald Tribune*]. The American Women's Voluntary Services and the Red Cross each rushed two large mobile kitchens to the scene to serve hot coffee to the rescued and the rescuers, many of whom were chilled to the bone from the ice-cold spray from fire hoses.

Then, at 2.35 a.m., as searchlights shone on her great hulk, the *Normandie* slid over in fifty feet of water and mud, with remarkably little noise, on to her port side. The great funnels of the ship halted just three feet above the surface of the water. At 3.00 a.m., a second fire was seen to leap from a point behind the rear funnel. A fireboat pressed forward to pour yet more water into the ship and extinguished it within an hour.

As the sun rose on the grey hulk, it was a sad sight for all to see. The *New York Times* reporter on the scene noted that where the navy grey paint had 'cracked and blistered away, it revealed the black and red of the pre-war *Normandie* – the only touch of the ship that was, in a setting for which she never had been built.' Less than two months after Hitler declared he would strike first against America, one of the Allies' biggest troopships was wrecked. It seemed the Nazis had claimed a major victory – but any talk of sabotage was immediately dismissed.

The following day, the naval authorities seemed pretty clear about what had caused the disastrous fire. Edward J. Sullivan of Greenwich Village was on board as a friend of a carpet manufacturer given a contract for refitting the ship. He saw the fire start:

> It happened in the grand salon on the promenade deck. One of the men had an acetylene torch. He was cutting down some decorative steel work. Another fellow was holding a shield for the sparks – it was about two by three feet. In the

> background were stacked some bales of what appeared to be excelsior [wood shavings used for packing]. The sparks were flying but they'd hit the shield and bounced back.

The workman then turned off the torch, but some of the sparks from the last shower got round the shield. One of the men yelled 'fire' as the flames ignited the bales. In a flash, the fire leapt up the stack to the ceiling.

Navy Lieutenant Henry Wood took charge of extinguishing the fire, but he did not have any water hose to hand. It was a full eleven minutes before the emergency services were called. By then, none of the crew or workmen could do anything about putting out the fire. Along with the fire-fighters and police, FBI agents and a sabotage investigation squad were on the scene. Rear Admiral Andrews backed up Sullivan's view of what started the fire:

> The fire was started by sparks from a blowtorch of a worker in the grand salon. The sparks ignited the wrapping of a life preserver. The hoses were let out but the fire spread rapidly and within a few minutes there was so much smoke that the men in the compartments had to get out.
>
> Due to the list of the ship it was thought better at first to sink her, that is, to open the sluice valves and let the seawater in. She was not very far from the bottom and it was thought best to give her enough weight to put her on the bottom. It was later decided, on the advice of technical experts, not to sink her. Instead water was pumped into the starboard side amidships.

Despite the appearance of having controlled the destruction of the liner, the result was that America's greatest troopship was out of action – and would remain so for the rest of the war. She was sold for scrap in 1946. That was a $56 million naval asset wiped out.

Journalists asked Andrews whether the fire was the result of sabotage. 'I can only repeat', he said, 'that, as far as I know, the fire started in the grand salon and I have no knowledge that it broke out, as has been reported by newspaper men, in three or four places at once.'

The government investigation that followed reinforced the official navy version of events. The FBI and New York District Attorney Frank S. Hogan worked with a team of twenty assistants to question over seventy witnesses. A navy court of inquiry was established under Rear Admiral Lamar R. Leahy. The final report concluded that the burning of the *Normandie* was caused by civilian incompetence. It pointed the finger at a stray spark from a workman's acetylene torch setting alight a nearby pile of life preservers. But it was the action of the fireboats that was the fatal error. So much water was poured into the top decks that it made the ship top-heavy. Pumping machines could not remove the water quickly enough and the ship rolled over onto her port side. Frank Hogan put it succinctly: 'Carelessness has served the enemy with equal effectiveness.'

That was the official government report, but many people refused to believe it. The fire was too intense to be an accident. The *Normandie* was a major target for enemy action. Many suspected it was the work of Nazi saboteurs. But could they achieve such a blow against the US?

German spy penetration of the New York docks went back to World War I and Franz von Rintelen's string of attacks. The FBI's round-up of the Duquesne spy ring demonstrated that German saboteurs were back in town just months before the burning of the *Normandie*. It is possible that a renegade spy could have escaped the mass arrests and set fire to the troopship as a final act of defiance in line with Nazi wishes. It is also possible that there were other unidentified spy rings operating in New York. Maybe FBI surveillance was not as perfect as it was represented and it had missed some vital agents. Certainly, the breaking of the Duquesne spy ring was not the end of German spy activity in America.

In May 1942, less than four months after the burning of the *Normandie*, two German U-boats set sail from France to America. On board were two teams of highly trained saboteurs – Germans who had lived in America before the war. Their mission was to strike at crucial American industrial infrastructure. It was Operation Pastorius, named after Franz Daniel Pastorius, the sixteenth-century leader of the first immigrant Germans to the United States.

The chief instigator of this operation was Adolf Hitler himself. He was furious at the arrest of the Duquesne spy ring and his anger rose when he was told by Admiral Wilhelm Canaris, head of the Abwehr, that there were no other Nazi secret service agents operating in the United States. Hitler's response was to order another immediate sabotage mission to the US. Canaris personally did not favour such an operation, preferring his agents to carry out espionage, but Hitler insisted on sabotage.

Colonel Erwin von Lahousen oversaw the operation. 'The German Admiralty staff', wrote Lahousen in his war diary for the middle of April 1942, 'had indicated that it is prepared to land our agents from U-boats on the eastern coast of the United States. The aim of the operation is to strike at one of the main bottlenecks in the American war economy, to sabotage the US production of aluminum.'

Later, the targets were widened to include factories, railways and the Hell's Gate Bridge across New York harbour. Eight agents were recruited for the mission. One team of four saboteurs was led by Georg Dasch, a German-American who had served briefly in the US Army, and the other was headed by Eduard Kerling, a keen member of the Bund.

The first U-boat to reach the American coast was *U-202* on 13 June. Its team of Nazi saboteurs came ashore three miles east of its target beach on Long Island at Amagansett. While three of them began burying their crates of explosive, their leader, Dasch, bumped into a US coastguard. Dasch kept his cool and the US coastguard presumed he had stumbled on a secret American operation. Dasch handed him a $100 note. The coastguard took the money, saluted, and disappeared into the mist.

The second German submarine, *U-584*, landed four more saboteurs on 17 June near Jacksonville, Florida. Dasch planned to rendezvous with their leader, Kerling, in Cincinnati, at the beginning of July and start their campaign. They were going to blow up factories, railways, and bridges from the East Coast to the Mid West.

The saboteurs managed to evade discovery until they reached New York. But when Dasch arrived in the city, he had a change of heart and decided to betray his colleagues. It may be that he had always intended to do this from the very beginning of the plot. He had contacts with left-wing groups in Germany who had suffered under the Gestapo. On 18 June 1942, Dasch confessed all to the FBI. They had already heard from the surprised coastguard and quickly swooped on the rest of the saboteurs.

It was another success for the FBI – but it clearly showed that the Eastern seaboard was still vulnerable to enemy action. Coming so soon after the Duquesne spy ring and the burning of the *Normandie*, public suspicion linked the sinking of the liner with German sabotage. It was a link that suited the government and the FBI just fine – serving to remind Americans of the ever-present threat posed by spies in their homeland. Hoover made just this point in a public announcement.

'Other saboteurs may try to come to our shores', he said. 'They must be stopped. We ask every citizen to immediately report any information regarding espionage, sabotage or Un-American activities to the Federal Bureau of Investigation.'

Hitler was even more furious when he heard of the failure of Pastorius. He summoned both Canaris and Lahousen to his headquarters on the Russian Front on 30 June 1942. 'I want to know', said Hitler, 'how it is possible for such an appalling catastrophe as this to happen. We had the same awful mess a year ago, when treachery led to the arrest of thirty of your agents in America. Now it has happened again. I demand an explanation.' At first, Canaris said nothing in front of Hitler's tirade, but then he pointed the finger at the Nazi party members on the mission.

For a moment, Hitler was speechless. 'All right; if that's so, it's all the worse', he raged. 'You must never send loyal members on such an expedition again. Next time you can send Jews and criminals.'

But there were no more German sabotage operations against the United States. Hitler's own statement that the only two missions sent were intercepted by the FBI means that it cannot have been German saboteurs who attacked the *Normandie.*

Of course, this was unknown in the United States and the belief that the *Normandie* was destroyed by accident or foreign sabotage remained prevalent for over thirty years after the disaster. But, curiously, after the burning of the liner, there were no more major fires on the New York waterfront. Over the next three years, hundreds of Allied ships safely left New York harbour. Had the FBI been totally successful, or could it be that some other factor was in operation?

In 1975, a controversial book was published – *The Last Testament of Lucky Luciano* by Martin Gosch and Richard Hammer. It purported to be based on the direct confessions of the chief mobster. In the book, Lucky Luciano made a sensational claim:

> This big French luxury ship, the *Normandie*, was sittin' at a pier on the West Side of Manhattan, and accordin' to what Tony [Anastasio] and Albert [Anastasia] was told, the government was workin' out a deal with that guy de Gaulle to take it over and turn it into a troopship. Albert figures that if somethin' could happen to the *Normandie*, that would really make everybody crap in their pants.

> It was a great idea and I didn't figure it was really gonna hurt the war effort because the ship was nowhere near ready and, besides, no American soldiers or sailors would be involved because they wasn't sendin' 'em no place yet. So I sent back word to Albert to handle it.
>
> A couple of days later, I heard on the radio where the *Normandie* was on fire and it didn't look like they could save her. That goddam Anastasia – he really done a job. Later on, Albert told me not to feel too bad about what happened to the ship. He said that as a sergeant in the army he hated the fuckin' Navy anyway.

Luciano was wrong that it would not have a big impact on the war effort – but he was right that it scared the government into making a pact with Luciano and the Mafiosi who controlled the New York docks. The deal had been in the making ever since 7 December 1941, or, as Luciano put it, 'When the Japs bombed Pearl Harbor and Roosevelt declared war, I got my second break . . .'

Luciano got his lawyer Moses Polakoff to set up a meeting with Meyer Lansky and Frank Costello at his prison in Dannemora in December 1941. Luciano ran his plan past them. It centred on his nemesis Thomas Dewey becoming governor of New York. When Dewey got in, he would get Dewey to get him out of jail. How? He would do the government a big favour. He had read in the newspapers that the Navy Department was nervous about sabotage along the Eastern waterfront. With Luciano's labour connections, he could promise to protect the docks from any sabotage. 'I could see Lansky start to smile while I was layin' it out', remembered Luciano, 'because he was the first one to see what I was getting at. He said, "Charlie, I get it, I get it. It's terrific. How can Dewey turn down a patriotic hero?"'

Frank Costello said he had contacts with Naval Intelligence based at Church Street and could set up the whole deal. But Luciano knew that some front-page demonstration of naval vulnerability was needed to get the government coming to him for help.

For a month he brooded about what this could be, then one of his chief hit men came up with the scheme. Albert Anastasia was a prolific murderer for the mob. Early on, he worked in the Brooklyn docks and became a key figure in the International Longshoremen's Association, the East Coast dock workers' union – a position maintained by his brother Tony.

Anastasia liked killing and when it looked as though he might be put on trial for murder, he wiped out witnesses and their families to protect himself. When Luciano wanted to kill his rivals in the Castellammarese War, it was Anastasia who leapt at the chance of killing Joe the Boss – he was one of the four-strong murder squad. Later, in 1942, Anastasia was drafted into the US Army where he served as a technical sergeant teaching soldiers at a camp in Pennsylvania how to be longshoremen. He served with distinction and was even awarded US citizenship at the end of his stint in 1944. But before this, in January 1942, it was Anastasia who came up with the solution to Luciano's problems.

Albert and his brother Tony knew that Naval Intelligence agents had been checking out the docks and talking to everyone about increased security. So, reasoned Anastasia, why not give them something to really worry about by torching the *Normandie*? Luciano thought it was a brilliant idea and gave his sanction to it.

In the 1979 book of his recollections – *Meyer Lansky: Mogul of the Mob* by Dennis Eisenberg, Uri Dan, and Eli Landau – Meyer Lansky corroborated Luciano's story that it was Anastasia who sabotaged the *Normandie*:

> I told him face to face that he mustn't burn any more ships. He was sorry – not sorry he had had the *Normandie* burned but sorry he couldn't get at the Navy again. Apparently he had learned in the Army to hate the Navy. 'Stuck-up bastards' he called them.

The burning of the *Normandie* sent a chill wind through the corridors of Washington. The Port of New York handled nearly half of all US foreign trade. Two hundred cargo docks, warehouses and piers in Manhattan, Queens, New Jersey and Brooklyn covered nearly eighty miles of coastal frontage. It had to be protected – whatever the cost.

The story of how the US government struck a deal with Lucky Luciano and his criminal associates to defend America's East Coast against sabotage is recorded in the Herlands Report of 1954. This was an investigation carried out at the direction of Thomas E. Dewey to record the exact detail of the contacts between US Naval Intelligence and New York's Mafia mobsters. The US Navy was not happy with its findings and the report remained secret for many decades afterwards. It is still unpublished.

Just twelve years after the events it records, William B. Herlands, Commissioner of Investigation, made the case for the US government talking to top criminals:

> The Intelligence authorities were greatly concerned with the problems of sabotage and espionage. Suspicions were rife with respect to the leaking of information about convoy movements. The *Normandie*, which was being converted to war use as the Navy auxiliary *Lafayette*, had burned at the pier in the North River, New York City. Sabotage was suspected.

The burning of the *Normandie* is mentioned several more times in the Herlands Report as a pivotal point in US domestic naval strategy, but only in the context of foreign sabotage. There is no suggestion that the Mafia torched it to provoke negotiations. Herlands went on to say:

> Commercial fishing fleets were suspected as sources of fuel and supplies for enemy submarines. While our Intelligence authorities had most of the suspected pro-Nazis spotted, they were not as well prepared with respect to certain elements who were sympathizers of Mussolini and pro-fascists.

Later in the report, Herlands mentioned Operation Pastorius:

> These fears became more acute when in June of that year, German agents trained in sabotage techniques, were actually landed at Amagansett, Long Island. They carried quantities of explosives and maps and plans for the destruction of strategic installations.

Captain Roscoe C. MacFall was Chief Intelligence Officer of the Third Naval District, which included New York and New Jersey. It was his idea for naval agents to talk to underworld contacts who might be able to help him secure the docks. MacFall got the backing of Rear Admiral Carl F. Espe, Director of Naval Intelligence.

> The outcome of the war appeared extremely grave [said Espe]. In addition, there was the most serious concern over possible sabotage in the ports. It was necessary to use every possible means to prevent and forestall sabotage and to prevent the possible supplying of and contact with enemy submarines.

But did Naval Intelligence not have any doubts about the morality of dealing with known criminals? Lieutenant Anthony J. Marsloe, who was assigned to the Third Naval District Intelligence Office, was clear on this:

> The exploitation of informants, irrespective of their backgrounds, is not only desirous [*sic*], but necessary when the nation is struggling for its existence.
>
> Intelligence, as such, is not a police agency. Its function is to prevent. In order to prevent, you must have a system; and the system, in its scope and latitude must encompass any and all means which will prevent the enemy from securing aid and comfort from others . . .
>
> By any and all means I include the so-called underworld.

Marsloe claimed that this process began as early as December 1941 – *before* the burning of the *Normandie*:

> The discussion was a continuing one. It started in December and carried on throughout the course of the first quarter of 1942 implemented specifically with the names of so-called underworld personalities as well as District Intelligence personnel assigned by Commander Haffenden to the implementation of this mission.

Commander Charles R. Haffenden was Marsloe's commanding officer and would be the dominant personality running the project in the Third Naval District Intelligence Office. Before being called up for duty, Marsloe had been attached to the District Attorney's Office, New York County, under the direction of Governor Dewey. During his discussions from December 1941 onwards, Marsloe said:

> Commander Haffenden, in general terms, outlined to me a plan of action which he was then contemplating putting into execution involving the enlisting of the so-called underworld as a means of obtaining information in a counter-intelligence sense and also as a means of preventing espionage and sabotage within the jurisdiction of the Third Naval District . . .

At first, Marsloe was not so sure it was such a good idea. 'I felt a certain amount of skepticism', he recalled, 'because I felt that since they had not been good citizens it was doubtful as to whether they would be of constructive service to our war effort.' He then discussed the plan with a senior colleague who had served in the FBI and he convinced

Marsloe that every means available to the armed forces and the government should be used to protect US installations. In the meantime, Haffenden's superiors were already taking the project further.

On 7 March 1942, just a month after the burning of the *Normandie*, Captain MacFall of Naval Intelligence met with Frank Hogan, the District Attorney, in his office. Hogan was currently involved in investigating organised crime on the waterfront and introduced MacFall to Murray Gurfein, in charge of the District Attorney's Rackets Bureau. Gurfein had been one of Thomas Dewey's most able investigators and was part of the original team that put Luciano behind bars. During the war, he led a double life. Aside from his civilian work for the District Attorney, he was also a lieutenant colonel in the US Army and was later chief of the Psychological Warfare Division at the Supreme Headquarters Allied Expeditionary Force (SHAEF) in Normandy in 1944.

In the DA's office, MacFall outlined the problems faced by Naval Intelligence. His specific fear was that enemy submarines might be refuelled by fishing boats or former rum-running ships owned by ex-bootleggers whose loyalty might be bought. Hogan replied that it was true that the underworld had advance information of many illegal activities and thought this might be useful.

'But can these people be trusted?' wondered MacFall.

'Many of these racketeers are loyal to America', said Hogan, 'and are not pro-Mussolini.'

The meeting ended with Hogan and Gurfein pledging to do everything in their power to help MacFall and Naval Intelligence. It was also agreed that Gurfein would act as representative of the District Attorney's Office and that Commander Haffenden, who was not present at the first meeting, would be the representative for MacFall and Naval Intelligence.

At a second meeting on 25 March, Haffenden met Hogan and Gurfein. Haffenden was a navy veteran of World War I. Just turned fifty, he was a tough, fearless figure who enjoyed dealing with underworld figures. He would later demonstrate his physical bravery by volunteering to be a beachmaster during the invasion of Iwo Jima, where he was wounded by enemy shellfire. In 1942, he was in charge of B-3, the investigations section of the District Intelligence Office.

Haffenden suggested the possibility that underworld leaders might be willing to cooperate in the war effort by helping to gather information useful to Naval Intelligence. Hogan agreed the idea was worth pursuing and Gurfein recommended they get the operation moving by contacting Joseph 'Socks' Lanza.

This was in line with Marsloe's view that Haffenden had been considering this since the start of the year. Marsloe soon after went to Hogan's office where:

> . . . in general terms the plan was outlined; and to the best of my belief, Mr Hogan stated that he would place the facilities of his office at the disposal of the Navy in order to gain maximum benefit from any information or intelligence that such characters might possess or have the means to ascertain.

At the top of their list of useful 'characters' was Socks Lanza. He was the Mafioso who ran the Fulton Fish Market. Not one fishing boat landed in New York without paying him a $10 tribute, not one truck left without paying him $50. He got his nickname from 'socking' anyone who got in his way. He was a powerful and brutal mobster who made even tough union representatives think twice about crossing him. He was also a close ally of Luciano.

Murray Gurfein suggested contacting Lanza through his attorney, Joseph K. Guerin. They met the following day at Guerin's Wall Street office. He was currently representing Lanza on a charge of extortion and conspiracy, a case being prosecuted by the District Attorney. Guerin suggested meeting Lanza later that day. At 11.30 p.m., Gurfein picked up Guerin and Lanza at 103rd Street and Broadway. The taxi drove to Riverside Park where Gurfein talked to Lanza and Guerin on a bench at midnight. The secrecy of the meeting was Lanza's idea. He did not want people to see him talking to someone from the District Attorney's office, in case they thought he had turned informer.

Gurfein told Lanza what he had said to his attorney:

> It's a matter of great urgency. Many of our ships are being sunk along the Atlantic coast. We suspect German U-boats are being refuelled and getting fresh supplies off our coast. We think it's fishing smacks that are a source of resupply. You know the people engaged in commercial fishing. You can find out how and where the submarines are being refuelled.

Lanza nodded and said he would try to secure the desired information. Gurfein asked Lanza if he would help Naval Intelligence. 'Sure', he said, 'I'll help the war effort. I got contacts in the fish market and fishing boat and barge captains and seamen all along the Atlantic Coast.'

A week later, Lanza and Gurfein had a second secret meeting, but this time it was in the more luxurious surroundings of the Hotel Astor. Their contact wore a naval uniform – it was Commander Haffenden. He had three hotel rooms as his office. Before the meeting got underway, Gurfein made it clear that Lanza was volunteering his help to the Navy and that no promise had been made by the District Attorney's Office in exchange for such cooperation. Everyone agreed. They got straight to the point.

'I hear you're willing to help us', said Haffenden. He then went over his fears of enemy submarines and suspicious waterfront activities. Lanza said he had no problem with helping the government and would be 'glad to ferret out the information about the suspected refuelling and resupplying of submarines and to ascertain whether fishing smacks were involved.'

'You let me know where you want the contacts made', said Lanza, 'or what you want, and I'll carry on.'

The meeting lasted only thirty-five minutes and Lanza gave Haffenden a series of telephone numbers where he could be reached. Several days after this, Lanza got a call to see Haffenden at his Church Street office and went there by himself, without his attorney. He signed in the visitors' book and was given a security badge allowing him to enter Haffenden's office. 'I want to get some of our men on some of the fishing smacks', said Haffenden. This meant getting fishermen's union cards for Naval Intelligence agents. Lanza said he could do this. From then on, Haffenden and Lanza met on a regular weekly basis.

Captain MacFall, Chief of Naval Intelligence in this area, later commented on this project:

> Some of the larger fishing fleets had their own ship-to-ship and ship-to-shore telephones, including codes used to guide the ships of one fleet to places where the catch was good. Utilizing these ships and their equipment and installing similar telephone equipment on fishing ships that did not themselves install such equipment, Naval Intelligence worked out a confidential cooperative arrangement and code with them as part of the submarine look-out system.
>
> Inasmuch as many Italians worked in such commercial fishing fleets and in the waterfront districts in the fish markets, their cooperation with Naval Intelligence was considered

> valuable. Haffenden told me that he was active in this phase of our work and that the underworld contacts he had developed were helpful in that regard.

The operation went further. Lanza spoke to Hiram Swezey – blind since the age of seven – who ran a fleet of trucks moving fish from Long Island to the Fulton Fish Market. Haffenden wanted civilian agents on some of these trucks picking up information. Lanza got union books for the agents and they went to work for Swezey. Swezey also introduced naval personnel to groups of fishermen and asked them to report any unusual sightings. Sometimes these fishing boats picked up maritime wreckage or parts of aeroplanes – even human remains. All this was reported to Naval Intelligence. Lanza also placed civilian agents as observers on fishing boats operating from Long Island, New Jersey, North Carolina, Virginia and Maine.

To help him with his naval business, Lanza recruited a mobster friend called Ben Espy. Together, they took a 'fishing trip' in the summer of 1942 from Maine to North Carolina. They stopped off at Boston, New Bedford, Nantucket, Block Island and Virginia Beach, gathering a list of names and addresses of people who might be useful to Haffenden and his agents. Lanza was enjoying himself. The secret mission kept his mind off the criminal charges hanging over him.

Lanza was not only talking to Naval Intelligence. He was clever enough to know that he had to keep his Mafia overlords informed as well, as Meyer Lansky recalled:

> Joe Socks did the right thing by coming to me. He knew I'd give him the right advice. Both of us went to see Frank Costello, who had been best man at Joe's wedding . . . Gurfein's move had been even shrewder than he realized, because Lucky and I were close to Lanza ourselves. We got him out of a lot of trouble when he was a boy, and he never forgot how we helped him.

Lanza was coming to the same conclusion. If Naval Intelligence was going to score a real victory on the Eastern waterfront, than the king of the fish market could not supply it by himself. On 16 April 1942, Lanza went to his attorney and told him he was having difficulty in getting information from certain Italian-born figures in the New York underworld. He suspected he was not getting their whole-hearted cooperation because they knew he had an indictment pending against him. With all the questions he was asking, they figured maybe he was working as an informer for the DA. It was then that Lanza came up with the big idea:

> Luciano could be of great assistance. If he came into this picture, I'd get all the cooperation from various people in the City of New York. He'd send some word out to Joe Adonis or Frank [Costello]. The word of Charlie [Luciano] would give me the right of way.

The message was clear. Get Luciano on board and the whole Eastern seaboard would be protected for good. It was a tall order.

Luciano had been New York's Public Enemy No. 1 and his 30–50 year sentence in jail was Thomas Dewey's greatest triumph. Could the US government really put this to one side and strike an alliance with the chief of America's Mafia?

Chapter Seven

Luciano's Deal

In early 1942, the war in the Atlantic was going badly for the Allies. In the ten months January–October 1942, 521 Allied ships were lost to enemy action. Packs of Axis submarines were operating without hindrance in the north-west Atlantic, hunting their prey close to the US East Coast.

In January 1942, a Norwegian oil tanker was torpedoed just sixty miles off the coast from Montauk Point, New York State. In the same month, U-boats sank a US merchant steamer, a Latvian freighter and a US tanker off North Carolina. These were just a few of the twenty-one vessels lost in that month. In February, off Cape May, New Jersey, a US destroyer on patrol duty was torpedoed and sunk – along with twenty-six more ships that month. On 23 February 1942, President Roosevelt had to admit on radio that the situation was not looking good. 'We have most certainly suffered losses', he said, 'from Hitler's U-boats in the Atlantic as well as from the Japanese in the Pacific – and we shall suffer more of them before the turn of the tide.' The roll call of destruction would peak in May with 102 losses and June with 111 lost ships. In April 1942, all lights visible from the sea along the waterfront areas of Brooklyn, Queens and Richmond in New York City were turned off for the duration of the war.

It was a time for strong action and the pressure was on Naval Intelligence to secure further results in its campaign to protect the East Coast. But, as Naval Intelligence agents spread their enquiries beyond the immediate waterfront, they became aware of Joseph Lanza's limits as a fixer. They needed someone with greater authority in the underworld – and that person, undoubtedly, was Lucky Luciano.

> Lanza was extremely valuable in making contacts at those various piers [said Lieutenant Commander Maurice Kelly]. But our responsibility was all over the Port and we found places where Socks Lanza did not have direct contact . . .
>
> We had to seek the cooperation of somebody that had an over-all control or interest. Because it was found out early in the stage of this thing that union officials and people in illegal operations along the waterfront had as much influence with conditions on the docks as the shipping people themselves, and in many cases, more.

Police Inspector Howard Nugent had lunch with Commander Haffenden and the naval officer told him that Lanza was providing him with good information on the activities of the offshore fishing fleet but they had to get the 'okay from Charlie Lucky' to have Lanza go further. Nugent told Haffenden to talk to the chief of prisons in New York State.

It was left to Murray Gurfein to make the move to get Luciano on board. In April 1942, Gurfein contacted Moses Polakoff, the attorney who had defended Luciano against Thomas Dewey in 1936. Polakoff had served in the US Navy in World War I and was sympathetic to the naval cause, but his first reaction was to say he was no longer interested in the Luciano case. He did not care to discuss the mobster any further. So Gurfein had to work a little harder. 'This is rather important and I wish you'd come to see me', he said. 'If you put it that way', said Polakoff, 'I'll be in to see you.'

At the District Attorney's office, Gurfein told Polakoff that Lanza was already working for US Navy Intelligence and if Luciano could be involved then the operation could be widened. 'We want to set up a network of informants among the Italian element concerning any information about sabotage', explained Gurfein. 'We want the help of Italian fishermen who operate fishing fleets, concerning any possible enemy submarines off our shores.'

'On an occasion like this', said Polakoff, 'if I can be of any service to you or the Navy, I am glad to do so. But I don't know Luciano well enough to broach the subject with him. But I do know a person who I have confidence in and whose patriotism, or affection for our country, irrespective of his reputation, is of the highest.' That person was Meyer Lansky.

That afternoon Polakoff phoned Lansky and then called back Gurfein. 'Mr Lansky, who knows Luciano better than I do, volunteers to do all he can to accomplish the result desired.' Lansky was pleased to receive the call. According to him and Luciano, the whole procedure up to this point had been a dance to get the two sides talking. This was finally happening, as he later described:

> Mr Polakoff called on me and told me that the Naval Intelligence was very much interested in getting Italians that could be helpful in the war effort. He was seen by the District Attorney and he had a conference with Mr Gurfein, and he told me that he would take the responsibility if I would come into the picture and go to Charlie 'Lucky' and ask his assistance to solicit Italians that could be helpful in various parts in this City pertaining to watch out for sabotage or anything else, that it would be a duty to the country.

Gurfein, Polakoff and Lansky all met for breakfast at Longchamps Restaurant on 57th Street, between Fifth and Sixth Avenue. 'I told Gurfein that I loathed Adolf Hitler', recalled Lansky, 'and that I was a patriot. I was grateful that America had given me a home and that America had been good to me through the years.' But then he warned Gurfein. 'We have to be very careful in making any moves because Mussolini is very popular with some Italians in New York.'

'The government is fearful of sabotage', responded Gurfein. 'We want to get some prominent Italians to get active in a movement to stop sabotage. It is a duty to our country.' Lansky agreed. Then the name of Charlie Luciano came up.

'Can we trust him?' said Gurfein.

'Sure you can', said Lansky – and then in a typically Mafia afterthought added, 'his whole family is here – his mother and father and two brothers and sister with children.'

Lansky proposed seeing Luciano in jail with Polakoff to discuss the matter. At this, Polakoff winced.

'Snow's still on the ground up there', he said, 'and travelling is too hard.' They then discussed transferring Luciano from Dannemora to a place where it would be easier to interview him.

At the end of the meeting, Lansky remembered that Gurfein made it clear to them that no compensation was to be offered to Luciano and that it was strictly a duty to their country. They then went along to the Hotel Astor where Lansky and Polakoff were introduced to Commander Haffenden in his office. On his desk was a dossier containing information on every aspect of Lansky's criminal career.

Haffenden knew he was a major Mafia figure, but he needed his help. He told Lansky:

> I'm going to ask you to keep what I say a complete secret. I'm risking the lives of many men by mentioning it. A very large convoy of American troops is shortly going overseas from here. I want their safety to be absolutely guaranteed. We've got to make sure no word of this leaks out from the men who work the docks.

Haffenden admitted that they were still rattled by the burning of the *Normandie*. He knew the Mafia ran the docks and wanted their help. He knew also that Lansky had been active in battling Nazis on the streets of Manhattan. He told him to think of the Jews suffering under Hitler in Germany. Lansky needed no reminding and pledged his support:

> Mr Haffenden told us where we were weak. Where he felt the Government needs lots of assistance such as the waterfront; pertaining to loaders of ships; employees on the docks; receiving knowledge as to fishing boats – whatever they do in their movements outside; and he wanted people that could be of assistance in that way so that nothing is brought out to any submarines. He was afraid that they were getting fuel out and they may have gotten notes of movements of important loading – just where things were being loaded. And then he went on to other assistance that he may need such as hotels; that they have suspicion of different Germans or Italians; that he would want to get assistance in there of the employees to be able to report these things.

Lansky was happy to oblige and used his union connections to help with watching hotels. He told Frank Costello to cooperate and Anastasia too. He told Socks Lanza to offer the Navy only low-level help on the waterfront – they would take care of everything else. According to Lansky's recollections, Lanza then asked him how much money he should ask from the Navy for his services. 'You're going to be a patriot', said Lansky. 'You do it for nothing. Even your expenses have to come out of your own pocket.' Lanza accepted the situation as it was. Two brothers, Dominick and Felix Saco, were hired by Commander Haffenden to act as liaison agents with Lanza.

Then Lanza met a problem in the docks. He had already explained this to his attorney but he also told Lansky:

> Lanza told me that the Italian people around there thought that he had a personal motive [he was indicted for a crime]. They didn't believe him that it was a movement that Italians should get interested; and he asked me to take him up to Charlie Luciano, and if Charlie Luciano would send word to these people he thought that resistance would stop.

In the meantime, the official procedure started for moving Luciano from Clinton Prison at Dannemora to Great Meadow Prison at Comstock. It was a far more convenient and comfortable prison, but the authorities went out of their way to make the point that Great Meadow was still a maximum security institution. 'The word "meadow" in the name of Great Meadow is not descriptive', said the Herlands Report.

John A. Lyons was the New York State Correction Commissioner and it was up to him to authorise the prison transfer. Commander Haffenden ordered one of his agents to present a written request to Lyons and then destroy it after he had read it. Several witnesses later testified that the letter said that Luciano's transfer was in the interest of the United States – making it easier for the mobster to furnish Naval Intelligence with information to help with the war effort. Lyons had no problem with the proposed transfer. He would do it if stopped the sinking of Allied ships and saved the life of 'at least one American abroad'. He went further. He instructed the Warden of Great Meadow, Vernon Morhous, to waive the usual fingerprint requirements of visitors to Luciano and that they should be allowed to talk to him in private.

In order to avoid any publicity, Luciano was transferred along with a number of other inmates from Dannemora to Great Meadow on 12 May 1942. It was time to put the deal directly to Luciano.

Some time between 15 May and 4 June 1942, Lansky and Polakoff made their first visit to Luciano to discuss the Naval Intelligence business. Since every subsequent meeting was precisely dated, it is surprising that the date of this initial meeting is not recorded. They took the train to Albany and then drove sixty miles to Great Meadow prison. According to Polakoff and Lansky, Luciano stretched out his arms and shouted: 'What the hell are you doing here? I never expected to see you fellows here.' Apparently, he had no idea why he had been transferred either. They then explained to him the Navy's need for his help.

Luciano remembered this first meeting somewhat differently. He claimed that Haffenden and probably Gurfein – 'Dewey's guy' – were at the meeting and he spoke to them directly. Lansky says that Luciano spoke to his mobster associates and then Lansky relayed the information to the government. What both agreed on is that Lansky brought a hamper of food to the meeting, as Luciano remembered:

> Before I even had a chance to say hello to anybody, I spot a table in the middle of the room loaded down with all kinds of cold cuts – just like the table we used to have in the back room of Dave Miller's Delicatessen. So I said, 'Fellas, before we talk, you'll have to excuse me', and I made a dive for that table. It was Lansky's idea to load it up with all the stuff he knew I liked, and he even had them kosher green pickles and the Dr Brown's Celery Tonic I loved . . . The taste of them pickles was almost as good as freedom.

Lansky explained that by cooperating with Navy Intelligence, Luciano might well get a reduction of his sentence. Otherwise he would have to wait until 1956 for his first chance of parole. Luciano said he was happy to help the government. He knew the important people on the waterfront and if he asked them to get interested in the war effort – then they would. But he had one major reservation. He was not a citizen of the United States and he knew that a warrant of deportation had been lodged against him. 'When I get out – nobody knows how this war will turn out – whatever I do', he said, 'I want it kept quiet, private, so that when I get back to Italy I'm not a marked man.'

Lansky corroborated this story: 'We convinced Charlie that it was a duty of us to give assistance', he recalled. 'Charlie agreed with one exception: to keep this secret because he had a deportation warrant attached to his papers and if he were ever to be deported, he might get lynched there [in Italy]'. He feared the punishment for breaking *omerta.*

Haffenden later reassured Lansky that he had a code system. Contacts were referred to by numbers and no names would be revealed. With that agreed, Luciano gave Lansky the authority to talk to all other mobsters in New York. Word was to go out that Luciano okayed the project to help Naval Intelligence secure the docks.

The Herlands Report recorded that Lansky's function was to act as a liaison between Luciano and other Mafiosi. Lansky told Naval Intelligence:

> There'll be no German submarines in the Port of New York. Every man down there who works in the harbor – all the sailors, all the fishermen, every longshoreman, every individual who has anything to do with the coming and going of ships to the United States – is now helping the fight against the Nazis.

It was a guarantee backed by Lucky Luciano.

The Herlands Report recorded at least twenty meetings between Luciano, Polakoff and Lansky between 15 May 1942 and 21 August 1945. But it also says that many more meetings involving other associates of Luciano were not recorded. Some of the mobsters seeing Luciano were Lanza, Frank Costello, Mike Lascari, Mike Mirandi, and Willie Moretti (the man who first welcomed Joseph Bonanno to America).

Polakoff found these numerous journeys to and from Great Meadow tedious. 'We slept in Albany or Glens Falls', he said, 'and got to the prison early in the morning. The visits were usually concluded by 1 o'clock so that we could travel back to Albany and make a train back to New York and get in about 8 o'clock or so.' Visits usually started at 9.30 or 10.00 a.m. and Polakoff would be excluded from the whispered conversations by sitting at a table at the far end of the room, usually reading a newspaper. It is likely that Luciano was discussing more than just ways to win the war – but was administering his criminal empire. It is little wonder that Polakoff asked if visitors could see Luciano without him. The answer was a firm 'no' – he was there to be an insurance against any violation of prison rules. That was Polakoff's contribution to the war effort.

In these dealings, Luciano himself claimed a more hands-on approach. When he later spoke to undercover FBI agent Sal Vizzini in 1959, there was no mention of Lansky:

> One day the warden calls me in his office and there's a navy commander with him. They want to know if I'll get the boys into a meeting and set up a kind of organization that will watch out for any screwy stuff going on around the docks. I called a meeting of longshore guys right up there in the warden's office and we set up just what they wanted.

According to the Herlands Report, however, it was Lansky who operated as Luciano's intermediary in this operation. Lansky had regular meetings with Haffenden in New York and discussed in detail how the Mafia could best help the war effort. Together, they discussed more efficient ways of loading and unloading ships; how to prevent strikes; how to keep troop movements secret and how to secure the area against sabotage. On one occasion, Haffenden suspected there were German and Italian enemy agents staying at certain hotels:

> He wanted waiters that could be trusted [said Lansky] to mix up in the union office and to hear what the different waiters were talking about as to conversations that sailors or any military men may have been in their different stations. He also thought that we may have to get in waiters and place them in certain restaurants and hotel lounges. One of the places he mentioned was the Pierre Hotel. He also told me about a place in Brooklyn – some sort of seamen's club – but we never had a chance to complete the mission because it got out in the newspapers.

Lansky got Johnny 'Cockeye' Dunn out of prison to act as his enforcer on the piers. Everyone was frightened of Dunn. When he walked into a dockside bar, everyone shut up. He was there to ensure that no one blabbed about troop movements or gave out details about secret missions. He had strong connections with the freight handlers' union on the waterfront.

One time, Haffenden got information on possible German agents staying at a waterfront hotel. Dunn went to investigate and the two men promptly disappeared. 'They'll never bother us again', said Dunn. Naval Intelligence asked him to clear with them beforehand any further such terminations of enemy activity. Despite that, according to Lanksy, Dunn was soon working directly for Haffenden:

> Dunn's job was to be a watchdog on the piers to have entrusted employees amongst the loaders . . . to make friends with the crew and to stay with them to get reports if there was any bad men around the crowd. Men that may lend themselves to sabotage or leakage. He also got friends along the waterfront in the bar rooms. If any of the crews got drunk and they would talk something that you would feel is subversive, to report to him or whomever else he placed on that to assist him on that.

Dunn became concerned about the way ships were being loaded in the docks. He thought bombs could be placed on them and passed this on to Haffenden.

Another enthusiastic helper was John McCue, released from Sing Sing after serving ten years for murder. He was the right-hand man of Joseph Ryan, president of the International Longshoremen's Association. When Navy men reported difficulties with certain dockyard workers, McCue broke their arms or legs to ensure future compliance.

So effective was the Mafia network of enforcers and informers that Meyer Lansky claimed it was he who first got information about Operation Pastorius – the landing of German agents by submarine at Long Island. He said he was approached by the brother of an Italian fisherman who had seen the four agents clamber out of the U-boat and row ashore. Lansky then told Haffenden who passed on the information to the FBI.

To spy on Nazi sympathisers in New York, Lansky persuaded associates of his who owned restaurants in Yorkville to hire German-speaking Navy agents as waiters to listen in on conversations. So intimate did the relationship get between Lansky and Haffenden that Navy agents ended up servicing Mafia-run vending machines in clubs. 'So we had naval officers being collectors for the Mafia', said Lansky. 'They handed over the money they collected and were always honest in their dealings. I think this must be the only time the US Navy ever directly helped the Mafia.'

Socks Lanza continued to help Naval Intelligence after contact had been made with Luciano. He visited him several times in jail and got his seal of approval. 'Joe, you go ahead', said Luciano. 'I will give word out and everything will go smoother.' Lanza noticed the difference straight away: 'Costello was helpful in the way that he would OK me to go and see people where I got the right of way through Charlie.' When Lanza approached Costello with a project for Naval Intelligence, the Mafioso would consider it and then say 'It's a good thing and you go along with it.'

Lanza often introduced Naval Intelligence agents to his associates on the waterfront, saying they were 'okay, regular guys'. This meant they could go about their business without being asked awkward questions. That included surveillance operations on suspicious figures on the piers or ships. Lieutenant Commander Maurice Kelly, a cop in civilian life, was one of these investigators and he noticed a distinct change in mood on the waterfront following the Navy's contact with Luciano:

> There was a decided and definite cooperative approach to all those people after that. There was no hedging. We met the assigned person we were designated to see on the particular pier – because Commander Haffenden would lay the plans for you. They spoke straight from the shoulder. They assisted you in obtaining the information you wanted to obtain. They would finger people for you. Watch out for certain baggage – whatever problem was at hand – and it was full and whole-hearted cooperation.

Before Luciano's involvement, confirmed Kelly:

> We ran in to great difficulty in obtaining reliable informants along the waterfront . . . Because of the make-up of the people that work these piers – they were suspicious of any investigators and it was part of their being that they just refused to talk to anybody, war effort or no war effort.

To ensure that the relationship between the US government and the underworld was working correctly, wire taps were authorised to monitor telephone calls to and from Lanza's headquarters at Meyer's Hotel, in the heart of the Fulton Fish Market at 117 South Street, Manhattan. The wire taps corroborated a number of missions carried out by Lanza for Haffenden. Sometimes they sounded faintly ludicrous. A printing plant in Harlem was producing and distributing subversive literature so Haffenden asked Lanza to help place agents in relevant locations. This included providing union cards for agents working undercover as hat-check girls in a Harlem cabaret club.

This close relationship served the Mafia very well as it ensured their grip on various enterprises. It also consolidated their domination over the East Coast longshoremen's union. For some time, Harry Bridges, a tough union leader who ran the West Coast longshoremen's union had been a threat to them. He was trying to clean up activities in the East and he made a move on the Brooklyn waterfront. There were rumours he was organising a strike there. Haffenden phoned Lanza.

'How about that Brooklyn Bridge thing?' he said, meaning Harry Bridges. 'I don't want any trouble on the waterfront during the crucial times.'

'You won't have any', Lanza reassured him. 'I'll see to that. I'll give you a ring. We'll get together.'

Bridges tried to hold a union meeting at Webster Hall – but Lanza got to him first. He gave him a beating. He did not bother coming east again. When Haffenden phoned Lanza again about this matter he did not ask for details, as the wire tap records confirmed.

'How about the waterfront condition in Brooklyn?'

'Bridges' men were stopped', said Lanza. 'We saw to that. Everything is under control.'

'Swell', said Haffenden.

'There was peace on the waterfront', noted Lansky. 'It was kept with rough methods. But that's what the Navy asked us to do and that's what the Navy got.'

Captain MacFall, Chief of Naval Intelligence in New York and along the East Coast, knew he was taking a risk by employing gangsters but considered it worthwhile. He also kept it to himself and his department, as he told the Herlands investigation:

> The use of underworld informants and characters, like the use of other extremely confidential investigative procedures, was not specifically disclosed to the Commandant or other superior officers as such use was a calculated risk that I assumed as District Intelligence Officer. It was my responsibility to use my best judgement as to the ways and means of getting information in which Naval Intelligence was interested . . .
>
> From time to time, Lt Commander Haffenden (who worked directly under me) gave me significant information about waterfront activities that came through the underworld. It developed that some of these informants had previously been members of a gang headed by one named Charlie Lucky Luciano, a notorious underworld gangster, in jail under a long sentence. Lt Commander Haffenden also informed me that Luciano still had influence in his underworld organization and had given orders for his henchmen to assist the District Intelligence Office . . .
>
> When underworld sources were used or informants turned up by underworld characters, their names would not be kept and no filed records were maintained of their information, as their activities and identities were considered extremely confidential.

According to the Herlands Report and the many Naval Intelligence officers cited in it, there is no doubt that Luciano, Lansky, Lanza and their mob associates helped them. They provided assistance and information that kept the East Coast docks working efficiently. They provided a front line of intelligence against any agents sent by Hitler or Mussolini to sabotage Allied shipping. The end result was that Allied convoys could carry on their vital job of moving soldiers and supplies to Europe to fight the war. That this was achieved by gangsters who used violence and illegal methods is true, but that aspect of the operation is not admitted in the US government report. That information comes from the personal memoirs of the gangsters involved – Lucky Luciano and Meyer Lansky. Today this might seem morally dubious, but at the time, in 1942, it made good sense, as the Herlands Report concluded:

> No practical purpose would be served by debating the technical scope of Luciano's aid to the war effort. Over and beyond any precise rating of the contribution is the crystal-clear fact that Luciano and his associates and contacts during a period when 'the outcome of the war appeared extremely grave', were responsible for a wide range of services which were considered 'useful to the navy'.

Meyer Lansky had his own take on the affair. 'If they had wanted to', he said, 'the Mafia could have paralysed the dock area.' He asked Haffenden what would happen if there was a shutdown. 'Without the supplies we're sending to Russia and Britain', said the Naval Commander, 'the war would go on a lot longer. It could even change the course of the war.'

'So', said Lansky in his memoirs, 'in the end the Mafia helped save the lives of Americans and of people in Europe.'

When asked openly by the Herlands investigators what good had been achieved by the 'Luciano project', he stumbled a little. 'I cannot give you any specific results', said Lansky, 'but I don't know how much has been avoided that if this didn't happen – I don't know how much sabotage this has stopped, and I feel it should have stopped plenty. I feel that it was a great precaution.'

In February 1943, Lucky Luciano hoped to capitalise on his contribution to the war effort. A motion was made in the Supreme Court, New York County, to modify the sentence imposed on Luciano. It came before Justice Philip J. McCook, the judge who had originally sentenced Luciano in 1936. The judge denied the motion but in his summing up, Justice McCook did hold out some hope for Luciano:

> Finally, we reach the argument that the defendant has assisted the Government in the war effort. Following the precedent in

> the Metropolitan matter, the authorities have been interviewed, privately, in the public interest. As a result, the court is able to conclude that the defendant probably attempted to assist them, and possibly with some success . . . If the defendant is assisting the authorities and he continues to do so, and a remains a model prisoner, Executive clemency may become appropriate at some future time.

'The nature of Lucania's [sic] aid to the war remained a mystery', said a *New York Times* report of the February legal plea:

> Mr Wolf [Luciano's attorney] was not at liberty to disclose what he described as a military secret, but told Justice McCook that the cooperation of his client had been sought by the military authorities, and had been given without 'any thought of consideration or hope of consideration'.
>
> He said he would call two 'high ranking military officials' to appear privately before the court, and declared later that they had conferred with Justice McCook, but that their testimony could not be made public.'

The US government wanted Luciano to stay in jail. There was still a lot more fighting to be done in the war. Besides, if Luciano had been released he would have been deported immediately to wartime Italy, which would not have served him very well.

But did Luciano and the Mafia have any more help to give? Could they take a more direct role in the action? As Allied troops won victories in North Africa, they came closer to the homeland of the Mafia – Sicily.

Chapter Eight

Putting a Contract on Hitler

In prison in Great Meadow, Lucky Luciano liked to follow the progress of the war. On one wall of his cell, he stuck a huge map of the war zone in Europe and noted every victory and every setback. He became a great fan of the aggressive General George S. Patton and raged at General Eisenhower for not giving him more control of the fighting.

By early 1943, Luciano was getting as impatient as Soviet leader Josef Stalin for the Allies to open a second front. As he saw it, the sooner the war was over, the sooner he would be out of jail. With a lack of action in Europe, Luciano finally ran out of patience. He summoned two of his top hit men – Tommy Lucchese and Joe Adonis. 'I told 'em somethin' hadda be done with this guy Hitler', said Luciano. 'I said that if somebody could knock off this son of a bitch, the war would be over in five minutes.' The Mafia hit men looked serious, looked at each other – then laughed. Luciano hit the roof:

> What the hell are you laughin' at? We've got the best hit man in the world over there – Vito Genovese. That dirty little pig owes his life to me and now it's time for him to make good on it. He's so fuckin' friendly with Mussolini and that punk son-in-law of his, that Count Ciano, he oughta be able to get close enough to Hitler to do it.

A prison guard rushed over to the cell to see what the noise was all about. Luciano was beside himself. Why not kill Hitler? The Mafia could get to anyone. Then, suddenly, he too saw the funny side and calmed down. His suggestion was not the first time a Mafioso had considered assassinating top Nazis.

Benjamin 'Bugsy' Siegel was the other half of the 'Bug and Meyer mob' – the Jewish gang formed by Meyer Lansky in the Lower East Side. Working together in their teens, they carried out contracts for bootleg gangs and made their own pile from smuggling liquor. As Lansky became more of an administrator of crime, Siegel liked to carry on with the killing. When Lansky linked up with Luciano, Siegel became a main hit man for him and was another part of the team that killed Joe the Boss.

Siegel was a dynamic personality with film-star looks and when he was sent to California in the late 1930s to take care of business for Luciano and Lansky, it was no surprise he started moving in celebrity circles. He mixed with Jean Harlow, Clark Gable, George Raft, and Cary Grant. One of his many glamorous girlfriends was Countess Dorothy Taylor di Frasso.

Countess di Frasso was the heiress to a fortune created by her father in the leather business. She had married a penniless Italian count and they had an open relationship, with her spending much time in California while he lived in Italy. In 1938, she decided to invest some of her fortune in a new explosive material called 'Atomite'. Bugsy Siegel witnessed a test of this material in the desert and thought 'if I'd only had some of this stuff in the old days'.

The countess contacted her husband in Italy who thought that Mussolini might well be interested in buying this new weapon. In fact, Il Duce so much liked the sound of it that he sent the countess an advance of $40,000 and invited her to demonstrate it in Italy. Di Frasso travelled with Bugsy Siegel and they stayed at her husband's family home – Villa Madama – just outside Rome. Unfortunately, when the day came to test the new explosive before Mussolini and his ministers, the button was pressed and there was only a wisp of smoke. The failure angered Mussolini who demanded his money back. He also punished di Frasso by expropriating part of her husband's villa.

As Siegel and the countess nursed their wounds, they noticed new guests of Mussolini arriving at the Villa Madama – senior Nazis Hermann Goering and Joseph Goebbels. The Jewish Siegel took an instant dislike to the arrogant Nazis. He had fought street fights with their kind – Bund members – in New York. 'I saw you talking to that fat bastard Goering', he told his lover. 'Why do you let them come to our building?'

'I've known him for a quite a while', she said. 'I can't really tell him to stay away if he wants to come down here on a social call.'

'I'm gonna kill him', snarled Siegel, 'and that dirty Goebbels too.'

'You can't do that', the Countess panicked.

'Sure, I can', reasoned Siegel. 'It's an easy set-up the way they're walking around here.'

The countess said that if Siegel did that then her husband would be shot too – by Mussolini. Siegel relented on his proposed double murder, but if they had been carried out – along with Luciano's contract on Hitler – then the Mafia might really have changed the course of World War II.

Siegel was not the only Jewish gangster who wanted to do his bit for his country and his people. Dave Berman built a gambling syndicate in Minneapolis and became a mobster associate of Bugsy Siegel when he invested a million dollars in a Las Vegas hotel. But at the age of thirty-eight in 1942, he was happy to give it all up to go and fight the Germans. He wanted to 'kill ten Nazis for every Jew'. Berman was turned down by the US Army as being too old and a convicted felon, but he joined the Canadian Army and was wounded in action in Italy, receiving an honourable discharge in 1944.

Vito Genovese – Luciano's chosen hit man for Hitler – was sixteen when he first came to the Lower East Side from Naples in 1913. He got friendly with Lucky Luciano and together they embarked on robberies and burglaries. When Luciano graduated into more organised crime, Genovese followed him, running brothels and selling heroin.

Heroin was a relatively new drug in the 1920s. Invented in 1874, when it was synthesised from morphine by the chemist C. R. Alder Wright in London, the drug was then marketed from 1898 by Bayer Pharmaceutical in Germany. *Heroin* was, until the company let it lapse, a Bayer trademark, just like *Aspirin*. Bayer had tested it on their workers. They loved it and said it made them feel 'heroic', hence the trade name. Heroin was sold as a cough medicine and a highly effective painkiller. By 1899, Bayer was producing a ton of heroin a year and exporting it to twenty-three countries. It proved especially popular in the United States, but then reports came through of users becoming hopelessly addicted to it.

It became a recreational drug in New York and all along the East Coast where some users – 'junkies' – collected junk metal to sell to support their habit. Bayer stopped making heroin in 1913. The following year, the use of heroin without prescription was outlawed in the US and in 1919 doctors were banned from prescribing it. By then, there were thousands of addicts and both Jewish and Italian gangsters stepped in. By 1925, Luciano and Genovese were New York's chief suppliers of smuggled heroin.

Intriguingly, an FBI memorandum of 28 August 1935 quotes a Bureau of Narcotics circular saying that Lucky Luciano accompanied another gangster called Jack 'Legs' Diamond to Weimar Germany in the summer of 1930.

> It was believed [said the FBI] that a conspiracy existed to smuggle narcotics from Europe into the United States. Diamond was arrested in Germany and deported, and the statement was made by the Narcotic Bureau that they believe the resulting publicity disrupted the plans of Diamond, Luciana [*sic*] and the other associates . . .

Three years later Hitler and his Nazis may well have disrupted the plans themselves.

In the Castellammarese War, Vito Genovese supported Luciano's strategy and was one of the four hit men who shot dead Joe the Boss. With the death of Maranzano shortly after, Genovese shared in the crime boom enjoyed by Luciano and his associates.

In 1932, Genovese met an attractive woman called Anna Petillo Vernotico – but she was married. Weeks later, her husband was found strangled. Both his killers were later eliminated. Genovese was ruthless and would kill anyone to get what he wanted. With the arrival of Thomas Dewey, the heat was turned up on New York's leading gangsters and Genovese made contingency plans for his escape. He put hundreds of thousands of dollars in a Swiss bank account and re-established contacts with criminals in Naples.

In 1937, with Luciano sent to jail, and accusations of murdering a fellow mobster, Ferdinand Boccia, hanging over him, Genovese fled to Italy. As a senior American mobster with lots of money to spread around, he became close to the Fascist regime and even friendly with Count Galeazzo Ciano, Mussolini's young foreign minister and son-in-law. It was Ciano who advocated the Fascist alliance with Hitler and signed the Berlin–Rome Axis agreement in 1936. But Hitler's invasion of Poland, conducted without consulting Italy, infuriated Ciano and he tried to take Mussolini out of any military commitment. Events overtook them both with the fall of France, and Mussolini decided to enter the war on the German side on 10 June 1940.

Fascist party secretary Achille Pisani introduced Genovese to Ciano and the count encouraged the American gangster to invest some of his fortune in an electricity power plant in Nola near Naples. This investment was used to put pressure on local businessmen to deal with him – or face losing their power. Genovese also donated $250,000 to raising a Fascist Party building in Nola. In return for this generosity, the mobster was made a *commendatore* – the highest rank that could be held by a civilian in Fascist Italy.

Luke Monzelli was a lieutenant in the Carabinieri who had been assigned to follow Genovese during his time in Italy:

> Vito Genovese obviously received his award because of his sizable contribution to the Mussolini monument at Nola [said Monzelli]. Mafiosi do all kinds of good works in Sicily. They build orphanages. They offer scholarships to children of the worthy poor. They do many favours for the clergy.
>
> Quite properly they expect their deputies in Parliament to see to it that they are recognised in the New Year's list which is similar to that made up every year for the Queen of England who distributes titles to esteemed subjects . . .

However, Luciano disapproved of Genovese's association with the Fascists, saying:

> When the war started he [Genovese] didn't have to live in a country that was an enemy of the United States; there was plenty of safe places for a guy with money. But he was just rotten greedy . . .
>
> We heard Vito had gone big into junk. Anythin' that easy for him was hard to pass up, even if it meant betrayin' his own country.

Luciano claimed that Count Ciano was a cocaine addict and was so hooked on Genovese's supply that he even flew the gangster to Istanbul in his private plane to secure a batch of drugs, bringing it back to refiners in Milan. Genovese set up his own drug-trafficking route that included flying heroin over to North Africa and then shipping it eventually to America from there. This was fine when Rommel and his Afrika Korps were in command of the area, but Genovese was furious when the Allies won the war in North Africa and closed off this route.

To ingratiate himself further with Mussolini, Genovese decided to help him with a problem faced by the Fascists in New York since the

1920s – Carlo Tresca, editor of the virulently anti-Fascist newspaper *Il Martello*.

> It drove Mussolini nuts [said Luciano]. So what does that prick Genovese do? He tells Mussolini not to worry about it, that he, Don Vitone, would take care of it. And, goddammit if Vito don't put out a contract from Italy on Tresca . . .

The contract went first to Tony Bender who passed it on to an ambitious Brooklyn hoodlum called Carmine Galante. On 11 January 1943 at 9.40 p.m., the 68-year-old Tresca had just left the office of his magazine at 96 Fifth Avenue. He wore a big black hat and long flowing cloak and was accompanied by a fellow political exile, Giuseppe Callabi, when suddenly a dark saloon pulled up on the curb. 'A man got out', said the *New York Times* report, 'and fired three shots at close range at Tresca. Then the assassin jumped back into the automobile and it fled, going west on Fifteenth Street. Mr Callabi took cover.' Tresca was shot in the head and back. He stumbled a few steps towards his attacker, then collapsed in the gutter on Fifth Avenue near the northwest corner at Fifteenth Street.

The *New York Herald Tribune* described the scene in more detail:

> The Fifth Avenue intersection was dark in the dimout. There was little traffic, and few people were about. As Mr Tresca and Mr Calabi [*sic*] turned the corner onto Fifth Avenue the killer suddenly materialized in the dimout, whipped out a gun and shot four times.
>
> Two bullets went wild, but one struck Mr Tresca in the head, passing through his cheeks, and another lodged in his back. He fell into the Fifth Avenue gutter, the oversize hat he customarily wore dropping beside him, and was dead when Mr Calabi bent over his friend.

The assassin ran across Fifteenth Street to a waiting car, which sped away towards Union Square. When the police arrived, they found an empty revolver cartridge near the body and then 100 feet away, behind a row of trash cans, they found a fully loaded .38-calibre Colt revolver. Did it belong to a second assassin waiting in the shadows or was it Tresca's?

Tresca had carried a gun back in 1931 to protect himself against Fascist assassins but accidentally shot himself in the leg. Ironically, back then, Tresca celebrated the Mafia as anti-Fascists. In return, Sicilian bootleggers threatened New York Black Shirts with dire retribution if they touched Tresca. The full story was told in the *New York Herald Tribune*:

> In 1931, when Mr Tresca was leading an anti-Fascist movement among Italians here, he was approached by an ex-bootlegger who told him he had been paid to assassinate him. The bootlegger was a fugitive from justice and needed money to return to Italy. If Mr Tresca would give him the money, he said, he would forget about the murder.

News of the threat got back to the local Mafiosi who knew that Tresca was much valued by the Mafia back in Sicily who liked his anti-Fascist stance. So a mobster called on Tresca and invited him to a conference of local hoods. When he entered the room, the would-be assassin was on his knees, trembling. The hoods told him to kiss the hand of Tresca and never threaten him again. For the moment, Tresca was under the protection of the Mafia.

Mussolini's vendetta with Tresca went all the way back to the early 1900s when they had met in Switzerland as young Socialist exiles. They argued bitterly and their parting conversation went like this.

'Well, Comrade Tresca, I hope America will make you over into a real revolutionist.'

'I hope, Comrade Mussolini, that you'll quit posing and learn how to fight.'

In America, Tresca became renowned as a revolutionary. His beard, spectacles, broad-brimmed hat and cloak made him the cartoonists' epitome of the bomb-throwing anarchist. He was arrested thirty-six times and whenever there was a suspicious explosion, the bomb squad contacted him. 'They ask me what I know', said Tresca, 'but I never know anything. So we have wine.'

Over 5,000 people attended Tresca's funeral, a non-religious service held at the Manhattan Center on 34th Street. Both anti-Fascists and anti-Communists gave eulogies. At first, Communists were thought to be the most likely killers as, in recent years, Tresca had been attacking Stalin for his murderous hold on power. He had also banned Communists from entering the anti-Fascist Mazzini Society and the government's Italian-American Victory Council. But Magistrate J. Roland Sala claimed, just two days after the slaying, that Tresca was assassinated unquestionably by an agent of Mussolini.

On the same day, the 35-year-old Carmine Galante was arrested and held as a material witness. A month later, when Galante was brought before Supreme Court Justice Philip J. McCook, he was told that he was continuing to be held because of a violation of his parole. The police needed more time to build a case. When the judge then said that his case would be heard by another colleague because he was joining the army, Galante shouted out: 'I hope you mow down the Japs, judge.'

However, the police could get no direct evidence to link Galante with the murder and he walked free. They kept a phone tap on him for the next four years, but they still got nothing. Genovese was never prosecuted for ordering Tresca's killing.

During the Herlands investigation, one witness, Charles Siragusa, claimed he had a source within the New York County District Attorney's office who had received information that Lucky Luciano knew the identity of the three men who murdered Tresca. The source said that Luciano 'offered to disclose the identities of these murderers in return for outright parole and permission to remain in the United States. Mr Dewey was alleged to have rejected this offer.'

Joseph Bonanno's approach to war was different to that of Luciano and Lansky. Admittedly, he did not have to profess a patriotic interest in the war because he was not in a situation where he needed to work a deal with the US government. He maintained a low profile and spent part of the war period out of New York in Tucson, Arizona, where he lived quietly with his family for several winters. There, his main inconvenience was wartime rationing of food and gasoline and the commotion caused by his wife losing a coffee pot.

Bonanno's view on the war was that it wasn't his battle. In his old Sicilian world, nationalism was not favoured by men of Tradition. They had fought against Italian and other foreign rule for centuries. 'Our fighting is personal, direct, man-to-man', he said.

Bonanno registered for the draft at the start of the war but said he was not called up because he owned a dairy. In 1945, Bonanno became a naturalised citizen of the United States. At the citizenship ceremony held in Brooklyn, he was asked by the Federal commissioner: 'If you become a citizen and have to fight against Italians, what will you do?'

'My duty is to fight for my country', he answered carefully.

'But what if you are sent to fight in Italy?'

'I would do my duty', he insisted. 'But in my heart', he thought later, 'I would feel bad about killing Italians.'

There is, of course, an inconsistency in this. Italians were foreigners to a Sicilian – and he did not mind killing them in a gang war either. What he really meant, in typical Sicilian style, was that he did not subscribe to fighting in any war on behalf of a nation. He fought only his private wars. In that, he most definitely maintained the tradition of old Sicily – an attitude left behind by other New World gangsters.

Joseph Valachi was a low-level Mafioso, serving as a 'soldier' to Vito Genovese. He functioned as a hit man and made money from loan-sharking and the numbers racket. When the war came, he was thirty-nine. The shift to a war economy had its effect on him along with the rest of the Mafia in New York. Many of his lower-end workers, 'runners', could earn more money working in war production factories and they drifted away from crime. With plenty of jobs and money around, the poorer members of the community stopped borrowing from Valachi and stopped playing the numbers lottery game.

Valachi had invested some of his ill-gained money in a clothes-making factory and this won a contract to produce military orders. It was not enough for Valachi and he looked around for some other money-making scam. He considered selling heroin, but his potential partners were arrested trying to bring in morphine from Mexico. Instead, he found a new opportunity in exploiting the wartime black market in fuel ration stamps. 'I thought it was penny-ante stuff', he said at first. 'Then I find out how them pennies can mount up.'

The owner of his local garage knew he was connected and asked him to get some ration stamps. Valachi met another low-ranking mobster called Frank Luciano (no relation to Lucky) and got 10,000 gallons-worth of stamps from him. As the middleman, Valachi made $189. It wasn't a huge sum, but Valachi didn't have to do much to get it. His next transaction with Frank Luciano was for ten times as much – and they struck up a partnership.

The ration stamps they sold had to be genuine. They could not pass off fakes as this was like handling counterfeit money and would attract too much attention. Instead, vast numbers of stamps were obtained by breaking into the local branches of the Office of Price Administration (OPA). This was generally left to gangs of burglars who passed the stamps on to the Mafia. Such an upsurge in the theft of stamps encouraged some OPA officers to put them in banks, but others joined the boom and sold them on to gangsters. At one time, it was estimated that some 250,000 gallons of gasoline a day was being diverted on to the black market. Eventually, the government had to issue a national appeal saying that the 'lives of our boys in uniform depend on millions of gallons of gasoline.'

Valachi did not care about that. The money was starting to roll in. Sometimes, as the stolen stamps bore serial numbers, they were considered too hot and would be dumped by the mobsters on unsuspecting middlemen. In one day, stamps representing eight million gallons were shifted in such a way. The vast amount of stamps temporarily depressed the market and dealers lost a lot of money, but Valachi didn't expect any of them to complain to the Mafia. By the end of the war, he had made over $200,000 from selling on black market stamps. 'It was the best business I was ever in', said Valachi, 'some of the big dealers made millions out of it, and it lasted right up to when they threw the A-bomb on the Japs.'

One of the biggest ration stamp dealers was Lucky Luciano. He ran the business from inside his jail with the help of Meyer Lansky and Frank Costello. Apart from dealing in gas, they also cornered the meat market, as Luciano remembered:

> Tommy Lucchese had taken over a lot of the restaurants that [Dutch] Schultz used to control, and the outfit was not only supplyin' meat but we was sellin' 'em the stamps so they could buy it. Frank [Costello] told me we had a good lock on about 400 gas stations where we bought a piece in each one all the way from New York to Louisiana.

The extent of the secret war fought between the OPA and the gangsters ripping off ration stamps was finally revealed in August 1945 in a newspaper report. Counterfeit stamps had been detected early in the war by the use of black lamps and chemical tests. It was stolen genuine stamps that were the most difficult to trace. These stamps were taken from filling stations or distribution companies in which the fuel companies had deposited used stamps after pasting them on sheets, known as 'bingo sheets' in the black market. Said the report:

> Some of the black market gangs – the cruder element – steamed the ration stamps off sheets which their men had stolen or bought them from free-lance thieves. These stamps became known as 'steam-offs' by Federal agents, who later spotted them on other sheets during routine inspections at the OPA ration currency verification center here.

Some of the cleverer mobsters got wise to this, understanding that the steam produced chemical changes in the stamps, which could be easily spotted by government experts.

> One of the black market 'master minds' made use of the laws of physics to break the laws of rationing [quipped the reporter]. He knew the effect of extreme cold on the glue of the 'bingo' sheets would cause the stamps to pop right off the paper. Thus were 'pop-offs' born.

Household fridges were not cold enough for this operation and so mobsters rigged up freezers to make the stamps come off instantaneously. OPA investigators foiled this by discovering that the quick freezing made tiny changes in the dimensions of the stamps and so, with delicate measuring equipment, they could detect the criminal stamps. With such high-tech methods, the OPA claimed, over three years, to have saved an estimated 25,000,000 gallons of gasoline that otherwise would have gone to the black market. This victory was probably news to the Mafia who were more than happy with their profits from wartime ration stamps.

'That was some business until the war was over', said Luciano.

Chapter Nine

Recruiting the Mafia

The decision to invade Sicily was made in Casablanca, Morocco, in January 1943. The decision makers were Winston Churchill, Prime Minister of Great Britain, and Franklin D. Roosevelt, President of the United States. Roosevelt wanted the Soviet leader Stalin to attend the conference but he was busy overseeing the Russian defeat of a German army at Stalingrad. It was the turning point of World War II. Churchill had won his own victory over Nazi Germany in North Africa with the defeat of Rommel's Afrika Korps at El Alamein two months earlier. 'Before Alamein we never had a victory', Churchill wrote later. 'After Alamein we never had a defeat.'

With success developing also in the Pacific, the US Joint Chiefs of Staff wanted to carry on the momentum and launch their long proposed cross-Channel invasion of France. They had been ready to go a year earlier, but Churchill was cautious and argued they should land a force in North Africa instead. Roosevelt agreed. This time, at Casablanca, the US Chiefs of Staff pushed again, impatient to win the war in Europe with a direct assault on Nazi Germany. Roosevelt knew that Stalin wanted a second front opened in Europe to take some of the pressure off his forces, but again, he came down on the side of Churchill and the British Chiefs of Staff who argued for more time to build up the Allied forces. They preferred to assault the soft underbelly of Axis Europe by attacking Mussolini's Italy.

The argument raged for the ten days of the conference. US Naval Commander-in-Chief Admiral Ernest King said that all US forces should be deployed in the Pacific if France was not to be invaded. Eventually, on the insistence of General George Marshall, it was agreed that a planning staff was to be set up to prepare for an invasion of France, but the operation would not take place until 1944. Churchill, Roosevelt, and the British Chiefs of Staff had won the debate.

It would be the last time that Churchill's personal influence on Roosevelt would determine Allied strategy in the war. As General Albert Wedemeyer, chief of US Joint Staff Planners, summed it up: 'One might say we came, we listened and we were conquered.'

In the meantime, once the Allied forces had taken Tunisia and won the war in North Africa, there was to be an immediate invasion of Mediterranean Axis territory. But where exactly should they strike? Churchill recorded his thoughts in his history of the war:

> I was myself sure that Sicily should be the next objective, and the Combined Chiefs of Staff took the same view. The Joint Planners, on the other hand, together with Lord Mountbatten, felt that we should attack Sardinia rather than Sicily, because they thought it could be done three months earlier . . .
>
> I remained obdurate, and, with the Combined Chiefs of Staff solid behind me, insisted on Sicily. The Joint Planners, respectful but persistent, then said that this could not be done until August 30. At this stage I personally went through all the figures with them, and thereafter the President and I gave orders that D-Day was to be during the favourable July moon period, or if possible, the favourable June moon period.

At the end of the Casablanca conference on 24 January, President Roosevelt addressed the press and told them 'peace can come to the world only by the total elimination of German and Japanese war power . . .' This meant that the Allied powers would only accept an unconditional surrender from Germany, Italy and Japan.

Churchill backed up this statement, but it has since been criticised for prolonging the fighting at the end of war. As a result of it, went the argument, German forces felt they had nothing to lose by carrying on fighting. This meant that Allied forces would face strong resistance from German forces in any invasion of Europe – and that included Sicily. Any extra-military assistance to help reduce the intensity of this resistance would thus be very much appreciated.

The US Navy always believed the main struggle of the war was in the Pacific and its leaders were irritated by what they considered distracting issues in Europe. This lack of interest in the European theatre of operations compounded a lack of intelligence in the Mediterranean area. Rear Admiral W. S. Pye made this clear in a speech to graduates at the Naval Training School in New York on 16 March 1944:

> In the present war the situation in regard to intelligence differs greatly from the last war, particularly in the Pacific. In the Atlantic, too, especially in North Africa and Italy, we found that we lacked much information required for the most effective planning.
>
> We should not be too critical because of the unavailability of such latter information, for up to three years ago or less, no one could have foreseen our need for information on the coasts of North Africa and Italy.

They had just not expected to be fighting in the Mediterranean. Traditionally, this sphere of influence belonged to the British and the Royal Navy. As a result of the decision at the Casablanca conference, US Navy Intelligence had to work hard and fast to gather the information needed for a successful invasion. Interestingly, Pye added another excuse for a lack of intelligence preparedness – snobbery:

> A combination of a shortage of officers, the cost of a large intelligence organization and a feeling among many Americans that intelligence duty is somewhat akin to spying and, therefore, in time of peace is an undignified and unworthy occupation.

Despite these excuses, US Naval Intelligence set about the task of preparing for the invasion of Sicily – Operation Husky – with speed and imagination. The officers chosen for the mission came from the Third Naval District – the same men who had been helping Haffenden and MacFall secure the New York docks. The fact that both operations involved making contact with Italian-speakers from criminal organisations was no coincidence.

Lieutenant Anthony J. Marsloe was appointed senior officer of a group of four Naval Combat Intelligence officers sent to North Africa in May 1943 to take part in Husky. A graduate of St John's University Law School, Marsloe had served under MacFall in the District Intelligence Office from February 1942 and knew all about the contacts with Lanza and Luciano. He was one of the most ardent defenders of the policy of talking to the Mafia, as he told the Herlands enquiry:

> Commander Haffenden's theory was correct. Yes, the theory was correct because it neutralized the possible use of the underworld by the enemy; and the underworld was used as a possible means of obtaining information in order to aid our war effort.
>
> Every available source of information which can be used to prevent, as well as to apprehend, those who are a potential or actual danger during an emergency or outbreak of hostilities is warranted by the unusual circumstances.

The other members of Marsloe's team included three more officers from the Third Naval District Intelligence Office: Lieutenant Joachim Titolo, Lieutenant Paul A. Alfieri, and Ensign James F. Murray. Titolo was a practicing attorney who also served as Deputy District Director of the OPA in its battle against mobsters exploiting the black market in ration stamps. He also received a letter of commendation for his role in investigating the German saboteurs who landed at Amagansett, Long Island. Alfieri would serve as Chief Investigator of the Waterfront Commission of New York Harbor. All of them understood very well the workings of the New York underworld.

On 24 May 1943, Commander Haffenden became directly involved in the invasion effort when he was appointed Officer-in-Charge of 'F' section in the Third District Intelligence Office. It was also called the 'Target' section and was concerned with gathering strategic intelligence on Sicily and Italy.

This process had begun informally in the latter part of 1942 when Haffenden saw the value of gaining information from Italian-speaking New Yorkers now that American forces were to be fully engaged in the Mediterranean. Operation Torch landed over 50,000 American troops in North Africa in November 1942.

> Numerous Italians of Sicilian birth or background and their relatives [said the Herlands Report] were enlisted to provide Commander Haffenden and his assistants information about the terrain, harbors, etc, of Sicily in anticipation of the Allied invasion there. Through these contacts and informants, the names of friendly Sicilian natives and even Sicilian underworld and Mafia personalities who could be trusted were obtained and actually used in the Sicilian campaign.

Commander Haffenden later told the Kefauver Senate Committee enquiry into organised crime that this was a substantial process involving 146 investigators gathering information from thousands of sources.

Marsloe described his own involvement in the research:

> It is my recollection that B-7 Section, or Counter-Intelligence Section, as well as the Investigation Section, was engaged in a continuous search for logistic information concerning the enemy; and because of my personal knowledge of Sicily and the dialects of Sicily, from time to time various personalities, otherwise unidentified, were sent to me by Commander Haffenden. These men were interviewed and photographs, documents, or other matters of interest were taken and in turn given to Commander Haffenden . . .
>
> Speaking to Commander Haffenden it was my understanding that this was part of the plan created by him and that these men in turn were being sent by his underworld contacts.

Meyer Lansky became involved in this process, taking numerous Italians to both the Astor and the Church Street HQs to meet Haffenden. 'Prior to our attack on Sicily', he recalled, 'the conversations ran of their knowledge of the coastline and the contour of the land off the coast.'

Haffenden wanted to know about all the channels around the island and pulled out a big map for Lansky's Italian contacts to comment on – pointing out their villages and what they knew about the surrounding landscape, as Lansky remembered:

> The Navy wanted from the Italians all the pictures they could possibly get of every port in Sicily, of every channel, and also to get men that were in Italy more recently and had knowledge of water and coastlines – to bring them up to the Navy so they could talk to them.

Lansky brought in prominent refugees from the island, including a former mayor of a major Sicilian town. 'He was brought through these gentlemen that visited Charlie Luciano', said Lansky. 'They solicited his assistance and he wanted to be of assistance and he was going to bring others. I brought him to the Naval Intelligence at 90 Church Street.'

Socks Lanza was also called in to help on this front, bringing in Italian-Americans with useful information about Sicily. One of these contacts was Vincent Mangano, who had run an import–export business between Italy and the US. Joe Adonis – one of the four killers of Joe the Boss – was asked to accompany Mangano to Haffenden's office, so maybe there is a suggestion of some enforcement here. Lansky makes this more clear in his recollections:

> Sometimes some of the Sicilians were very nervous. Joe [Adonis] would just mention the name of Lucky Luciano and say he had given them orders to talk. If the Sicilians were still reluctant, Joe would stop smiling and say, 'Lucky will not be pleased to hear that you have not been helpful'.

Adonis arranged for many useful contacts to provide information on Sicily. On one occasion, he 'sort of' kidnapped a man who had been mayor of a village in Sicily. Mangano was said by Lansky to be the chief contact between the Mafia in the United States and its parent organization in Sicily. 'Joe [Adonis] really worked very hard', said Lansky, 'to show he could be a patriotic American. He found some Italians we didn't even know existed.'

Moses Polakoff was roped in as well and brought in his own Italian contacts. Those who only spoke Italian were passed on to Haffenden's staff of translators. Lieutenant Marsloe was in charge of the linguistics sections. He spoke Italian, French and Spanish and understood the many Sicilian dialects that came up in interrogations.

Part-way through this project in January 1943, Socks Lanza was taken out of the team. He was arrested and sentenced to 7½–15 years for extortion and conspiracy. The main accusation was that Lanza was a 'racketeer czar' who had operated a shakedown scheme to get control of union funds. It came as a shock to other mobsters who thought their enthusiastic help for the war effort would shield them from such retribution.

When Socks Lanza stood before Judge James Garrett Wallace, nothing was said about his war work or even alluded to. His lawyer argued for leniency, saying he had been an asset to the community, but when he elaborated on this by mentioning his hard work on behalf of his union – the same union he wanted to loot – Judge Wallace broke in and said 'He was an unmitigated nuisance to the community.'

It had been clear from the start that Lanza's help would not be traded for leniency, but it left a bitter taste in the mouth of many of Lanza's friends. By then, Naval Intelligence probably felt they had had the best of Lanza anyway. Lansky was convinced it was the work of Thomas Dewey – he had just become governor of New York and wanted to demonstrate his anti-Mafia credentials by sending to jail one of its leading figures.

Despite the removal of Lanza, the Navy's work continued. Most mobsters had little alternative but to continue with their assistance, especially if they were connected with Luciano, as it was still his only chance of any reduction of his sentence.

Captain Roscoe MacFall, overall commander of the Third District Intelligence Office, was kept fully informed of the entire research procedure and commended Haffenden for his handling of it:

> Prior to the landing of US forces in North Africa, and also subsequent to that time, the District Intelligence Office concentrated a considerable portion of its forces on the collection of strategic intelligence on the North African theatre and the Mediterranean basin . . . It was felt that, since Mussolini had been responsible for the expulsion of many Sicilians, persons of Sicilian origin, might be willing to aid Naval Intelligence.

This was a direct reference to Cesare Mori's campaign against the Mafia in Sicily in the 1920s and how many of them had relocated to the United States. It was these people the US Navy wanted to speak to, said MacFall:

> Haffenden would report quite frequently to me that he and the men under him were interviewing large numbers of persons of Italian birth, and that many of these informants came to Naval Intelligence through the instigation of Luciano.

All this information was recorded on the big wall map Lansky saw in Haffenden's office. George Tarbox was the civilian artist responsible for charting the information. He produced a large map of Italy and Sicily, with transparent overlay drawings showing the information from numerous reports, all given reference numbers. When it was finished, it was three feet wide and four feet long and mounted in a wooden frame. This and other maps were later destroyed after the invasion.

> A great deal of similar data [concluded MacFall] was sent to the headquarters of Naval Intelligence in Washington DC.

> While the names of certain classes of informants were then kept, such as banking house personnel and records, businessmen, etc, it was not deemed necessary or desirable to record permanently the names of underworld informants or persons coming through them.

Captain Wallace S. Wharton was on the receiving end of all this information in Washington. He was head of the Counter-Intelligence Section, Office of Naval Intelligence, and was particularly interested in potential sabotage and espionage activities in Italy. Haffenden visited him personally at least once a month, as Wharton recalled:

> On the occasions when Commander Haffenden gave names to me, he told me that he had obtained these names from his contacts in the underworld. The names of the individuals in Sicily who could be trusted turned out to be 40% correct, upon eventual check-up and on the basis of actual experience.

Other crucial intelligence passed on by Haffenden to Wharton in Washington included the names of Sicilians who might be friendly to US armed forces in the event of an invasion. Throughout this research process, Luciano was regularly mentioned by Naval Intelligence officers as a helpful presence, guaranteeing the free flow of information from Italian-Americans. Luciano himself, however, denied the existence of this dimension of his wartime alliance with the US government:

> As far as my helpin' the government was concerned, then or even the following year when they said I helped 'em open up Sicily for the invasion by gettin' the cooperation of the Mafia guys to help the American troops, that was all horseshit.
>
> It would be easy for me to say there was somethin' to all that, like people have been sayin' for years and I've been lettin' 'em think, but there wasn't. As far as me helpin' the army land in Sicily, you gotta remember I left there when I was, what – nine? The only guy I knew really well over there, and he wasn't even a Sicilian, was that little prick Vito Genovese. In fact, at that time the dirty little bastard was livin' like a king in Rome, kissin' Mussolini's ass.

This contradicts an earlier statement in which Luciano quoted Vito Genovese's letters to him, saying 'the most important thing he said was that in Sicily my name was like a king . . . in Sicily they thought of me as a real number one guy. And that set me to thinkin' how I could give

Dewey the legitimate excuse he would need to let me out.' Clearly, he had considered his reputation in Sicily as a source of leverage with the US government.

Meyer Lansky had yet another view of Luciano's involvement:

> Lucky came up with a plan that I thought was pretty wild, but I passed it on to Haffenden . . . He wanted to join up with the invading army. He thought he could go in as an ordinary soldier and be a kind of liaison or scout. He said he was ready to go with the first troops.
>
> He thought his presence would guarantee Sicilian cooperation. He didn't want anybody to think he was just trying to get out of prison; he was ready to risk his neck to prove his point. He said he was prepared to be parachuted into the island . . .

Lansky laughed at that – he had a vision of Luciano landing on top of a church. He toned down Luciano's proposal but he did put it to Haffenden, saying maybe they could land Luciano by submarine. Haffenden took the idea to Washington but said his superiors turned it down. In fact, Captain Wharton later testified that such an offer had been made:

> Haffenden told me that Luciano was willing to go to Sicily and contact natives there, in the event of an invasion by our armed forces, and to win these natives over to the support of the United States war effort, particularly during the amphibious phase of an invasion.

Wharton said that Haffenden argued strongly for Luciano to go to Sicily, saying he could go to Governor Dewey and get him to pardon Luciano, releasing him to travel to Sicily via a neutral country such as Portugal. He also claimed that Luciano suggested the best place to invade Sicily was the Golfo di Castellammare, near Palermo, home to many leading Mafiosi.

Wharton considered the idea but later rejected it. He commended Haffenden's enthusiasm and imagination but sometimes felt his ideas were not always balanced by good judgement. Naval Intelligence was happy with the information they were getting from Luciano and didn't want to attract any more attention by releasing Public Enemy No. 1 from prison on a secret mission. That was certainly Lansky's take on why such a mission was rejected.

In the light of this bizarre proposal, why then did Luciano deny any involvement in the projected invasion of Sicily? It may well go back to his realisation that if he was released from jail he would be deported to Italy, and he didn't want anyone over there viewing him as a collaborator with a foreign invader – however friendly that nation might be.

That Frank Costello might have been trying an alternative route to get Luciano out of jail was revealed by Federal Narcotics Agent George White. He testified to the Kefauver Senate Committee enquiry into organised crime in 1950 that he had been approached by a drug smuggler called August Del Grazio. He claimed he was acting on behalf of two attorneys and Frank Costello. Del Grazio told White that Luciano was a principal member of the Mafia and had many useful connections in the Italian underworld. 'The proffered deal', recalled Senator Kefauver, citing White's testimony, 'was that Luciano would use his Mafia position to arrange contacts for undercover American agents and that therefore Sicily would be a much softer target than it might otherwise be.' Luciano's price was to be his parole and that he would then go to Sicily to make the arrangements.

Lansky denied the involvement of either of these two gentlemen in the 'Luciano project'. 'I never knew of George White', he said, 'and I still don't know of August Del Grazio.'

In May 1943, after several months preparing for the invasion of Sicily, it was time for Haffenden's task force to leave the desks of New York and join the soldiers in North Africa. Marsloe recalled:

> Commander R. Thayer came to New York and spoke to me concerning a mission to be made up of selected personnel having intensive law-enforcement background and experience with particular emphasis on Italy – language qualifications – to land with the combat troops and perform certain essential services.

With just two hours' notice, he left for Washington for further briefing. Marsloe was joined by Titolo, Alfieri, and Murray – all young naval intelligence officers keen to trade the streets of Manhattan for some real action abroad. Two other linguist officers travelled with them. They spent two days in Washington studying reports and on 15 May they flew via Newfoundland and Iceland to Scotland, and then on to the Mediterranean. In North Africa, at Mers-el-Kebir, they were given intensive commando training with the Counter-Intelligence Corps of the US Army. They were also brought up to date with all the latest information on Sicily. 'We were the beneficial recipients of intensive indoctrination in North Africa from sources such as American and British monographs on the area', recalled Marsloe.

So far, this story has focused on the American dimension of the relationship between the Mafia and Allied Intelligence – the so-called deal between Luciano and the US Navy to help the war effort. But, it must be emphasised, that the Americans were not the only nation willing to make a pact with the devil to win the war. So were the British.

One of the British reports that Marsloe and his team read was the 1943 *Handbook on Politics and Intelligence Services* for Sicily. It was prepared by the North African branch of the British Secret Intelligence Service (SIS, also known as MI6). It was based on a variety of information sources, including the interrogation of Axis prisoners of war. Among a list of key Sicilian personalities mentioned in the report as possible contacts for the Allies was Vito La Mantia.

The British intelligence report described him as 'head of a Mafia group, but escaped arrest at the time of Mori's round-up through the refusal of his followers to speak'. The report described La Mantia as 'very anti-Fascist and, if still alive, might supply valuable information: uneducated but influential: was last reported as the manager of a property belonging to the Mafia in Via Notabartolo, Palermo.' Another influential Sicilian mentioned was a man called Le Pape. He was said to be a 'leading lawyer of independent views: used to defend the Mafia; lives in Palermo.' From this, it seems the British had no problem in making contact with leading Mafiosi in Sicily in order to help their invasion. This was not only an American idea.

In general, the same report was sceptical of the success of Mori's regime in the 1920s. 'As to the Mafia', it concluded, 'there are some indications that it was not completely destroyed by Mori's savage purge . . .'

This was a view backed up by a report of 9 April 1943 prepared by the Joint Staff Planners for the US Joint Chiefs of Staff. It was entitled *Special Military Plan for Psychological Warfare in Sicily*. The Joint Staff Planners (JSP, but also called Joint Planning Staff) were a new advisory organisation combining US military, naval and air personnel. They set out a plan to undermine Axis forces in Sicily.

The JSP analysis made much of the social connections between America and Sicily, referring to Italian-American veterans of World War I living in Sicily. 'Links between Sicilians in America and their relatives in Sicily', they said, 'have been maintained through mutual assistance associations which customarily bear the name of the Sicilian town from which its founders emigrated.' 'There have also been reports of a resurgence of the Mafia', said the JSP, defining it as a 'secret organization for securing vengeance'. In the next sentence, the JSP mentioned a report of a whole Sicilian town that had revolted against the Fascists. So many had been involved in the unrest that the Fascists could not arrest them all. In their conclusion, the JSP said that 'Sicilians are temperamentally susceptible to our psychological warfare agencies; they are war weary, and ferment for revolt exists.'

Their suggested lines of action included the organisation of dissident elements for active resistance. Their methods to accomplish this involved the infiltration of Sicilian-Americans onto the island to gather information on the condition of both the civilian and military populations, and to establish communications between Sicily and their headquarters in North Africa.

Some of the personnel required for this mission included Marsloe and his Naval Intelligence team, as well as others who had undergone selection and training in the United States and North Africa 'with proper language qualifications for use in Sicily as organizers, fomenters, and operational nuclei in the conduct of guerrilla warfare.' The JSP *Special Military Plan for Psychological Warfare in Sicily* gave further detail about preparing dissident elements in Sicily for active resistance. It described the 'Establishment of contact and communications with the leaders of separatist nuclei, disaffected workers, and clandestine radical groups, e.g., the Mafia, and giving them every possible aid.' That included 'Smuggling of arms and munitions to those elements', the 'Organization and supply of guerrilla bands', and the 'Provisioning of active members of such groups and their families.'

The JSP, it appears, was strongly recommending the arming of Sicilian Mafiosi and would encourage them to carry out sabotage on bridges, railroads, roads, and military installations. In retrospect, it is a sensational admission, but at the time the Mafia were considered just another dissident element.

The JSP plan was sent for approval to the Joint Chiefs of Staff in Washington DC. General George Marshall, chairman of the American Joints Chief of Staff, was at the top of the list for receiving the report.

In the light of the revelations contained in this secret plan, it cannot now be said that no one at the very highest level knew about US government proposals for collaboration with the Mafia. It was not just a US Naval Intelligence project engaged in at a relatively low level of command. It was understood and recommended by the very highest too – the Joint Chiefs of Staff.

The *Special Military Plan for Psychological Warfare in Sicily* was approved by the Joint Chiefs of Staff in Washington on 15 April 1943. It was then passed on to the Commanding General, North African Theater of Operations, in Algiers – General Dwight D. Eisenhower.

The message was clear. The Mafia were to be deployed in the conquest of Sicily.

Chapter Ten

Mafia Resistance

The 1943 SIS Sicily *Handbook* made it clear that the British, along with their American allies, were happy to talk to Sicilian Mafiosi if it would help their cause. The 1943 JSP *Special Military Plan* revealed that the Allies would arm and support the Mafia in a guerrilla war against the Axis forces. But were Sicilians already engaged in a secret war against their occupiers?

Violent encounters were mentioned by Sicilian prisoners of war. In a British Interrogation Report of 28 May 1943, a PoW from Palermo said that he had seen drunken German soldiers shouting insults at locals. Fights would break out and sometimes Sicilians would be shot in brawls with the Germans. German soldiers in Palermo were said to molest the local women. The JSP plan reported further action:

> Trouble has resulted from relations between German soldiers and Sicilian girls. German officers and soldiers have been killed or injured and the Germans now go out at night only in groups of three or more.

Evidence of this new sense of threat felt by the Germans was provided by an order from Field Marshal Albert Kesselring, German Commander-in-Chief in Italy, captured by an Allied agent in June 1943:

> German troops in Sicily may only leave their quarters in parties; side arms must always be worn. The troops are to be given detailed instructions in a suitable form, first, that no provocation of the Sicilian population must occur – on the contrary every possible form of assistance must be afforded to

> the population – and secondly, that any attack which may be made against German soldiers by the civil population, must however be repelled by the sharpest measures, if necessary by force of arms.

'The Germans heartily reciprocated the dislike felt for them', said the SIS *Handbook*, 'and referred to the Sicilians as "unfriendly, wild barbarians".'

That Sicilian attacks might be part of a resistance movement was suggested by Foreign Office correspondence in December 1941. It came from an anonymous Polish source living in Sicily:

> In Sicily people are wearing the Union Jack under the lapels of their coats and anxiously awaiting a British landing. Their relations with the central authorities in Italy are illustrated by the fact that no Italian officer or official not speaking the Sicilian dialect can venture to leave his lodgings at night without running the risk of being stabbed in the back. The authorities are well aware of this and are endeavouring to break what they call 'Sicilian resistance' by transferring all Sicilians, employed in the army or the civil service, to Lombardy or the Alpine provinces.

Further evidence of organised discontent was recorded in a British Foreign Office report sent by telegram to the Prime Minister and British Chiefs of Staff in October 1941. It described an angry crowd in Palermo tearing up ration cards and burning down the town hall. Severe food shortages were believed by the Sicilians to be due to the dispatch of foodstuffs to Germany.

This picture of a demoralised Sicily was matched in a US Joint Intelligence Committee (JIC) report prepared in Washington DC in the same month and sent to the War Cabinet Offices in London. It quoted the American Embassy in Rome as being of the opinion that a British landing in Sicily might actually be welcomed by the local population.

That the Mafia themselves were involved in a resistance movement was claimed in a *Memorandum on conditions and politics in Sicily* prepared by the British Political Warfare Executive (PWE) in August 1942. A copy was later passed on to the Foreign Office.

> Although the Mafia was 'officially' suppressed by Mussolini in 1929 [said the PWE], recent reports indicate that it is still active to-day. German soldiers in Sicily are picked off at the

> rate of almost one a day, according to Count Sforza, the former Italian Foreign Minister . . . No Italians are taken as hostages or shot, he said, because Hitler and Mussolini desire to maintain the pretence of 'good relations'.

Count Carlo Sforza had a meeting in Washington in June 1942 with Dean Acheson, Assistant Secretary of State. Sforza presented himself as the leader of Free Italians and claimed there were numerous Italians ready to join an underground movement in the kingdom.

The idea of a Mafia resistance was also mentioned by Vanni Buscemi-Montana, a prominent anti-Fascist based in New York and vice-president of the Federation of Sicilian Societies in America. In July 1942, he submitted a five-page report to the US government, which was passed on to the Office of Strategic Services (OSS). He made a distinction between the two generations of Mafiosi on the island:

> Mussolini's war against the old Mafia was supported by the young Mafia and was motivated mainly, from one side, by political reason, and from the other side, by economic reasons, for the young Mafia, already in Fascist uniform, intended to supplant the old mafia and organize its own rackets without any fear of competition.

He said that members of the old Mafia then emigrated to Tunisia and America, but that anti-Fascist underground groups remained in Sicily. They were located throughout major towns, including Palermo, Trapani, Castellammare, Caltanissetta and others. Buscemi-Montana argued:

> These groups, the old Mafia, and thousands of soldiers who have deserted the army and are hiding in the country, are responsible for the killing of so many German officers in Sicily . . . The strongest opposition and deepest hate against the Nazi and the Fascist in Italy is today in Sicily.

Buscemi-Montana suggested an action plan that could involve Sicilian-American groups. They could organise radio broadcasts encouraging Sicilians to start a guerrilla war against the German occupiers and the Italian Fascists. It would be in the spirit of the famous medieval Sicilian Vespers in which locals rose up to attack their French rulers. That this level of discontent could rapidly escalate to a more political dimension was picked up by the PWE:

> Confidential reports dated September 1941 hinted at a separatist movement in Sicily . . . The resentment of the four million Sicilians living under the German yoke had been crystallised into a movement for separation from a nation which had delivered them to this subjection. They were preparing for the first favourable opportunity to revolt and declare themselves independent of Italy.

This referred to a confidential report describing an attempt to set up an independent republic in Sicily. The attempt was made in an unspecified small town and was crushed by soldiers after only a few days. This backed up other references to Mussolini's crack-down on dissidents within the Sicilian government in August 1941 when Sicilian civil servants were shifted *en masse* to the mainland.

> Separatist tendencies in Sicily [concluded the SIS *Handbook*] received a certain stimulus from Italy's entry into the war. The Sicilians, besides harbouring a certain dislike of the mainland, were reluctant to be dragged into hostilities. A few sources state that the Sicilians would even welcome the Allies as their advent might enable them to achieve their independence. There is however no confirmation of this.

The SIS assessment badly underplayed this. The Separatist movement would become a major force in war-time Sicily – and the Mafia would be directly behind it.

On an everyday level, the most annoying aspects for ordinary Sicilians of Sicily's involvement in the war were widespread food shortages. For some Sicilians, the situation was desperate. 'He who has no money goes to bed hungry', wrote one woman quoted by the PWE, '. . . and the children are crying and won't listen to reason. You can imagine what a state I am in. I spend my life running round the streets looking for supplies.'

This situation, much like the fuel shortages in the US, was exploited by the Mafia through their control of the black market. That this then created a climate of wider discontent with the Axis occupation can be seen as an unintended but strong element of dissidence due to Mafia activities.

The British SIS *Handbook* reported a Sicilian peasant returning from military service at the end of November 1942:

> I am not going to sow either wheat or oats, only broad beans. Being mobilised has ruined me. I do not intend to work myself to death now. The mule that I sold for 5,000 lire when I was called up would cost me 16,000 or 18,000 lire to buy now. Today you cannot buy for 1,000 lire what once you could have bought for 100.

Sicilian prisoners of war complained of a lack of supplies, stating that the Germans were removing food from the countryside. An anonymous Sicilian writing in the London *Observer* in July 1943 blamed the poor food situation on Mussolini's failure to address fundamental agrarian problems:

> It is not the first time that Sicilians have had the sad opportunity of experiencing the consequences of Fascist bluff. Mussolini . . . promised water to the peasants afflicted by drought, but the peasants saw nothing except newspaper stories of the irrigation schemes. He promised agrarian reform, in order to redeem Sicily from the surviving feudal distribution of land, but when the beginning of the great work was officially announced, Mussolini declared war, and Sicily became a war zone.
>
> The semi-feudal regime of Sicily is reflected in the famous illegal bands of 'mafia' which Fascism first boasted to have suppressed, and then simply made Fascist. The 'mafiosi' are the relics of feudal landlords' personal bodyguards and still keep up a sort of code of honour mingled with a love of trouble.

If Mafiosi had ever been turned Fascist, as the author claimed, it was only a temporary conversion. Now that Mussolini no longer commanded the respect of most Sicilians, the Mafia were back in control of their own destiny.

British and American intelligence agents were keen to exploit the rebellious atmosphere in Sicily. The British hoped their traditional influence among an older, English-speaking aristocracy and merchant class might prove effective, but times had changed. The SIS *Handbook* had to admit that many more Sicilians had family connections with immigrants in the USA and that many of these returned to invest their money in their native towns and villages. The Americans played hard on this relationship. A 1941 FBI interview with a Bavarian lawyer who had lived in Italy for six years before coming to New York revealed a common theme:

> The Italians love and admire the Americans [said Dr Conrad H. – during his three hour interview in Madison Avenue]. Many of them have been in America and went back to Italy after having gained some modest wealth which they are now spending with their families. The man in the street in Italy thinks that America has not joined the war because she thinks Hitler will win: but the moment America does go in with the Allies, the Italians will think that Hitler's chances have gone down so much that a change of front would be possible.

Two years later, US Joint Planning Staff had clear plans for exploiting the American link and Sicilian economic chaos. They stressed that Italy's involvement in the war had dangerously weakened the agricultural economy of Sicily. The government demanded more food, while a shortage of artificial fertiliser, usually coming from North Africa, resulted in smaller crops. As a result, many poorer farmers hoarded their products, preferring to sell them for higher prices on the black market. When they were arrested and punished for doing this, it sparked off riots.

To turn this into a weapon, the JSP suggested 'Creation of the belief among Sicilians that millions of dollars in remittances have been accumulated by Sicilians in the US for the relief of Sicily', and, 'Development of the conviction that food-ships are waiting to be rushed to Sicily'. It was a cynical suggestion – but no more than arming the Mafia.

Such information was passed on to all Allied Intelligence agents stationed in North Africa. Lieutenant Marsloe and his naval agents, along with officers from other Allied intelligence organisations, were all fully informed. They were impatient to get on with the job.

There was a strong feeling among the Mafiosi of Sicily that here, at last, might be an opportunity to set up an independent realm of their own – a Mafia kingdom in the middle of the Mediterranean. But, for the moment, the Mafia were happy to go along with the Americans and the British in their war against Hitler.

As the Allies prepared for the invasion of Sicily, there was much discussion about what would happen when they defeated the Axis troops and had to govern the island. The Mediterranean was an area of strategic interest to the British because of their long-established naval bases and their imperial route to India via the Suez Canal. British aristocrats had connections with Sicily going back at least 200 years. But the Americans also had considerable interest in the area – not just to rein in the imperial pretensions of the British. They had a large immigrant population of Italian-Americans and that meant concerned voters.

An American proposal distributed among Allied diplomats in May 1943 argued that the chief officer of the Allied Military Government, Occupied Territory (AMGOT) in Sicily should be British, but that his deputy should be American. It then went further:

> In view of the friendly attitude of many of the inhabitants of Italy toward the United States, and in consideration of the great number of American citizens of Italian descent, the President is of the opinion that the Allied Military Government should be given, particularly in the lower offices, as much of an American character and as large a proportion of American personnel as is practicable, with the purpose of facilitating our Allied war effort in Husky and in other areas that may be occupied at a later date.

A copy of this proposal was sent to Britain's Ambassador in Washington, Lord Halifax, and he sent his own comments back to the Foreign Office:

> Italian communities in New York were already beginning to lay down the law about administration of Italy. Italian communities here had an intimate knowledge and connexion with Huskyland [Sicily] and quite unimportant appointments might have reactions here (for instance it would be known at once if one of our 'anti-Fascist' appointees was a Mafia man as was not unlikely).

The decision to give the Allied invasion of Sicily an American emphasis had already been discussed by Churchill and Roosevelt in April 1943. In a telegram of 14 April, President Roosevelt gave his approval to the appointment of General Alexander as Allied Military Governor of Sicily. Alexander was British, but, the president insisted:

> In view of the friendly feeling toward American [*sic*] entertained by a great number of citizens of Italy, and in consideration of the large number of citizens of the United States who are of Italian descent, it is my opinion that our military problem will be made less difficult by giving to the

> Allied Military Government as much of an American character as is practicable.
>
> This can be accomplished at least to some extent by appointing to the offices of the Allied Military Government a large proportion of Americans.
>
> I believe that this Military Government should be represented to the world as a definitely joint Allied control and that there should be no 'senior partner'.

The next day, Prime Minister Churchill responded:

> I entirely agree with you that the utmost advantage should be taken of American ties with Italy, and that at least half of the officers of the Allied Military Government should be American and, further, if in any case or district it is found that American pre-eminence is more useful to the common cause, this should at once be arranged. The two Flags should always be displayed together and we should present a united and unbreakable front in all directions.
>
> All the above is of course without prejudice to the United States being supreme throughout the whole of French North Africa and my continuing to be your lieutenant there. I hope I have given satisfaction.

Unusually subservient, Churchill was playing his balancing act well, but his true feelings about American dominance came out in an earlier reprimand to his minister in the Middle East, Harold Macmillan. Macmillan wanted to dampen down Foreign Office references to imperial concerns in the Mediterranean. 'To be quite frank', Macmillan said in a telegram of 28 February 1943, 'I do not like the terminology of paragraph 4 regarding vital British interests in the Mediterranean. This is the old empire stuff that they [the Americans] hate so. We can get what we want without treading on these particular toes.' Churchill strongly disproved of Macmillan's craven attitude. He growled:

> With regard to your paragraph 2, it is a great mistake in my opinion to be shy about defending with the Americans (quote) vital British interests in the Mediterranean (unquote). I do not like your expression (quote) old empire stuff (unquote) which also seems to argue an apologetic outlook. In my experience which is considerable Americans respect Englishmen who do not hesitate to take a firm line about their country's rights and the British Empire.

Despite his obsequious posturing as Roosevelt's 'lieutenant', Churchill was, at heart, the old imperial warrior. This underlying national rivalry concerned some American intelligence agencies in the months leading up to the invasion of Sicily.

In 1942, Max Corvo was a 21-year-old American-Sicilian living in Middletown, Connecticut. His father had left Sicily in 1923 after refusing to accept the Fascist regime on the island. He made contact with the anti-Fascist Italian community in Chicago and New York and started his own anti-Fascist newspaper circulated widely in Connecticut.

Max Corvo volunteered for military service before Pearl Harbor because he wanted to carry on the anti-Fascist struggle of his father. At first, he was given a clerical job at the Quartermaster Training Center at Camp Lee, Virginia. Fortunately, Corvo managed to convince his superior officers that he had plans for pursuing underground warfare in Sicily and he was dispatched to Washington DC where he was introduced to various military intelligence officers. At the very end of his three-day pass, Corvo entered a building housing the Office of Strategic Services (OSS).

OSS was the brainchild of William Donovan, a US Attorney and veteran of World War I, winner of the Medal of Honor. In the 1930s, one of Donovan's clients was Winston Churchill – then merely a British MP without political power – but come 1940 this put Donovan in a useful position and he acted as a special ambassador between Roosevelt and Prime Minister Churchill. In wartime London, Donovan had access to the headquarters of Britain's Secret Intelligence Service, and met its commander, Major-General Sir Stewart Menzies.

By the time Donovan returned to the US, it had been decided to appoint him head of a new super intelligence agency – one that would span the globe, and reach deep into the hot spots of enemy territory. It was sorely needed but there was an element of opposition – J. Edgar Hoover, Director of the FBI. Hoover was already building his own intelligence empire with agents operating abroad. Hoover considered Donovan little more than a privileged amateur.

Donovan, as skilled in diplomacy as intelligence, suggested a tactful compromise. His new intelligence agency would not tread on the toes of the home duties performed by the FBI and nor would it supplant the Army's and the Navy's own intelligence sections. The compromise seemed to suit Hoover.

In July 1941, Roosevelt appointed Donovan head of a new foreign intelligence agency, calling him Co-ordinator of Information. A year later, with America at war and Donovan in uniform, he was appointed head of the Office of Strategic Services. It turned out to be the forerunner of the CIA.

OSS did not get off to a smooth start. When Donovan needed crucial information to help Eisenhower with the Allied invasion of North Africa – Operation Torch – he authorised a series of burglaries on the Spanish Embassy in Washington. When Hoover heard of it, he was furious at this action on home soil – his territory. The Joint Chiefs of Staff were forced to intervene to shield Donovan from the wrath of the FBI. Donovan's reaction was sharp. 'The Abwehr – the German secret service', he said, 'gets better treatment from the FBI than we do.' It was just the first of many turf wars between US intelligence agencies.

When Max Corvo entered the OSS building in July 1942, his timing was a little premature. North Africa and the Mediterranean were still considered a British problem, but his contacts with anti-Fascist groups in New York aroused the interest of OSS officers and his pass was extended to allow him to travel to New York and gather further information. A month later, Corvo was invited to go back to Washington and join the Italian Secret Intelligence (SI) section of OSS.

Corvo was given a training course in basic commando skills based on that used by the British Special Operations Executive (SOE). It was intended as a test of endurance and physical courage and included training in the use of explosives and unarmed combat. When he returned to his desk, his first main task was to recruit more Italian personnel to OSS, but he was in competition with the British Secret Intelligence Service as it too had been recruiting in New York among anti-Fascist exiles.

Corvo spent the next few months making contacts with leading anti-Fascists throughout the US. He worked with the Socialist Girolamo Valenti, the editor of *La Parola*, and they spoke to all kinds of expatriates, including academics, lawyers, and union leaders, but they did not speak to anyone belonging to the underworld.

> The decision to prohibit all contact with anyone having ties with the crime syndicates was made at an early date [recalled Corvo], when several efforts by OSS/Treasury sources were made to have me meet 'Lucky' Luciano who, at that time, was at Dannemora and was offering to place his ostensible contacts in Sicily at the government's disposal.

> On those occasions I explained to Brennan [chief of the Italian section at OSS] that we could gain nothing from such a tie and that the relationship might prove to be embarrassing in the future. I pointed out that the Mafia had been practically stamped out by Mussolini . . .
>
> The proponent of the meeting with Luciano was a Major White who had formerly served with the Treasury department and was simply passing on the information for whatever interest we might have.

Brennan accepted Corvo's assessment of the lack of usefulness of Luciano and the Mob and encouraged him to carry on with his work with Valenti. Corvo's supreme boss, William Donovan, head of OSS, shared his lack of interest in making contact with Mafiosi. He wanted no part of a deal with mobsters and considered the Mafia 'a supranational conspiracy without any allegiance to the United States.'

In September 1942, in New York, Corvo had a meeting with the Jewish-Italian radio broadcaster Lisa Sergio. She had worked for the Fascists, broadcasting Mussolini's speeches in English, but she left Italy in 1938 when anti-Semitic laws came into force. When Corvo returned to his hotel room, he was jumped by two men with guns. They frisked him for a weapon, then introduced themselves as agents of the US Army's Counter-Intelligence Corps (CIC). They believed Corvo was a Fascist spy and took him down to Naval Intelligence headquarters at 90 Church Street.

Corvo was interrogated for a night and a day. An OSS employee entered and told him off for not reporting to him on his arrival in New York. He was then returned to Washington where he underwent disciplinary action.

Eventually, a year later, Corvo made contact with Lieutenant Joachim Titolo of Naval Intelligence who explained the background to the incident. Titolo knew Lisa Sergio who told him that she was suspicious of Corvo, believing he might be a Fascist agent sent to track her down. Titolo then informed the CIC who brought in Corvo for questioning.

This is Corvo's view of the incident. But it might equally have been US Naval Intelligence exerting its strength in a field of activity it considered its own – especially in New York. It might also have been a slap on the wrist for Corvo's official rejection of their use of Luciano – presumably his disapproval of their methods had got back to them.

As the possibility of an invasion of Sicily grew through 1942, Corvo took part in a research drive intended to gather as much information as possible on Sicily. Even eighteenth-century British Admiralty charts were brought into use to help construct an accurate relief map of the island. World War I veterans, Spanish Civil War Garibaldi Brigade volunteers, university professors, all were contacted for their specialist knowledge.

What is notable about this process is that Corvo and his Italian section were intent on creating their own body of information on Sicily separate from that used by British intelligence – and separate from that gathered by US Naval Intelligence. They were also keen on diminishing the British influence in post-invasion Italy. Corvo feared that a British initiative to create a government-in-exile headed by Count Sforza in Tripoli would be detrimental to US interests in the region and worked hard to scupper the project. Corvo was satisfied when this resulted in a decline in British influence in the Italian refugee network in New York.

In 1943, the OSS Italian section worked on plans to insert undercover agents into Sicily. They listed information on safe contacts on the island and targets for sabotage. OSS wanted to recruit a legion of Sicilian-speaking troops – including anti-Fascist volunteers and prisoners of war in North Africa – who could spearhead the Allied landings. It was the first operational plan devised by OSS – and it did not mention the Mafia as a key part of their strategy.

Max Corvo's son, William, who has studied his father's wartime career, has emphasised the lack of OSS involvement with the Mafia:

> The reality is outlined in a number of documents with the Max Corvo archive which include the detail of OSS radio traffic between OSS Italy and OSS Africa. These documents are sequentially numbered and dated and cover the entire period of the Sicilian invasion and occupation. They clearly show no contact with so called 'Mafia' leaders.

In March 1943, the first eleven-man group of OSS agents was sent out to North Africa by direct order of William Donovan. Lieutenant Max Corvo arrived in Algiers in late May. Colonel William Eddy was in command of the OSS operation but Corvo was appointed second-in-command of any projected mission to Sicily. Annoyingly for Corvo, he discovered that OSS agents in the field were entirely dependent on the British for their transportation.

As Operation Husky approached, OSS was still keen to land its agents on the island before the invasion, but Allied Headquarters had other plans. In fact, a US State Department memorandum going back to March 1943, approved by General Marshall and President Roosevelt, had already decided against the idea of a Sicilian-American legion going in:

> In conducting the operations a definite policy should be adopted not to make use of volunteer military units of Italians in exile, or separate units constituted from Italians naturalized as citizens of any of the United Nations. Italians now resident abroad would, upon their return to Italy as separate units of the occupying forces, be looked upon with suspicion (even as traitors) . . . The formation of special Italo-American units, even within the American forces, is inadvisable for the same reasons.

Just days before Husky, Corvo was told that the OSS mission had been cancelled because it might alert the enemy. 'I was saddened', said Corvo, 'that lack of transport and operational support had deprived us of the opportunity to contribute our intelligence efforts to ease the burden placed on the Allied invasion forces.' Then came the news that they would not even be in the first wave of Allied troops to land on the island:

> It was incomprehensible to me that the OSS should have been given such meagre information about both the planning and execution of the invasion of Sicily. It was particularly difficult to understand in view of the fact that we had the only pool of manpower and expertise in the US Army which was familiar with both the language and terrain and that our planning was so advanced.

Corvo and his OSS agents had lost the race to land on Sicily.

The Counter Intelligence Corps (CIC) provided the biggest group of US intelligence officers involved in the Allied conquest of Sicily but is the least well known. It was its officers who would be the first to enter many of the towns and villages controlled by the Mafia in western Sicily. The CIC officers, mainly young college graduates, were given instructions to operate in advance of the main military units. Some eighty of them had been assembled for Operation Husky. Happy to work with other intelligence agencies, including the British, they did not think much of the OSS. OSS men 'worked independently and at times at cross-purposes with the CIC', said CIC commander Major

Edward L. Ray Jr. 'Their accomplishments in the CI field are believed to have been negligible if not nil.'

Sicily would be the beginning of a major rivalry between these two US intelligence agencies. All their skills – plus those of US Naval Intelligence – would be tested to the maximum in the forthcoming operation.

Chapter Eleven

Operation Husky

Operation Husky swung into action on the night of 9/10 July 1943. A vast Allied armada of 2,500 ships and landing craft surged towards the south-east tip of Sicily. On board were 181,000 men belonging to two great armies – one was Lieutenant General George S. Patton's US Seventh Army; the other was General Sir Bernard Montgomery's British and Canadian Eighth Army.

Lieutenant-Colonel Gerald Wellesley was with the British contingent:

> On the night of the assault, no one went to bed properly as the first breakfast for the first assault troops was at 12.30 a.m. and as we lay some miles off shore we could see the tremendous bombardments and bombing of the towns on the east coast of Sicily which preceded the actual landings.
>
> The first landings took place about 3 [a.m.] and we heard from the returning landing craft that there had been little opposition, though a few losses from land mines. I had breakfast at 3.45 and actually jumped on shore from the assault landing craft about 9 carrying all my kit, which I continued to do for a mile and half up hill to the 'Personnel Assembly Area'.
>
> This was a lovely almond orchard filled with large rocks. The whole landing went like clockwork and it was wonderful to see the tanks and large lorries driving down the ramps to the beach and moving off.

Despite a gale earlier in the night, the winds had dropped and the amphibious landing has gone remarkably well for the British. They quickly moved all their troops and equipment on to the beaches and inland. By midday, Wellesley remembered:

> The Germans had found out where we had landed and for the rest of the afternoon and most of the night we were bombed and machine-gunned. Periodically I had to leave our nice shelter to get news of how the battle was going as my instructions were to enter Syracuse as soon as possible after it fell.

Syracuse was Montgomery's first target and his soldiers moved swiftly towards it. This was thanks in part to an advanced unit of glider-borne troops who landed near the key bridge of Ponte Grande. More than 200 airborne soldiers had been drowned as their gliders were released too early and crashed into the sea. Of the remaining seventy-three who made it to the bridge, sixty-five were killed or wounded holding it for the approaching ground forces. Wellesley described the scene:

> At every pill-box along the road the dead were still lying about, a ghastly sight for those not accustomed to battlefields. At first light the next day I heard that our troops had taken [Syracuse] at 9 the night before. We got a lift on a truck that was going in and by 9 in the morning I had met the Mayor and Prefect and had taken over the civil government of the place.

Wellesley was an officer of AMGOT – the Allied Military Government of Occupied Territory. It was later known simply as AMG. This organisation, headed by Major-General Francis Baron Rennell of Rodd, would rule Sicily for the next six months. It would be the front line for Allied dealings with the Mafia.

American forces landed to the west of the British on the southern coast of Sicily at Licata, Gela and Scoglitti. Associated Press War photographer Herbert White went in with the first waves of attack at Licata:

> Boy! Our American warships were crackerjacks – they knocked out every pillbox ashore! The infantry landing craft started for the beach at about 2.45am and our Navy poured it on each pillbox that tried to get tough. I would see a flash from a shore gun and immediately naval shells would start whistling over my head and smash the enemy into silence.

> Enemy bombers came over in the darkness, dropping flares before they let go with bombs, but they didn't hit a thing . . .
>
> After daylight I went ashore to see the equipment unloaded from my landing ship on tanks and it was a pretty exhibition of efficiency to see loads of artillery and vehicles and supplies moving from sea to land like an assembly line in a Detroit factory.

By the end of the day, White had seen only four American casualties – two dead soldiers and two dead sailors.

Among the first waves of assault troops that hit the beaches were the New York Naval Intelligence team of Lieutenants Anthony Marsloe, Paul Alfieri, Joachim Titolo and Ensign James Murray.

> We were broken up into two teams of two members each [said Alfieri]. Lieutenant Titolo and myself were assigned to the invasion of Sicily at Licata, and Lieutenant Marsloe and Ensign Murray were assigned to the invasion of Gela.

They were armed with all the information they had gathered in New York from Luciano and his mobsters and put it to use straight away, as Marsloe recalled:

> It was of tremendous help following the landing, because we gained an insight into the customs and mores of these people – particularly Sicilians – the political ideology and its mechanics on lower echelons, the manner in which the ports were operated, the chains of command together with their material culture which enabled us to carry out the findings and purposes of our mission.

Alfieri went further and explained how he used his Mafia contacts:

> One of the most important plans was to contact persons who had been deported for any crime from the United States to their homeland in Sicily, and one of my first successes after landing at Licata was in connection with this, where I made beneficial contact with numerous persons who had been deported . . . They were extremely cooperative and helpful because they spoke both the dialect of that region and also some English.

Meyer Lansky later told a story about one of Alfieri's first contacts being a man who Lucky Luciano had saved from the electric chair. The man had fatally shot a policeman on the Lower East Side when he was sixteen. The boy's mother was a cousin of Luciano and pleaded with him to organise his escape. Luciano sent him out of New York via Canada to Sicily. In Sicily, the cop-killer became the head of his local Mafia and kept up links with other criminals deported from the States. Alfieri saw this man when he landed in Licata.

'I was told that "Mafia" and "Lucky Luciano" were passwords', remembered Lansky. 'Maybe that sounds crazy right in the middle of the war . . . but one of the agents told me later that those words were magic. People smiled and after that everything was easy.' Alfieri told his contact that he wanted to get to the headquarters of the Italian naval command. They identified it as hidden in a holiday villa set back from the beach. The local Mafioso then gathered his gunmen and they attacked the HQ, killing the German guards outside. Alfieri went inside and blew open a safe that contained valuable documents. In the safe, he found plans that outlined German and Italian defences on the island, plus their radio code-books. Most importantly, it also contained information on the Axis naval forces throughout the Mediterranean. Map overlays detailed marine minefields and revealed safe routes through them. It was a tremendous prize that saved many Allied lives.

For that Mafia-aided act, Alfieri was awarded the Legion of Merit. 'By his resourcefulness and daring devotion to duty', said the presidential citation, 'he made available information of great value in planning future operations, thereby contributing in large measure to the success of our invasion forces.'

Later, during the Herlands investigation, Titolo was asked if, in the invasion of Sicily, he made contact with members of the criminal underworld or the Mafia. 'We did, sir', was Titolo's direct answer.

Exhilarated by their capture of the Italian naval documents, Marsloe and his team now had to settle down to the more mundane work of gathering further information from the locals. They used their experience on the New York waterfront to deploy the local fishing fleets to their advantage. Said Alfieri:

> The original purpose of this Sicilian fishing fleet under the US Navy control was to acquire food for the Italians where the invasion had already been effective, but under the command of Lieutenant Titolo all fishing boat captains were instructed to report certain information which had high intelligence qualities, which assisted us greatly through those early troublesome days of the invasion.

In particular they located minefields and booby traps along the coast and in harbours.

The team then moved inland with the rest of Seventh Army. As they moved out of Licata, they passed hundreds of Italian prisoners. 'The Italian soldiers that were rounded up', noted Herbert White, 'sat rather glumly on the hillside watching the American Army whiz past them to the European second front. There must have been from 300 to 350 Italians in that batch of prisoners.'

As the Allies advanced into Sicily, they uncovered evidence of a profound lack of morale among Sicilian and Italian troops. Preliminary reports gained from interrogating captured soldiers painted a desperate picture of the Axis forces. Said an Allied HQ report of 17 July 1943:

> Morale very low and worse than that of PSW [prisoners of war] captured in Tunisia campaign. Most PSW appear heartily sick of War and happy to have been taken PW by Americans or British. In some cases invasion welcomed. Some PSW boasted of having given themselves up without firing a shot or resisted at all. PSW complained of lack of food and supplies stating that Germans were cleaning out countryside of all food.

On the US Seventh Army front in western Sicily, a message of 19 July said there were many accounts of Italians surrendering and indications that some had mutinied against the command of their German officers. Another report for the European Theater of Operations (ETOUSA) chiefs of staff, including supreme commander General Eisenhower, prepared at the Allied HQ in Algiers on 20 July, summarised the situation on the island:

> Authenticated cases are not merely Sicilian Coastal Divisions but also units of Neapolitan and Leghorn Divisions surrendering en-masse. Prisoner evidence confirms that 20,000,000 [leaflets] were dropped over Sicily before the invasion and softened up the morale. Suggest that you play up pro-ally morale of civilians and Italian troops in Sicily . . .
>
> First results of German prisoner interrogation, shows lowest morale yet encountered in German troops. The main features are Germans who hitherto regarded Italians as poor soldiers, now regard them as worse than useless, even

> betraying positions to enemy. Germans regard the defense in Sicily hopeless. They feel themselves sacrificed uselessly as in Tunisia and also hope German High Command does not intend to defend Italy. There is no indication yet, of a break in discipline, since Officers still retain their hold.

The Germans themselves were damning about the value of their Italian Allies. In a German campaign report produced by the *Hermann Goering* Panzer Division, they did not hold back with their criticism:

> In Sicily the Italians virtually never gave battle and presumably they will not fight on the mainland either. Many units in Sicily, either led by their officers or on their own, marched off without firing a single shot. Valuable equipment fell into the hands of the enemy in undamaged condition. The good intentions of some commanders and the good appearance of some officers and non-commissioned officers must not lead one to overlook the fact that 90 per cent of the Italian Army are cowards and do not want to fight.

With the Germans viewing their Axis partners in this light, it is little wonder that many Italian soldiers declined to die alongside them.

That the Fascists themselves were aware of a chronic breakdown in morale was revealed in a government radio broadcast made in Rome in the middle of July:

> Our enemies have once again resorted to threats. Roosevelt and Churchill have addressed an appeal to Italians asking them to rebel against the Italian Government. Italians have been asked to betray their cause and place themselves at the disposal of the invaders.
>
> [But, argued the broadcast] if Italy surrendered it would not mean that she would have found peace once again. The Italian people would still be in the war – they would be asked by the invaders to turn their weapons against Germany . . . Thus our country would still continue to suffer the horrors of war.

While the Americans appeared to be having a relatively easy time advancing across the island, the same could not be said for the British and the Canadians. As the Eighth Army advanced north along the east coast towards Catania, it met strong resistance. The Germans had chosen to defend their airfields at Catania and brought in the elite

Hermann Goering Panzer Division, including several Tiger tanks. The kind of fighting the British faced here shocked Lieutenant-Colonel W. I. Watson of the Durham Light Infantry. 'The enemy were always quite ruthless and fought with almost fanatical ardour at times' he reported. He saw German paratroopers shoot Allied wounded and stretcher-bearers, and when captured, these same Germans bared their chests anticipating they would be shot and shouted 'Mein Führer!'

General Harold Alexander, deputy Supreme Commander to Eisenhower, sent his own personal report of the fighting to Winston Churchill on 22 July:

> The battle around Catania is very fierce and the Germans are fighting bitterly in positions well suited for defence but we have killed a lot. 8th Army are trying to outflank them to the north by a thrust on Adrano by 30 Corps. This will be assisted by 1st USA Division . . . Remainder of 7th Army are progressing very well and are nearing Palermo . . . Reports are that Italian officers are deserting by getting into plain clothes and disappearing. All this is to the good and we can deal with these gentlemen later.
>
> I appreciate that Germans will hang on to Messina peninsula at all costs consequently I must have Palermo as a port through which to supply 7th Army which I shall bring into line north of 8th Army at earliest possible.

General Alexander understood that the Germans in Sicily were desperate to evacuate as many of their soldiers as they could to mainland Italy. This meant holding the British back from the port of Messina. The rest of the island was left to fend for itself. Thus, the Americans got an easier ride to Palermo, but they were then expected to turn eastwards and drive towards Messina.

A report of 25 July from 15 Army Group said: 'Intelligence in Western Sicily last Italian remnants being mopped up. Up to last night 42000 PW taken by 7 Army.' Later the same report said that '2 Corps [from Seventh Army] captured Gangi continued advance eastward along highway . . . Prov Corps captured Trapani and Castellammare and consolidated control Western Sicily.'

Gangi, of course, was the home of a notorious Mafia gang in the north of the island and the site of Mori's greatest victory over them. Castellammare was the hometown of many of New York's top gangsters, including Joseph Bonanno.

A report from Allied HQ in Algiers to the War Office in London on 27 July declared that all enemy resistance in western Sicily had ceased, but said that the British still faced a slow and determined German rearguard action up the east coast. The British and Canadians had drawn the short straw and would endure many casualties in the hard slog towards Messina.

As the Americans laid claim to western Sicily, they entered the realm of the Mafia. Their hold had always been at its strongest in the central and western regions of the island. Seeing the Americans arrive with their tanks and military hardware, the Mafiosi, at first, took the soft approach. Sergeant Jack Foisie, an army reporter for *Yank*, the US Army weekly news magazine, described an encounter he had in the village of Pollina, on a mountainside above the valley of Mazzara in north central Sicily. 'We drove the jeep straight up until the road became a stairway', said Foisie, 'we got out and climbed the rest of the way on foot. I had to duck several times to avoid the picturesque overhanging balconies – and I am not a very tall guy.'

They were greeted by the local Carabiniere, with a sword dangling from his side, who escorted them to the town hall. They met the local priest and the one-time Fascist representative who now 'looked a little seedy'. But soon their time in the village was hijacked by a man called Mauro Poliootto. He explained he had been to America and laid out for them some red wine, almonds and cheese. 'He apologised for the humbleness of the meal', said Foisie, 'showing me a small can of coffee beans. "This is all the coffee we've had for four years", he said. "I drink a cup once a year, on January 27, my saint's day."'

Foisie noted there was some rivalry between the priest and the Fascist and saw that the crowd of villagers around the American soldiers now looked to them for guidance. Foisie declared they were mere journalists but Poliootto took it upon himself to tell the priest and the Fascist that Foisie was just being modest and that all Americans were 'big shots'. Poliootto continued to try to demonstrate his quiet authority to the Americans by whispering instructions to them. 'The mayor's no good', he said. 'Get rid of him.'

Then, out of the crowd, came a tall man, 'a giant among the short Sicilians'. The man handed a note to Foisie. It was addressed to a house in Alhambra, California. 'You can deliver this note to my brother, yes?' said the tall man. Poliootto was immediately suspicious and asked

Foisie, 'What kind of document can these two men have in common?' The citizens of Pollina shifted their attention to the tall figure.

'We left them jabbering away', said Foisie. 'I shouldn't be surprised if he's the next Mayor of Pollina.'

The subtle jockeying for power here is fascinating and indicates the importance of American connections in post-Fascist Sicily. Whether any of these figures were local Mafiosi, we will never know.

A more robust assertion of Mafia power was demonstrated in Villalba. Socialist politician and journalist Michele Pantaleone, whose family lived in Villalba, is the source of this most famous story told about the Allied invasion of Sicily. According to Pantaleone, German and Italian resistance to the American advance inland in central Sicily was centred near Monte Cammarata. On the slopes of the mountain, goes his story, Axis infantry were backed by formidable 88-mm anti-tank guns and a detachment of German tanks. Norman Lewis, who later re-told the tale in English, added the detail that they were Tiger tanks. The Axis position commanded the road leading north to Palermo and was perfectly placed to strike the American convoy heading towards it. The nearest major towns were Mussomeli, to the south-east, and Villalba, to the east.

On 14 July, four days after the Allied landings, an American fighter plane flew over Villalba. 'The aircraft dipped so low', said Pantaleone, 'that it almost grazed the roof-tops and a strange banner or pennant could be seen fluttering from the side of its cockpit. The pennant was made of a yellowish-gold cloth and there was a large black 'L' carefully drawn in the middle.' The aircraft dropped a nylon bag into the town near the house of the local priest. It was handed to Carabiniere Angelo Riccioli who opened it. Inside, he found a small yellow flag with a black 'L' on it – just like the banner on the aircraft.

A second bag was dropped near a farmhouse belonging to Don Calogero Vizzini. Known as Don Calo, Pantaleone claimed Vizzini was the head of the Mafia of all Sicily. Other authorities have their doubts about this, but certainly he was an influential Mafioso in the region. The second bag was recovered by one of Don Calo's servants, Carmelo Bartolomeo, who took it to his master. He watched as Don Calo opened it. Inside, said Bartolomeo, was 'a foulard handkerchief which looked as if it was made of gold, exactly the same colour as the cloth hanging from the aeroplane'.

Don Calo knew exactly what it meant. The silk handkerchief was a traditional Mafia method of contact. It was like a password and on this one the black 'L' stood for Lucky Luciano. In response, Don Calo reportedly wrote a coded letter to Giuseppe Genco Russo, the second most important Mafioso in the area. 'Turi, the farm bailiff, will go to the fair at Cerda with the calves on Thursday 20th', wrote Don Calo. 'I'll leave on the same day with the cows, cart-oxen, and the bull. Get the faggots ready for making the cheese, and provide folds for the sheep.' 'Cows' meant the US Army, 'cart-oxen' meant tanks, and 'bull' meant the US commander. Don Calo was telling Russo to do everything he could to make the Americans happy and secure. That evening, the message was taken by horseman to the town of Mussomeli where Russo lived.

Five days later, on 20 July, a Sicilian, who preferred to remain anonymous, said he saw American tanks come along the road to Villalba:

> I rushed downstairs and shouted to the villagers. 'The Americans are coming! The Americans are coming!' So we went to meet the tanks. I picked up a broomstick and a white pillowcase. I made a white flag and went to meet the tanks at the village entrance. The tanks were approaching Villalba and a hollow voice was saying, 'Call Don Calo Vizzini, Call Don Calo Vizzini!'

Three US tanks entered the town of Villalba. One of them flew a yellow flag with the black 'L' from its turret. When the tanks stopped in the town square, an American officer climbed out of one of the turrets and spoke in the local Sicilian dialect, asking for the 66-year-old Don Calo.

> In due course Vizzini turned up [said Pantaleone]. In his shirt-sleeves, with his jacket over his arm, a cigar in his mouth and his hat pulled down almost over his big tortoise-shell spectacles, he elbowed his way through the crowd in his usual slow way as if he were encumbered by the weight of his bulky body.

Without a word being said, Don Calo handed over his yellow flag to the American officer. He was accompanied by one his nephews who had lived in America. 'The turret opened', recalled the anonymous Sicilian. 'Don Calo and his nephew climbed into the tank, leaving us in the lurch. As they left, they threw us handfuls of sweets and cigarettes.' The young Sicilian was a little annoyed to see the town's protector disappear with the Americans.

The next day, on the heights around Monte Cammarata, overlooking the road north to Palermo, where the Axis commander, Lieutenant-Colonel Salemi, hoped to pulverise the Americans, two-thirds of his troops had deserted. Left alone, the remaining Germans decided to withdraw in their tanks. Some of the Italian troops later claimed they had been approached by Mafia agents in the night who told them they were in a hopeless situation and should leave. They offered the soldiers civilian clothes and any other help to go home to their families. The following day, Salemi was intercepted by the Mafia and taken as a prisoner to the town hall in Mussomeli. The battle of Cammarata had been won without a shot being fired – or so Pantaleone claimed – thanks to the intervention of the Mafia.

The Americans pressed on to Palermo.

Who were the US soldiers at Villalba who took Don Calo away with them in their tank? The most obvious answer is that they were Counter Intelligence Corps (CIC) officers, operating, as usual, in advance of the main troop formations.

By far the largest US intelligence formation deployed in the invasion of Sicily, the CIC had played a dominant role since the very start, providing pre-invasion security in North African ports. Ten CIC detachments landed on the beaches with the first assault troops and advanced rapidly inland. In the first Sicilian towns they entered, CIC agents seized civil offices, Axis headquarters and communication centres, gathering enemy intelligence documents such as code-books and maps. But soon they were pitched into taking a grip on law and order, according to the official CIC history of the campaign:

> Town officials were taken into custody, informants were recruited; parish priests were utilized to gain the cooperation of the populace and to read proclamations. Town-criers and posters were also used to promulgate military regulations. Road blocks were set up, weapons collected, pillaging stopped, brothels checked . . . Because CIC Agents were often the first conquering officials to enter a town, Agents of the Corps often were forced to assume, by default, other tasks which properly were within the province of Civil Affairs.

Sicilian Mafiosi behind bars during a trial in the 1920s. An old church at Termini Imerese was converted to house mass Mafia trials.

A young Cesare Mori riding out in pursuit of Sicilian outlaws. Mori's presence on a raid was enough for some bandits to give themselves up straight away.

Sicilian bandit Pietro Albanese, one of the outlaws arrested in Mori's Madonie operation. This photograph was presented in court as evidence against him, but he claimed he was wearing fancy dress at a party.

Above: Cesare Mori in Fascist uniform as Prefect of Palermo 1925–9. It amused him that Sicilians called him 'a man whose heart is covered with hair'. Others called him simply 'the beast'.

Above right: Benito Mussolini, *Il Duce*, Fascist dictator of Italy, at the height of his power in the late 1930s. His humiliation by the Mafia in Sicily encouraged his war against them.

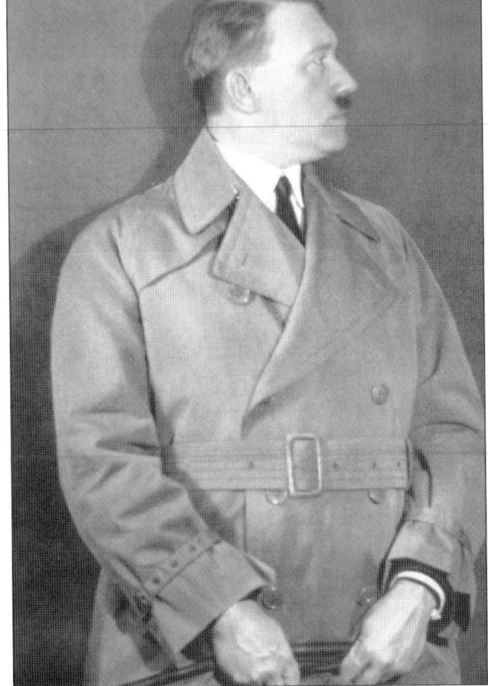

Right: Adolf Hitler photographed in 1935 in a trench coat and holding a horse-whip. The orginal caption reads '*Die Pietsche*' – the Scourge. Hitler liked to cultivate an image as the hard man of German politics.

Memorial concert in the town square at Misilmeri, arranged by Mori to honour the death of a young man who stood up to the local Mafia. Mori sits with other dignitaries on the stage behind the piano.

Giuseppe Bonanno was born in Castellammarese but left during Mussolini's crack-down on the Mafia. He later headed one of the five New York crime families.

Giuseppe 'Joe the Boss' Masseria was killed by Lucky Luciano's hit men in 1931, bringing an end to the so-called Castellammarese War.

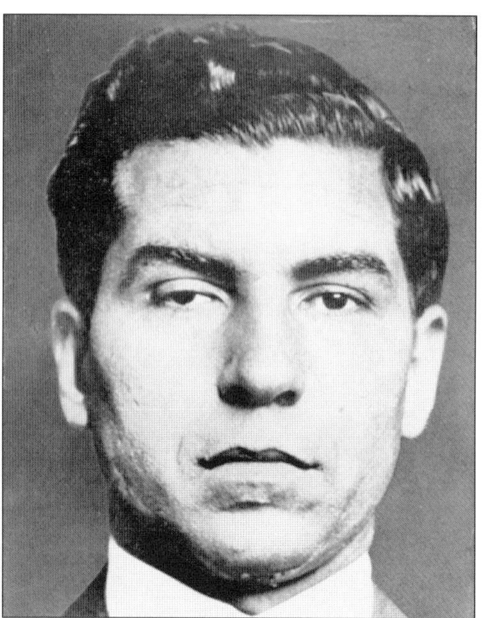

Charles 'Lucky' Luciano was born Salvatore Lucania near Palermo in 1897. He became 'Boss of Bosses' in New York in the early 1930s.

Meyer Lansky was Luciano's right-hand man and a key figure in the Jewish underworld. He fought against American Nazis during the 1930s.

Bugsy Siegel (*left*), early associate of Meyer Lansky, contemplated killing Hermann Goering and Joseph Goebbels during a trip to Italy. Siegel was later suspected of skimming Mafia money so his long-time friends Lansky and Luciano ordered his execution. His tagged foot is shown *below* in the Las Vegas morgue in 1947. *(Granger Collection, New York)*

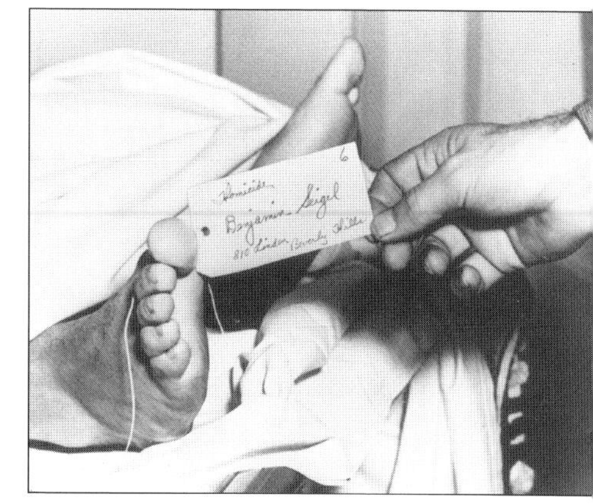

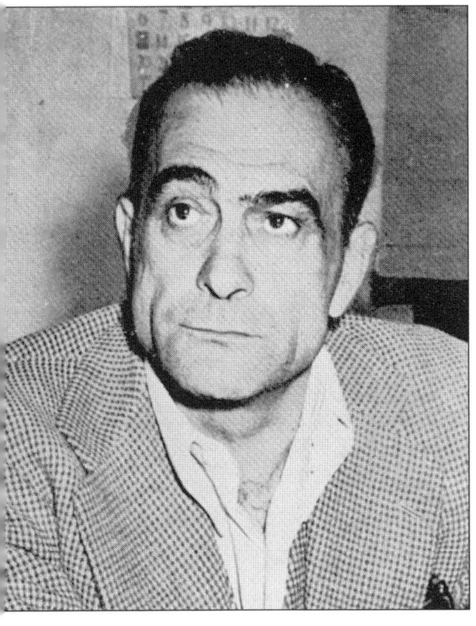

Vito Genovese served under Lucky Luciano before developing his own black-market empire in World War Two Italy. He later returned to New York.

Frank Costello helped run Luciano's underworld empire after he was jailed in 1936 and negotiated with the authorities for Luciano's release.

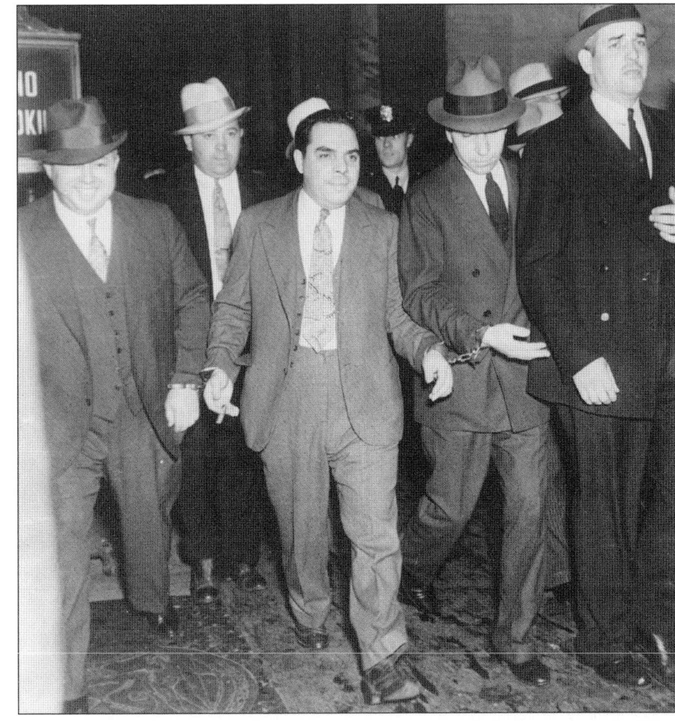

.ucky Luciano, handcuffed nd surrounded by New /ork police, is led to jail .fter being sentenced to 30–50 years' imprisonment n 1936.

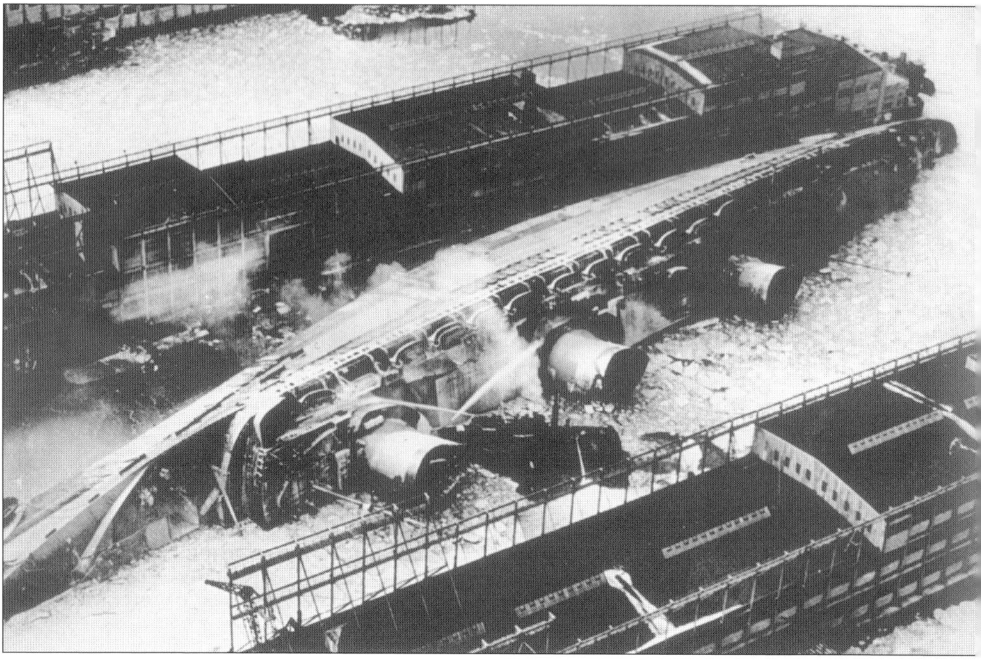

The luxury liner *Normandie* had just been converted into a troop ship when fire broke out on the vessel in February 1942 and she sank at New York's Pier 88. Some thought this was sabotage by Nazi or Fascist agents; others have pointed the finger at the Mafia.

Commander Charles Haffenden dictating notes in his office. He helped conceive and carry out the plan for US Naval Intelligence to work with the New York underworld in World War II.

Above: Allied chiefs plan the invasion of Sicily, 29 May 1943. *From left:* Eden, Gen. Brooke, Air Marshal Tedder, Adm. Cunningham, Gen. Alexander, Gen. Marshall, Gen. Eisenhower, Gen. Montgomery, and Churchill (*centre*). *(Enigma Books Collection)*

Right: French cartoon of 1942 depicting President Roosevelt and Prime Minister Churchill as gangsters. After Churchill once posed with a tommy gun, Axis propaganda liked to portray the Allied leaders as mobsters. *(Granger Collection, New York)*

Right: The Allied invasion fleet assembles off the Sicilian coast at Gela, 9 July 1943. The American forces met light resistance here during the first hours of the landing. *(Enigma Books Collection)*

Above: British soldiers prepare for their tanks to land on the beaches near Siracusa. *(Enigma Books Collection)*

Left: A Sherman tank drives past the hulk of a German Panzer. Some captured German armoured vehicles were later used by Mafia rebels in their battles with Allied and Italian troops. *(Enigma Books Collection)*

A GI gets directions from a Sicilian peasant near Siracusa. Allied troops on the island were generally given a friendly welcome as most Sicilians were happy to see the end of Mussolini's regime. *(Enigma Books Collection)*

British Eighth Army soldiers in bitter street fighting at Acireale on the way to Messina. *(Enigma Books Collection)*

Canadian Highlanders advance along the slopes of Mount Etna to attack German forces based around the volcano. The British and Canadians took the brunt of the fighting on the eastern side of Sicily in July 1943. *(Enigma Books Collection)*

Above: A poster welcomes the Allies to Palermo: 'The time of longed for freedom has arrived.' Leading Mafiosi immediately issued invitations to Allied commanders to meet with them. *(Enigma Books Collection)*

ERAZ. FASCI DI COMBATTIMENTO DI PALERMO

Camicie Nere e Popolo di Palermo!

Gli eventi di guerra hanno fatto della Sicilia la
tiera avanzata della Patria.
Siamo tutti in prima linea, al pari delle valo-
Forze Armate, che contendono al nemico le vie
nostro mare e del nostro cielo e presidiano il
ro suolo.
Memori di quanto i nostri padri operarono e
irono per l'unità e grandezza della PATRIA, noi
iamo qual'è il nostro dovere e la nostra responsa-
à in questa lotta di continenti.

LAVORARE significa COMBATTERE
RESISTERE significa **VINCERE!**

La ferocia nemica non ci scuote: siamo SICILIANI,
edienti alla legge dell'ONORE.
La NOSTRA VENDETTA SARA' LA VITTORIA:
essa, siamo pronti a combattere, con l'aratro e col
chetto, con la zappa e con la bomba, come la
rra vuole.

CAMERATI!

Arruolarsi nei ranghi del Servizio del Lavoro e
e Centurie "VESPRI„ è un impegno d'onore.
La PATRIA, la Grande Madre ci guarda.
Nel nome del RE e del DUCE, serviamola in ogni
nte, con le OPERE e con il SANGUE.

utta la SICILIA è in piedi. PALERMO è alla testa.

Above: A Fascist Party poster ordering the population of Sicily to resist the Allies, proclaiming: 'The ferocious enemy will not shake us: we are Sicilians obedient to the law of honour.' *(Enigma Books Collection)*

Left: A US half-track drives through the rubble-strewn streets of Palermo. The port was hit by Allied bombers before the invasion and some of this damage can still be seen today. *(Enigma Books Collection)*

General Walter Bedell Smith, Eisenhower's chief of staff, signs the armistice with Italy at Cassibile, 3 September 1943. General Castellano (standing behind his interpreter on the right) signed on behalf of the Italian government. *(Enigma Books Collection)*

Major-General Francis Baron Rennell of Rodd, Chief of Civil Affairs, Office of the Allied Military Government in Sicily, at his desk in front of a map of Sicily, 1943. *(Imperial War Museum)*

US Attorney Thomas E. Dewey was the nemesis of Lucky Luciano and set himself on his political career by sending the New York mobster to prison. This photograph of 1946 shows a still youthful-looking Dewey.

Salvatore Giuliano, notorious bandit leader in Sicily 1944–50. His bandit army worked closely with the Mafia and the Sicilian Separatist movement.

Don Calogero Vizzini, Mafioso of Villalba, who supposedly helped the Allies during their invasion of Sicily.

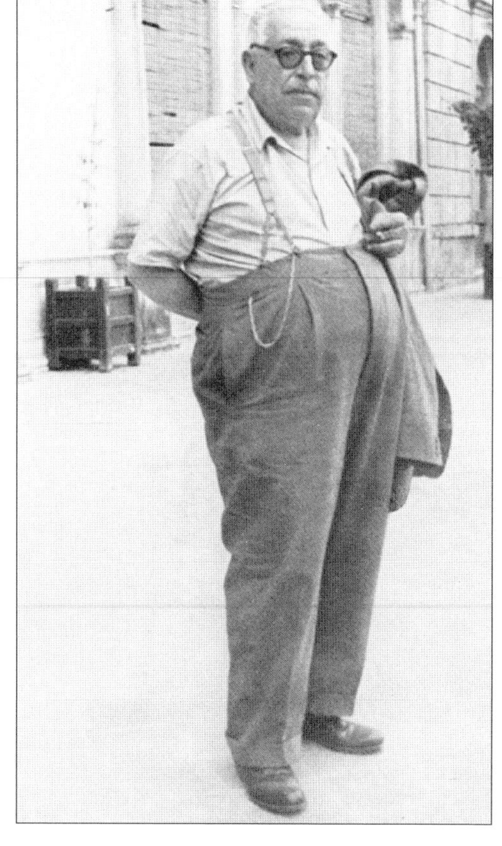

Castellammare del Golfo – home town of Joseph Bonanno, Salvatore Maranzano, and other leading Sicilian-born Mafiosi. The photograph shows the remains of the sixteenth- or seventeenth-century fortress at the end of the small harbour.

Statue presented to Lt-Col Bertram Hefford, a Metropolitan Police officer sent to Palermo to help restore law and order in wartime Sicily. *(Martin Gerrard)*

Last members of Giuliano's bandit gang being taken for trial in Palermo. The Mafia finally tired of Giuliano's outrages and helped the police wipe out his gang.

DETECTIVE DIVISION, BUREAU OF CRIMINAL IDENTIFICATION
CIRCULAR No. 68

POLICE DEPARTMENT
CITY OF NEW YORK

LIMITED TO DEPARTMENT CIRCULATION
PHOTO UNIT No 43060

WANTED AS THE ALLEGED VICTIM OF A KIDNAPPING

THE ABOVE PHOTOGRAPH IS ONE "JOSEPH BONANNO" MALE, WHITE, 59 YRS., WANTED AS THE ALLEGED VICTIM OF A KIDNAPPING.

AT APPROXIMATELY 12:20 A.M., OCTOBER 21, 1964, "JOSEPH BONANNO" OF 1847 EAST ELM STREET, TUCSON, ARIZONA, WHILE IN THE COMPANY OF HIS ATTORNEY, WAS REPORTED PHYSICALLY SEIZED IN FRONT OF 35 PARK AVENUE, MANHATTAN BY TWO (2) UNKNOWN WHITE MALES AND FORCED INTO AN AUTOMOBILE WHICH THEN SPED AWAY.

DESCRIPTION OF PERPETRATORS AS FOLLOWS:

#1 - MALE,WHITE, 6'2", 210 LBS., WEARING BLACK RAINCOAT, A DARK FEDORA, ARMED WITH A GUN.

#2 - MALE, WHITE, 6'0", 200 LBS., DARK CLOTHES.

GETAWAY VEHICLE WAS A BEIGE 2-DOOR SEDAN OF RECENT MODEL OF UNKNOWN MAKE, BEARING NEW YORK REGISTRATION PLATES.

ANY INFORMATION ON THE ABOVE, NOTIFY THE 13TH DETECTIVE SQUAD FORTHWITH: OREGON 4-0770 - OREGON 4-0771 - 777 3290.

Far left: Typical old narrow street in the hill town of Corleone, notorious centre for the Mafia in western Sicily. Until recently, most of the residents stayed indoors at night while local gangsters fought for control of the streets.

Left: Wanted poster for Joseph Bonanno as the victim of a kidnapping in 1964. It was part of the so-called Banana War between rival Mafia gangs in New York.

Above: The extraordinary baroque fountain in front of the municipal building in Piazza Pretoria where the Allies based their administration during the war years.

Above: Grand Hotel Et Des Palmes in Via Roma, central Palermo. This was Lucky Luciano's favourite hotel in Palermo and the meeting place for Joe Bonanno and leading Mafiosi in 1957. Inside, the décor has hardly changed since the mobsters stayed there.

Left: Lucky Luciano always liked to dress well. He is shown here during his exile in Italy. *(ullstein bild)*

Ucciardone prison in central Palermo – once known as 'Villa Mori' – the jail where many Mafiosi were held during the round-ups organised by Prefect Mori in the 1920s. It is still used as a prison today.

Plaque recently raised in the Giardino Garibaldi to commemorate New York detective Joe Petrosino, shot dead in the slums of Palermo by Mafiosi in 1909. It replaced an earlier plaque in the same Piazza Marina.

CIC officers were given certain guidelines, but the process of establishing order in a captured town was frequently left up to the initiative of the soldiers themselves. In Agrigento, which fell on 17 July, Lieutenant Jack B. Cameron, found himself dealing with a whole range of civic problems. In his monthly report of 31 July, Cameron listed the following CIC achievements: stopping rioting and looting; rounding-up remaining Carabinieri and placing them on police duty; ordering the local fire chief and firemen to collect dead bodies; asking the provincial vicar-general to calm the civilian population; and locating and guarding food and fuel warehouses. Soldiers were vital to all security demands and Cameron believed he needed as many as were available:

> Security dropped off more than 50% when Army guards were not used and to depend on whatever units that happened to be in the area to supply guards was poor security, for the ability of such units to make men available to CIC hinged on the fluctuations of the immediate tactical situation.

Sometimes CIC officers found themselves compelled to act as guards when they should have been pursuing their counter intelligence purpose. On their first day in Termini Imerese, nine local black marketeers were arrested and the Carabinieri were told to arrest anyone else they considered a problem. Understandably, CIC personnel were keen to hand over matters to the AMGOT officials as soon as they turned up.

The CIC officers who entered Villalba would have to have been attached to either the 45th Infantry Division or the 3rd Infantry Division, both operating in central western Sicily at this time.

The British Government's official narrative of the Allied invasion of Sicily, based on US and UK military reports, says that the US 3rd Division captured Mussomeli on 19 July and then captured the high ground north of Mussomeli on 20 July, including Monte Cammarata. From there, it advanced north-west to capture Corleone on 21 July.

The same source also says that 45th Division overcame a stand made at Vallelunga by an Italian battalion and two tanks. Vallelunga is the next town north of Villalba and this puts these US troops in the neighbouring area to 3rd Division. On 21 July, 3rd Division patrols reached highway 121 north of Lercara Friddi and contacted 45th Division. Clearly, the divisions were very close to each other and advanced groups from either could have entered Villalba.

The CIC official history of the campaign in Sicily, produced by CIC staff in the early 1950s, does not mention the Mafia and does not mention the incident at Villalba at all.

Further research at the US Army Military History Institute reveals that it was in fact the 180th Infantry Regiment (part of the 45th Infantry Division) that was operating in the area of Villalba and in particular the 45th Cavalry Reconnaissance Troop. This was a mechanised unit in armoured vehicles and it seems most likely it was their tanks that entered Villalba and invited Don Calo to join them.

The daily journal of the 45th Cavalry Reconnaissance Troop does mention their entry into Villalba, but nothing special is recorded. The entry for 19 July says they had an 'order given to find out what enemy forces were in vicinity of Vallelunga' – some ten miles to the north of Villalba. The strength of the enemy was reported as 200 Germans and five tanks. They were then told to reconnoitre Valladolma, also to the north of Villalba. No other major confrontation or enemy troop formation is reported. On the following day – the 20th – at 1.00 p.m., the daily journal of the 45th does mention 'contact made in Villalba with 3rd Division Patrol. (Two small Italian tanks had been abandoned by Italian and destructed [*sic*]).'

By now, however, Villalba was well behind other towns that had already been entered by advanced US elements and judged safe. Earlier that morning, Caltavurturo, some fifty miles north of Villalba, had been entered by the 3rd Platoon of the 45th Cavalry Reconnaissance Troop, while 300 enemy soldiers had already left it before their arrival.

The general Axis movement was backwards – the German line of resistance had been drawn far away to the east of the island before Messina. The 45th's tale of war for the 19th and 20th is of minimum resistance and captured prisoners. Villalba and Monte Cammarata were, according to the 45th, definitely not areas of potential Axis resistance that could only be defeated by an alliance with the local Mafia. In fact, on the date mentioned by Pantaleone, other American soldiers were already way ahead, past these towns, and on the way to Palermo. The only recorded point of conflict in the Villalba area was to the north at Vallelunga and consisted of just 200 enemy troops who were quickly overcome.

Turning to the reconnaissance reports of the 3rd Infantry Division, mentioned by the 45th as also being in the vicinity of Villalba, a similar story emerges. The operations report for the 3rd Cavalry Reconnaissance Troop for 20–21 July has the following entry. 'At 1500 the Division commander ordered the [1st] platoon to reconnoiter road Cammarata–S Stefano. Platoon moved 1545 completed mission and returned 2000. Road reported clear.' This road runs east to west along the northern slopes of Monte Cammarata and would presumably be the target area for any Axis ambush as suggested by Pantaleone. The road then forks at San Stefano, with one branch running north to Corleone and Palermo, the other continuing west.

It was only north of San Stefano that some Italian opposition was encountered by 2nd Platoon, covering the road to Corleone, but they drove the enemy away. The narrative of the operations of the 3rd Cavalry Reconnaissance Troop Mechanized adds some more detail to this entry:

> Lieutenant Gunter's [2nd] platoon came upon some Italians trying to establish a strong delaying position near San Stefano. Again it was a case of seeing the enemy before being seen. Lieutenant Gunter deployed his vehicles off the road and radioed that contact was imminent. He then proceeded to move back to apprise the infantry CO of the situation. The doughboys deployed, moved up, and attacked by fire. It proved to be a successful surprise action. The Italians were decimated and wiped out before they could offer any resistance.

The next entry in the operations report, for 21–22 July, has 1st Platoon immobile thanks to vehicle failure while 2nd Platoon is eighty miles to the north-west of Cammarata, near Chiusa Sclafani, where they came under fire from artillery, mortars and machine guns. They returned fire, knocked out some of the enemy defences, and took thirty-four prisoners. The road to Corleone was clear from that point onwards.

Again, the story is one of clear roads and rapid progress, with occasional skirmishes successfully won. According to all these US field reports, there was no major Axis position on the northern slopes of Monte Cammarata that could have provided any hindrance to the American advance to Palermo.

That the US visit to Villalba on 20 July may have been purely routine and had nothing at all to do with a bigger plot to use the Mafia in the campaign is further suggested by an account of the day's events by Luigi Lumia, a former mayor of Villalba, recorded in his later history of the town:

> At about 2 o'clock in the afternoon of 20 July three US tanks rolled into the town of Villalba. Trying to make themselves heard above the squeals of delight from the town's children, soldiers appeared from the turret of the tanks asking where the person in charge could be found – *il capo del paese*. Not long after, a procession of people with Calogero Vizzini at the helm made its way towards the tanks chanting: 'Long Live America', 'Long Live the Mafia', 'Long Live Don Calo'.
>
> The Americans asked whether there were any German troops in the area and on hearing that there weren't, they took *il capo del paese* [Don Calo] on board the tank together with Damiano Lumia who was acting as his interpreter. However, it wasn't easy for the tanks to leave again. The soldiers had to bribe the dozens of kids who were climbing all over the tanks with pieces of candy, chewing gum and even cigarettes in order to get rid of them and clear the streets of the crowds of people who had come out to see them.
>
> Eventually, after managing to shake off even the most die-hard supporters of Don Calo who insisted on clinging to the tanks, they were able to move off. The two men were then taken to Turrume-Tudia and questioned by a US official.

During the interrogation, it was revealed that an American jeep on patrol had come under fire a few days earlier at a road junction not far from Villalba. An American soldier was killed and the attackers were believed to be Italian soldiers hiding in olive trees near the hamlet of Lumera. The US infantry returned fire and their shots set fire to the dry fields. The fire spread quickly and ignited ammunition left by the Italians who had hastily retreated. The more the ammunition exploded, the more the Americans believed they were under attack from a major force. According to Lumia, this forced the Americans to send three tanks across the disputed territory to enter Villalba.

The source for Lumia's account appears to be Vizzini's interpreter, his nephew. According to the interpreter, Don Calo told the American that the Italians had fled and the firefight had been caused by exploding ammunition. The Mafioso assured him they faced no local enemy, but this answer just annoyed the American interrogator.

> He told Don Calo that there was no way it had all been for nothing and he took his rage out in a stream of obscenities that the poor translator deemed unfit to translate. Then,

> purple with rage, he [the American] shouted, 'Get out, get out!' like a madman. 'On foot?' asked the interpreter. 'On foot! On foot!' he yelled, trying to put an end to the conversation.
>
> After much shouting on one hand and much pleading on the other, the American, who had calmed down a bit, decided to accompany *il capo del paese* back to where he had come from in a jeep.
>
> It was already night-time and Calogero Vizzini, tired and brow-beaten, was driven back to his house, halfway between the Americans and the countryside. He told his interpreter not to tell anybody what had happened and then lay down in his bed and went to sleep. The American troops started up their march again.

And that was that, according to Luigi Lumia. The Americans merely wanted to know what opposition they faced and certainly did not treat Don Calo with any respect. In fact, Don Calo was thoroughly embarrassed by the whole incident. There is no hint here of any pre-arranged deal. So much for the great conspiracy.

Michele Pantaleone is the main source for the Luciano–Vizzini story and he, as an enemy of Don Calo, is a very biased source. Wartime OSS documents reveal that his family was in dispute with the Vizzini clan over a local property issue and this – along with him being a Communist and political rival of Vizzini – casts much doubt on his view of events. And yet his seductive tale of Don Calo has been endlessly repeated by others, especially Norman Lewis, who introduced it to English readers.

The fact is, it appears, it never actually happened.

The first soldiers into captured Italian towns in the British sector of the island belonged to Field Security sections. Captain J. H. Bickerton Edwards was a Field Security Officer (FSO) with the 51st (Highland) Division and he described his experience in Sicily:

> Usually upon entering a town the section became AMGOT; Police; providers of grain, food, news, relief, cigarettes and all the good things the Sicilians had been without for the last five years. FS, for the most part arrived several days – and sometimes weeks before AMGOT representatives;

> consequently, all the preliminaries of civil administration fell to their lot . . .
>
> The collection of arms from the civil population was a revelation. In Vizzini alone there were over 200 shotguns, ranging from ancient flint-locks to modern twelve-bores. Thousands of home-made cartridges, bombs, mines and pistols of every calibre were handed to us in that town.
>
> The only suitable store-room we could find was in the billet, and on one memorable occasion, the FSO, who for lack of space in the house was sleeping amongst all the armament, inadvertently set his bed alight by falling asleep with a lighted cigarette in his hand. There were a few anxious moments until the fire was quelled!

As in the American sector, the Carabinieri were quickly recruited and expected to maintain law and order under the Allies. According to Captain Edwards:

> The local CC.RR [Carabinieri Reali] were allowed to keep their arms – rifles only, and instructed to continue with their normal police duties. We found that they were quite willing to help us but that, in the majority of cases, they were inefficient and lazy. It was impossible to trust them completely; most of them had friends or relations in the district, and we often suspected – but never once proved that they tipped off some of the 'wanted' people . . .
>
> Many 'self-styled secret agents' and 'spies' came to offer their services to us. Again, for the most part, such men were simply airing personal grievances and never proved to be any great help. One man represented himself as having worked in Egypt as a British Agent, when, in reality, he had been a dope smuggler there . . . There are undoubtedly a number of rackets being organised and run on black market lines. These are flourishing. Such is the Sicilian outlook. Racketeering is their second nature. Was not Al Capone a native of Caltanissetta?

Actually, Al Capone's family came from Naples, but the link with US gangsterism was pointed. The British were undoubtedly aware of the Mafia but were intent on closing down their rackets rather than forging an alliance with them.

During the invasion and conquest of Sicily, Max Corvo considered the OSS was sidelined. As usual, he blamed the British:

> Even though 'Husky' was an Anglo-American operation, the British dominated the planning staffs and Whitehall wanted to direct and channel the various phases of the first assault on Europe, especially in an area that was considered one of primary British political and economic interest.

This bias would have been news to the British, from Churchill down, who had been compelled to accept an American character to the conquest of Sicily. Corvo put his finger more correctly on the OSS problem when he cited other US intelligence agencies:

> On the US side the traditional intelligence services such as G-2, CIC, and the Office of Naval Intelligence (ONI) often displayed open hostility toward the OSS because they did not understand its work and objectives.

There was an element of snobbery to this as OSS personnel were perceived to be from a middle-class elite – the agency was even nicknamed 'Oh So Social'.

British Vice-Consul Manley tells an interesting story about the OSS and its agents' first days on the island. In his *Report on Sicilian Separatism* – a political movement calling for the independence of the island and backed by the Mafia – he says that Separatist supporters claimed they made contact with the Allies at the time of the landings at Gela. 'Sicilian deserters from the Italian army carrying the red and yellow Sicilian flag', says Manley, quoting his Separatist sources, 'gave themselves up to the Allied authorities'. Manley doubted this and gave his own interpretation of events:

> What I think actually happened was that the OSS unit with the 7th US Army occupied the castle of Falconara near Gela for a few days. This castle belongs to the Barone Frassini Bordonaro, a relative of Lucio Tasca one of the [Separatist] leaders . . . As some of the Frassini Bordonaro family were in residence at that time they probably came into contact with the OSS officers, who no doubt discussed the local situation with them.

Max Corvo did, indeed, visit the castle, but he claimed the family of the baron had left and he only talked to the caretaker – he had no contact with any Separatists. Italian soldiers had used it as a base but fled before the Americans. He took over the castle and made it the first OSS headquarters in Sicily. Lucio Tasca, however, was a key Mafia figure on the island. Was a contact made between the two at this early stage?

With the fall of Palermo on 22 July, the Americans turned eastwards to join the British and Canadians. They were still fighting hard against the Germans based around Catania and the road to Messina alongside Mount Etna. Several small amphibious operations conducted by the Americans along the north coast helped to outflank the Germans and it was Patton and his Americans who arrived first in Messina on 17 August, beating General Montgomery by just two hours.

The casualties suffered by the Americans throughout the Sicily campaign were not slight, some 9,213 being killed and wounded. The British and Canadians lost 12,572 men. Axis losses were much higher at 156,000, but the vast majority of these were captured Italians. The German rearguard succeeded in holding off the Allies long enough for 53,000 Axis troops to escape to the mainland, along with 50 tanks and 9,800 other vehicles. The successful evacuation of so many enemy troops to Italy, to carry on the fighting, was judged to taint the overall success of the Sicilian campaign.

A major achievement of the campaign, however, was to end Benito Mussolini's rule in Italy. On the night of 24 July 1943, the Fascist Grand Council passed a vote of no confidence in Mussolini. They turned instead to King Victor Emmanuel to help them solve the crisis that had overtaken their country. The next day, the king dismissed Mussolini from power with a curt handshake at the door of the Villa Savoia in Rome and he was escorted by submachine-gun-carrying Carabinieri to Podgora Barracks. Il Duce's 21-year-reign had come to an end.

Victor Emmanuel chose Marshal Pietro Badoglio to establish a new Italian government without one Fascist member. Badoglio immediately began negotiations with the Allies and on 3 September agreed to an unconditional surrender in a secret armistice. It was not announced until the 8th, by when the Allies hoped to have their invasion of mainland Italy under control, but the Germans swiftly reinforced their troops and Badoglio and the king were forced to flee in a corvette to Allied territory in the south.

Hitler was furious with the Italians and ordered a complete German military occupation of their country. Field Marshal Albert Kesselring was made supreme commander of forces in Italy and rounded up many Italian soldiers, who had thrown away their uniforms and deserted, and sent them to forced labour camps. Hitler demanded that the new Italian government release Mussolini so he could restore him to power. The Italians refused and moved him to a mountain-top ski resort at Gran Sasso in the Abruzzi mountains – a sufficiently remote location, or so they thought.

Hitler instructed his top commando trouble-shooter Otto Skorzeny to rescue him. Skorzeny put together a 'Mission Impossible' team of German paratroopers and special forces troops and crash-landed gliders on to the mountain-top. They then stormed the hotel and bundled Mussolini into a light aircraft. The 6-foot 4-inch tall Skorzeny insisted on cramming himself into the cabin next to Mussolini and the aircraft lurched over the edge of the slope, nearly plunging into the valley floor, before the pilot regained control and flew them on to Nazi Germany.

Reunited with Hitler, Mussolini was instructed to head a new Fascist state based at Salo beside Lake Garda in north Italy. Badoglio and his government declared war on Germany on 13 October. The news was received badly by Hitler. A year before, over dinner with Grand Admiral Raeder, Hitler cockily declared: 'There's one very curious thing to note in all this; the side Italy is on invariably wins!' He was right about that.

Cesare Mori – nemesis of the Mafia – had never thought much of Mussolini's chances in a war against the Allies. When the war started, he followed its progress carefully, supposedly in British newspapers. On a rare visit to Rome he was heard to agree with the British view on the war and was denounced for defeatism – it was the last time he figured in public affairs.

Mori's wife died in early 1942 and he, heartbroken, died a few months later in July. His death received little coverage in the newspapers – he was yesterday's hero. And yet the forces that Mori had gone some way towards defeating were now on the verge of being unleashed. The Allies would have to deal with the hydra monster that Mori had almost slain.

Chapter Twelve

An English Lord against the Mafia

The work of AMGOT – the Allied Military Government of Occupied Territory – began almost immediately after the Allied invasion of Sicily. The day after the landings, Lieutenant-Colonel Gerald Wellesley took over the civil government of Syracuse. It took three more weeks of hard fighting before Wellesley could take command of the city of Catania, capital of the province of the same name in the east of the island. Then, he walked into a minefield of problems.

> Catania normally contains a quarter of a million people [reported Wellesley]. For three weeks it had been pounded by air, sea and land. There were 60,000 people in it when I took over administration. Of these, 12,000 were living in huge underground shelters without light and without sanitation. There was no food in the town and 20,000 houses were uninhabitable. At first there was water, but the Germans in their retreat cut the main and within twenty-four hours this failed.

Straight away, Wellesley organised an emergency delivery of 50 tons of grain. Royal Engineers started work on fixing the water supply and the Signals Corps restored electricity. The return of refugees who had fled the city put tremendous pressure on Wellesley who had to place them in barracks which his own soldiers had considered too insanitary to use. Garbage was piling up in the streets and there was a real fear of an outbreak of typhoid. At the same time, Montgomery was insisting

Wellesley clear the roads so tanks and lorries could move northwards in pursuit of the Germans.

> In Catania I had a staff of 6 Officers to help me [said Wellesley], and units of the Engineers and Signals to deal with water mains and wires. But imagine the position of a young and inexperienced AMGOT Officer, not speaking a word of Italian, entering a captured town alone. He finds hundreds of dead to bury, thousands of living to feed. There is no light, no food, often no water and often not more than one house in five habitable.

This was the challenge faced by AMGOT officers across Sicily. Fortunately, in the centre and west of the island the devastation of war was far less than it was along the east coast. There, trouble would come not so much from helping refugees but maintaining law and order.

Wellesley dealt with this in Syracuse by allowing the Carabinieri to be armed so they could prevent the looting of food stores. Even the archbishop of the city complained about the widespread theft, having had his own car stolen. Food queues had to be controlled, a curfew enforced and Wellesley had to settle a strike of grave diggers.

On top of this, political factions within Sicily were already seeking advantage over each other by putting their cases to AMGOT. In Syracuse, Wellesley was visited by an anti-Fascist group, while in Catania, that city's archbishop was 'a very unpleasant old man who has come to ask for the release of all the Fascists who have been interned. I am as civil as I can be but find it very difficult to get rid of him.'

In the middle of his work, Wellesley fell ill with a high temperature and was diagnosed with sand-fly fever. He rested briefly but then pushed on. Wellesley continued his work into September, but then it came to a halt. His nephew was killed during the Allied landings at Salerno on the Italian mainland on 9 September. He died childless and that meant Wellesley inherited his title. He was now the 7th Duke of Wellington – the inheritor of an illustrious military reputation that stretched back to the battle of Waterloo. Wellesley left his post in Sicily shortly afterwards and returned to England. His son remained on the front line in Italy and fought through to 1944 – he is the present 8th Duke of Wellington.

Before Wellesley left, he attended a meeting of senior AMGOT staff at their headquarters in Palermo in late August. He gave an upbeat account of the situation in his province of Catania. 'The popularity of the Allies is quite extraordinary', said Wellesley. He had witnessed flag raising demonstrations with cheers, which had impressed him greatly, and he found that all Fascist records had been burned. Another AMGOT administrator reported that already the Sicilians were forming political parties.

Lieutenant-Colonel Irish, responsible for the province of Caltanissetta, in the south of the island, said that 'In addition to the usual Independent Sicily movement he had come in touch with another organisation entitled Christian Democrats. One of the leaders with whom he had come in contact had hardly given him the impression of being either a Christian or a Democrat.'

Wellesley was not the only English peer to serve in Sicily. On 24 July, Major-General Francis Baron Rennell of Rodd arrived on the island. He had been appointed head of AMGOT in Sicily. Rennell and Wellesley knew each other well. Rennell's father had been British Ambassador to Rome and was godfather to Wellesley's son. Senior to Rennell was General Sir Harold Alexander, Deputy Commander-in-Chief of the Allied forces in the Mediterranean. He became Military Governor of Sicily, but it was Rennell, as Chief Civil Affairs Officer of the Occupied Territory of Sicily, who was expected to oversee day-to-day life on the island. An American, Brigadier General F. J. McSherry, was appointed deputy to Rennell.

The 48-year-old Lord Rennell was an impressive figure and would come to dominate the Allied administration of the island for the next few months. He did not tolerate fools and had sharp words for many of his colleagues. But he was generous too and praised those he considered worked hard and well. Rennell had been educated at Eton and Oxford and served in World War I in the Royal Field Artillery but was later seconded to intelligence duties in Italy. In 1919, he entered the Diplomatic Service, operating in Rome and Sofia. In 1924, he resigned to work in the City on the stock exchange and in banking. During this period, he took up exploring and visited the Sahara twice, making a study of the Tuareg nomads that won him the Royal Geographical Society's Founder's Medal for 1929.

Foreign service and exploration ran in the Rennell family. His father, James Rennell Rodd, the 1st Baron Rennell, was a senior diplomat in Rome and British East Africa, but he was also an archaeologist and published poet and moved in London's bohemian circles, being a friend of the artist James Whistler. An earlier ancestor was James Rennell, dubbed the father of oceanography, who, among his many achievements in the late eighteenth and early nineteenth centuries, charted the Gulf Stream.

Lord Rennell would need all his family skills of diplomacy, plus his personal courage as an explorer, to deal with the criminal forces ranged against him in Sicily in late 1943.

A draft directive for the Allied administration of Sicily was in circulation on 1 May 1943. It came from the Civil Affairs Division of the US War Department and was sent to the British War Cabinet for their comments. Politically, it proclaimed that all Sicilian prefects and mayors of major settlements should be replaced by Allied military officers. The local Fascist party should be dissolved and the entire Fascist party leadership removed from all posts of authority. This would mean, of course, there would be a rush to fill the political vacuum left by the Fascists – a process that would attract the Mafia. Economically, the directive promised rationing and a maximum prices system for all major commodities. Black market practices and hoarding would be punished severely. Again, any concerted effort by the Allies to stamp out the black market would bring them directly into conflict with the Mafia. So, on two fronts at least, a major confrontation with the Mafia could be expected.

When Lord Rennell arrived on the island, he made it his priority to break the black market. He also restricted the movement of civilians, setting up a system of permits. Cars were kept off the road, unless driven with a permit.

AMGOT headquarters was in Palermo. Under Lord Rennell, there were nine provincial administration units. They were run by Senior Civil Affairs Officers (SCAOs), five Americans and four British. Lieutenant Colonel Charles Poletti was SCAO for Palermo.

Poletti noted the different ways in which US forces used their Civil Affairs Officers (CAOs) in western Sicily:

> The General commanding the 45th Division from the first realized the value of keeping a Civil Affairs detachment with his advanced headquarters to take over the towns immediately after capture . . .
>
> The General commanding 3rd Division adopted a procedure somewhat different from that obtaining in the 45th Division areas. He was not embarrassed by the presence of a Corps Headquarters in his rear and retained control of his

> L of C [Line of Communications] from the beaches to his advanced troops . . .

Sometimes CAOs were the very first Allied agents into a Sicilian town. In a report of 31 July 1943, Poletti was proud of their closeness to the front line:

> Throughout the operations, we have kept a certain number of civil affairs officers at the very front. In fact, in several instances, where troops were pushing ahead fast and bypassing places, civil affairs officers entered towns before troops had actually occupied them.

This put them in close proximity to the local Mafiosi.

One British CAO faced the stiff challenge of establishing Allied control in the notorious Mafia hill-town of Corleone and its neighbouring communities. His first task was to end the black market by getting grain directly from the farmers to the town – without the local Mafia intervening to hoard it and sell it at higher prices. He reported:

> For transport I was assigned a Jeep and an American soldier as general aide and interpreter. I called together all producers and explained to them the situation, appealing at the same time for co-operation, many of them responded well, others ignored the appeal . . .
>
> When invited to open locked doors on the farm usually the excuse was 'I cannot find the key'. Our reply was three minutes to open the locked doors, if in that time they were not opened we cut them open neatly with the jeep axe. In the majority of cases we found large quantities of grain hidden away.

The British CAO was disappointed by the performance of the local Carabinieri and had to work largely on his own with his American assistant fighting the black market and searching for hidden guns. Every Saturday, he held a Summary Court at Corleone to try all offences against the Allied Proclamation. Black-market offences were punished by imprisonment. He was unimpressed by the performance of many of his towns' mayors and had to change some, but he was not the only Allied power in his region and described one intervention by the CIC:

> The CIC from Palermo (7th Army), as the result of some agitators in Balestrate, and quite unknown to me as CAO,

> swooped down on this sea-side town and after a few superficial enquiries put the Mayor and his Communal Secretary in the local prison and appointed new officials to replace them. The new Mayor resigned his functions after only 4 days of office.
>
> The Marshal of Carabiniere who gave me the information about this peremptory action, also informed me that members of the American Army came and released the former Mayor and Secretary. I informed the SCAO [Colonel Poletti] of what had taken place without my authority, and asked for some information. The matter was taken up to higher levels and the CIC were found to have acted 'ultra vires' and duly censured.

Poletti was aware of inter-Allied problems and mentioned this in his report of 31 July:

> There is grave danger of a lot of free wheeling on part of officers of AMGOT Hq. Confusion, misunderstanding and dispersion of responsibility will result. In my opinion, the provincial seat of government must be strengthened. Functions, previously stemming from Rome, will now have to be centered in the respective provinces.

This suggestion was music to the ears of the Mafia-backed Sicilian separatists.

Lord Rennell made his first detailed report on the Allied government in Sicily on 3 August 1943 in a confidential letter to a Colonel French:

> I do not wish you to think that anything has broken down yet, but I am acutely conscious of how near to breakdown we have been . . . The only thing which has not broken down or shown signs of breakdown as yet, is Anglo-American relations.
>
> The American officers in Amgot have done very well. This applies to the younger as well as the older. They have shown enterprise, ingenuity and tremendous keenness. They have generally exceeded expectations. The young British officers are generally up to expectations. The older ones are disappointing and are breaking down. I have one senior

> SCAO in charge of a province who has succeeded in making a first class mess already and one which has compromised the issue of wheat prices all over the island. This type of life is not an old man's job.

In the British House of Commons, Labour MPs were openly critical of the Allied administration established in Sicily. They questioned the use of the Carabinieri as police by AMGOT, believing them to be agents of the Fascist regime. Lord Rennell denied this strongly. He saw the restored Carabinieri as his principal weapon against the Mafia:

> In a country like Sicily where the Mafia is far from dead, it requires an intimate local knowledge which is only possessed by the Carabinieri to keep Mafia activities in bounds; as it is there has been a recrudescence largely due to the fact that in the first few days after the occupation of an area the Carabinieri were disarmed, which led to the unruly elements, for which Sicily is notorious, assuming that the local police force had been disbanded.
>
> The fact that they were not disbanded has checked what might have been, and may yet be, a serious menace to good administration. Both I and my officers, including the London police officers as well as the officers of both Seventh and Eighth Armies, are entirely satisfied with the behaviour of the Carabinieri as a whole.

Lord Rennell did, however, admit to early mistakes in the appointment of new town mayors to replace Fascist community leaders:

> The word Podesta has been abolished and replaced with the older Italian title of Sindaco who was elected but is now nominated by the Allied Military Government . . . Unfortunately owing to the zeal which Allied Military Government Officers have shown in the removal of Fascist Podesta they have fallen into the trap of appointing the most pushing and obvious person, who in certain cases are now suspected as being the local Mafia leaders.
>
> In certain parts of Sicily there is no doubt that the election of Sindaco will result in virtually unanimous voting for local Mafia leaders. It will take quite a long time for the Allied Military Government to weed out the good from the bad. I

am convinced that even if municipal elections had been possible, the elective system would have produced chaos.

In a second secret report of 20 August 1943, sent to the War Office in London, Lord Rennell drew attention to the volatile political situation on the island. From the first moment he landed, he was aware of certain elements calling for Sicilian Separatism:

> Within a few days of the occupation of Palermo a Committee for Sicilian Independence was formed. A manifesto was printed as a handbill and posters were put up in the streets. This was stopped and the persons concerned warned that all forms of political activity were forbidden . . .
>
> Among the leaders of the movement are, as might be expected, members of the Tasca family who have always been associated with Sicilian Separatism and have equally always been Anti-Fascists. Finocchiaro Aprile a pre-Fascist Under-Secretary of State and a Sicilian by origin is also in the forefront of the movement. He served in Italian pre-Fascist governments in the departments of War and Finance. He is somewhat garrulous and not very outstanding in ability . . .
>
> I have personally warned Alessandro Tasca and Finocchiaro Aprile. But I do not flatter myself that these warnings will have much effect; from the point of view of the leaders, the moment is clearly not one to be lost if they are to achieve anything.

British Vice-Consul Manley also noted that the Separatists were fast off the mark. Lucio Tasca was a prominent Separatist with links to the Mafia. Together with the Duchess of Cesaro, he was quick to contact the Allied authorities in Palermo, including Poletti. They wined and dined them, presenting themselves as leading anti-Fascists. Tasca's prize was to be appointed Mayor of Palermo, with a number of his Separatist friends gaining other public appointments.

Lord Rennell was under no illusion that the Mafia had their part to play in this movement. It is also clear that *he* viewed them as a major problem – he would not succumb to their dinner party offensive – and certainly had no intention or plan for working with them. He observed:

> The other element which may be of considerable importance is the Mafia. Many of the long sentences which were awarded

> in the trials which followed Mori's campaign have recently come to an end and many of the prisoners are probably once more at large.
>
> These who have not been liberated are probably still in convict stations or in compulsory domicile in the islands. Generally speaking these men will be reputedly, and really, anti-Fascists; but they are not people to whom clemency can safely be extended on the grounds that they are political prisoners who have suffered at the hands of the Fascists.
>
> While the Mafia is primarily a 'racket' organisation for blackmail, protection, and robbery, it formerly also played a considerable political part in elections. I would expect the Mafia to be associated with the Sicilian Independence Movement.

It is certain from Lord Rennell's tone that, as far he was concerned, the Allies owed nothing to the Mafia for any help given during the invasion. He should have known – he was the senior officer in charge of the Allied military occupation of the island. It is worth emphasising that point. He saw the Mafia primarily as a threat to Allied law and order – not a help in securing it:

> There is some evidence of Mafia activity increasing. There has been one murder of a land owner which looks like Mafia work. The aftermath of war and the breakdown of central and provincial authority provide a good culture ground for the virus.
>
> The only formation capable of dealing with the Mafia with proper support is the Corps of Carabinieri. These with Civil Affairs Police Officers and military patrols may be able to check a recrudescence of activity. I say deliberately 'may', because with the 'Omerta', or Sicilian code of honour, which precludes recourse of the injured parties even in cases of murder to the Government, it has been notoriously difficult to secure evidence of guilt, or even willingness to make charges.

With the senior military administrator in Sicily calling the Mafia a virus, it looked as though the Mafia could expect little mercy from the Allies.

In a report issued in October 1943, Lord Rennell repeated his belief that the Allies had been too keen to remove any trace of Fascism without thinking who would take over the administration of Sicilian towns:

> I also fear that in their exuberance to remove Fascist Podestas and Municipal officials in rural towns, my own officers have in certain cases by ignorance of local personalities appointed a number of Mafia 'bosses' or allowed such 'bosses' to propose suitably malleable substitutes.
>
> Here my difficulty resides in the Sicilian Omerta code of honour. I cannot get much information even from the local Carabinieri who in outstations inevitably feel that they had better keep their mouths shut and their skins whole if the local AMGOT representatives chooses to appoint a Mafioso, lest they be accused by AMGOT of being Pro-Fascist.
>
> The local Mafiosi, who of course had no love for the regime which persecuted the Mafia, are naturally not slow in levelling accusations of Fascist sympathies against their own pet enemies.

Here, we can see, from the evidence gathered by the chief Allied Civil Affairs Officer in charge of Sicily that there was no Allied conspiracy to put the Mafia back into power. Instead, through misunderstanding and administrative overstretch, the Allies – by mistake – allowed the Mafia to put themselves back into positions of power.

Corrections, however, were being made. In Palermo province, said Lord Rennell, a 'number of unsatisfactory municipal appointments made in the first few weeks have been removed, as have several suspected Mafiosi and bad characters who were appointed Sindaci of townships. Some remain to be removed.'

Lord Rennell also saw that the rebirth of the Mafia was being enforced by a campaign of murder:

> The fact of the matter is that while ordinary civil crime other than black market offences is at a satisfactory level except in Trapani province and in most provinces has been decreasing, homicide has undoubtedly increased in the provinces reported to be Mafiose [*sic*].
>
> Many of these homicides are of the Mafia type or bear indications of Mafia antecedents. In these cases arrests are infrequent and evidence unobtainable. In Agrigento province there were six homicide cases; arrests have been made in four cases but only in one which has Mafia antecedents has good

> evidence been obtained. In this case the witnesses have all been locked up to ensure their security and in order to ensure expedition the case has been transferred to an Allied General Court on which Italian assessors will sit. If a conviction is secured the effect on the Mafia in that province, where it has been rampant, may be considerable.

As a result of the Fascist operations against them, many Mafiosi were still locked in prison on punishment islands off the coast of Sicily. Lord Rennell was aware of this and careful not to make any further mistakes. All prisoners had their cases analysed and those awaiting trial for minor offences were released. But the wholesale release of prisoners awaiting trial for more serious charges was halted. 'The risk of releasing Mafiosi without investigation is not worth taking in present circumstances', said Lord Rennell wisely.

The same wary view of the Mafia was taken up in the *Narrative for Official History of Civil Affairs in Italy* written by D. S. Duff and intended as the British government's summary of the occupation of Sicily. Duff felt the weak point lay in American relationships with the Mafia:

> Stress must be laid upon the number of Mafiosi who managed to get themselves incorporated into the administration in the early days on account of their former trans-Atlantic residences (often enforced) and their knowledge of a certain amount of American gangster speech. They were incorporated into the [Allied] regime because a number of non-Italian speaking American officers discovered, quite rightly, that they were anti-Fascist, having frequently enjoyed enforced residence in Italy also, and on account of their sometimes elementary knowledge of English. While there was a lull in Mafia crime after the landing, it poked its ugly head up very quickly . . .
>
> Reports from local people indicated that Mafia activities had begun again now that the Fascists had gone, and it was necessary to take a firm line at the beginning. In Provinces there were a number of Mafia members released from prison, and some were still in prison. It was suggested that as many as possible should be deported.

From the British point of view, at least, it is clear that the Mafia in Sicily should be no friends of the Allies.

A London *Times* correspondent was in Sicily in September 1943 and he described the feeling on the streets of the newly liberated capital:

> Palermo, the capital of Sicily, has already the appearance of returning to normal. Much of it is illusory. The shops, for instance, succeed in making great display with little and tawdry material. The main streets are full of people, but in reality not much more than half the population has returned. You can get a tolerably good meal in certain restaurants, but the communal food situation is not good; there is a shortage that becomes more acute as the population returns, 'Following the food'.

The *Times* correspondent noted that there was a general distrust of government among the Sicilians, wherever it came from. 'There is perhaps more stubborn aversion to government in general', he wrote, 'in the interior of this island than there is on the mainland, for the spirit of the Mafia is not wholly dead.'

With shortages of food and other essentials, the black market in Palermo and elsewhere in Sicily was growing rapidly under Mafia patronage. Tough action was needed and it was up to AMGOT to deliver it.

On 10 September 1943, the *New York Times* printed a sensational story about an Allied clash with the Mafia near Palermo:

> The Mafia, Sicilian extortionist gang that fascism tried for years to rub out and then incorporated as one of its criminal appendages, has been smashed from the top. Two of its notorious leaders, Domenico Tomaselli and Giuseppe Piraino, and seventeen district bosses were nabbed in a joint British-American coup in which Scotland Yard had a hand.

With these gangsters behind bars, the Allied authorities had further leads on other leading regional Mafiosi, which it intended to follow up:

> The Mafia men already jailed and those on the way to joining them controlled the black market, which still has a stranglehold on Sicilian life. It follows that breaking the Mafia gang means breaking the black market.

The newspaper report claimed that the Allies had been helped by other Mafiosi who were anti-Fascist and wanted to see an end to Fascist-backed profiteering. Of course, what may well have been really happening was that one Mafia faction wanted to take over the black market in their area and so informed on those Mafia who had colluded with the Fascists. It was a classic take-over strategy using a third party to do the dirty work. The Mafia in both Sicily and America were not averse to using the authorities to knock out a rival on their behalf.

The military operation against the Mafia was said to have begun when the US 3rd Division was on its drive towards Messina and chose Castel d'Accia for its rear echelon headquarters. It was located inland from Trabia, about twenty-two miles from Palermo. The newspaper gave credit to Louis Bassi of Stockton, California, a 'technician in the special service staff', for discovering that the tiny hamlet was in fact a Mafia fortress. He investigated it by himself until he had enough evidence for an open and shut case against the racketeers and then reported it to his colonel.

The *New York Herald Tribune*, which also published the Associated Press story, added another dimension: 'A major who also had the distinction of helping Mike Fiaschetti bust the New York markets racket was drawn into the case from the food-supply angle and was in on the kill . . .'

Michael Fiaschetti – known as 'Treat-'Em-Rough Mike' – was an experienced anti-racketeer investigator in the New York Police Department. As deputy commissioner, he was credited with smashing a racket centred around the supply of artichokes in 1935. From this, it is clear that AMGOT took the problem of the black market in Sicily seriously enough to turn to specialist police agents to help them crack it. A subsequent newspaper article also commented on the affair:

> Dispatches from Sicily telling of the arrest of bosses and sub-bosses of the Mafia probably surprise most of us. That powerful criminal gang was thought to have been put out of business by the Prefect of Sicily, Cesare Mori, who died last year . . . Now we hear that the Mafia is caught running the black market. The Fascists hadn't suppressed it. They had annexed it. We are not told exactly on what basis, but presumably on some regular division of territory and profit. You feel a little sorry for the Mafia. It has got into trouble by keeping bad company.

Unfortunately, all these articles were hopelessly optimistic. The Allies had not smashed Mafia control of the black market in Sicily. They had replaced one set of bosses with another, apparently more pro-Allied bunch of Mafiosi.

In the swoop on the Mafia bastion at Castel d'Accia, the *New York Times* and the *Herald Tribune* reported the involvement of Scotland Yard – headquarters of the London Metropolitan Police – in the Allied assault. The London *Times* correspondent also noted the presence of the 'London bobby' on the streets of Palermo. 'Each department is staffed by equal numbers of British and American officers' he wrote, 'and British police officers are almost wholly drawn from the Metropolitan Police Force'.

As part of its readiness to face crime in Sicily, AMGOT had recruited sixty-five Metropolitan Police officers to patrol the streets of the occupied cities. AMGOT'S plan for law and order relied on re-establishing the Carabinieri as the main police force on the island. To use a military police corps would have been to go against the primary purpose of AMGOT, which was to maintain public order without diverting military manpower. The sixty-five London bobbies were intended to work alongside other specially trained Allied officers who would supervise the actions of the Italian police.

'The Metropolitan Police contingent proved itself astonishingly versatile in the role of Civil Affairs Officers, Supply Officers and in any other administrative job on which they were employed', said C. R. S. Harris, who served with AMGOT in Sicily and later wrote a government book on the subject. 'It would be no exaggeration to describe them as more responsible than any other element for such practical success in military government as AMGOT undoubtedly achieved.' Lord Rennell was also impressed by them:

> I am particularly pleased in the 8th Army area, with the good work of my police officers drawn in large part from the London (Metropolitan) Police. In spite of language difficulties and no foreign experience they have proved themselves adaptable and efficient and have got on well with the Carabinieri and the American officers with whom they are associated.

A later booklet, *The Metropolitan Police at War*, mentioned that 'Much of the work these officers were called upon to do was quite outside the normal range of police duties . . . However, a British bobby seems to able to turn his hand to most things, and they carried out their tasks, by all accounts, most efficiently.'

Most of the policemen sent to Sicily were older officers, some of them having seen military service in World War I. Bertram Hefford MBE was one of them. He was a 47-year-old Superintendent at Scotland Yard when he volunteered, much to the annoyance of his wife. He went to Palermo with a close colleague and joked that AMGOT really meant 'Aged Military Gentlemen on Tour'. Metropolitan police officers were given an equivalent military rank in AMGOT and Hefford was even promoted to lieutenant-colonel. After Sicily, he went to Genoa and then returned home as a Chief Superintendent, retiring in 1956. Hefford's family are the proud owners of two very impressive two-foot high statues presented to him by grateful Carabinieri. The inscription reads:

> The Italian Carabinieri, VI Brigade, being very grateful to Major Bertram J. Hefford, who in painful and difficult moments knew how to understand and assist them cordially and to infuse into them new self confidence and fortitude, offer this souvenir, Sicily, July 1943–February 1944.

Some younger Metropolitan policemen were recruited directly into the army. Corporal William Capp was a 24-year-old policeman in Islington when he was given the harsh choice of being either a rear-gunner in the RAF or an army commando. After commando training in Scotland, he ended up in Sicily in August 1943 in No. 2 Commando taking part in raids behind German lines. 'In Scaletta [on the way to Messina], we had to hold up a German train', he remembered, 'but a few of our blokes got hit by snipers.'

From Sicily, Capp went to Salerno where he took part in the landing that killed the then Duke of Wellington. 'They had tanks lined up on the promenade shelling us. We went in with 350 men and by the time we took a hill on the coast we had 73 of us left.' In northern Italy he captured a Tiger tank – 'a round got stuck up its barrel and its crew ran off, I still have the swastika flag from the tank'. After more raids behind German lines along the Dalmatian coast, Capp returned to Britain where he resumed his police service in 1946, clocking up thirty years as a bobby on the beat.

In his behind-the-lines raids in Sicily, did Capp ever work with the Mafia? 'No, we never heard of them', he said decisively.

At first, in Sicily, because the Carabinieri wore military uniforms, they were mistaken for Italian soldiers by the Allies. Some were taken as prisoners of war and shipped over to North Africa. AMGOT got these men released and dressed in civilian clothing but with police armbands. They then set about re-building their morale by arranging for Allied military police to go on patrol with them so as to raise their status in the eyes of the Sicilian public. SCAO Colonel Poletti described this process in his report of 31 July:

> At beginning of the occupation we proceeded slowly in rearming Carabinieri and local police. Thereafter it was ordered that they be rearmed at once because the population has little respect for a policeman without arms. We also pursued the practice of having one MP accompany two Carabinieri so that our soldiers would become accustomed to them.

'The restoration of the morale of the Carabinieri was the notable achievement of the Metropolitan Police officers,' claimed C. R. S. Harris, 'who managed to command not only the professional respect but, what was even more important, the personal loyalty of their Italian colleagues.' The same could not be said for the Agenti di Sicurezza Pubblica, the criminal investigation officers of the Italian police force. They had been closely associated with the Fascist regime and commanded little respect among Sicilians. Many of their commanding officers were interned by the Allies.

> The respect for the law had been considerably diminished [concluded Harris]. This showed itself in a number of ways at first, in a considerable increase in crimes of violence and of robbery, and an enormous increase in the whole range of black market offences, and, later, what was much more significant, in a revival of the Mafia . . . The removal of the heavy hand of Fascism gave rise to a freer use of the dagger and pistol – which Allied Military Government was wholly unable to prevent.

Lord Rennell sometimes had to intervene personally to break the rule of *omerta* in the countryside. On one occasion, Baron Genuardo, a wealthy landowner from Agrigento, was shot five times and stabbed seventeen times. The local Mafia were suspected of his murder and two suspects were arrested by the Carabinieri. To avoid the intimidation of a local jury, Lord Rennell had the case transferred to an Allied military tribunal. Death sentences were passed and rapidly carried out by a firing squad. It was a clear and strong message to the rest.

The English Lord had ordered his first strike against the Mafia.

Chapter Thirteen

Unwitting Tools of the Mafia

That the Mafia was back in action in Sicily was confirmed by early reports from Civil Affairs Police Officers (CAPOs). At their meeting held at AMG HQ in Palermo on 8 September 1943, a Major Smith gave a brief talk on the Mafia. 'Reports from local people', said Smith, 'indicated that Mafia activities had begun again now that the Fascists had gone, and it was necessary to take a firm line at the beginning. In Provinces there were a number of Mafia members released from prison, and some were still in prison.' It was suggested that as many as possible of these Mafiosi should be deported. At a second meeting of CAPOs, held a month later, it was recommended that the Mafia be dealt with on an island-wide basis. Any information about their activities should be directed to AMG HQ for a co-ordinated response.

A more complete picture of Mafia activity in Sicily was provided by a report prepared by an American Military Intelligence Officer, Captain W. E. Scotten, in late October 1943. He had served for three years as American Vice-Consul in Palermo and was called upon by the Commissioner of Public Safety at AMG HQ in Palermo to provide an account of the threat posed by the Mafia to the task of Allied occupation.

The Commissioner and his department wanted some evidence to hand to a higher authority so they could get full backing to deal with the Mafia. Copies of Scotten's memorandum were handed to Brigadier General MacSherry, Lord Rennell's American deputy, and to Harold Macmillan, British Resident Minister at Allied HQ in Algiers.

In his six-page memorandum, Scotten gives a detailed history of the Mafia in Sicily so as to explain their grip on the island:

> Whatever may have been the necessity or justification for Mafia in any given epoch, in our times it had degenerated into a criminal system, the object of which was to commit extortion and theft with impunity. To accomplish this, no method or means was neglected, ranging from threats and terrorism to outright murder, arson, kidnapping, and mayhem.

In order to protect itself, the Mafia had formed an alliance with various major landowners and this meant it became involved in island politics:

> As a matter of fact, Mafia, before the advent of Fascism, had reached the position of holding the balance of political power in Sicily. It could control elections, and it was courted by political personages and parties.

Cesare Mori's campaign against the Mafia had failed to root it out. His attack was directed mainly at its lower ranks and had sought to destroy the more notorious bandits and their gangs. It was headlining stuff:

> But the higher level of Mafia was not appreciably interfered with. According to the statement of many serious people in Sicily, Mori was ordered by Rome to slacken his efforts when it became apparent that a complete housecleaning would involve too many high-ranking professional and business people and even influential members of the Party . . .
>
> Thus it should be said that Mafia was only driven underground under Fascism; it was never stamped out in any sense of the word . . . Furthermore, to [my] certain knowledge, there were innumerable rackets, big and small, functioning under Mafia control, which the Fascist regime appeared either to tolerate or to be unable to wipe out. It seems as though the regime was satisfied with the suppression of the more outrageous aspects of the system and thenceforth refused to admit officially that Mafia existed any longer in the island.

It was a subtle and perceptive analysis of the Mafia's relationship with Fascism. In his research, Scotten spoke to CIC officers, the Political Intelligence Section in AMG, and local Sicilians. The feeling he got was that the Mafia was re-asserting itself:

> Reports are constantly flowing in, especially from the operatives of the CIC, that Mafia is becoming increasingly bold in many areas. Already our own courts have been obliged to deal with flagrant outbreaks in the province of Agrigento.

There was still a window of opportunity to crush the mobsters. Scotten recommended swift and uncompromising measures before they regained their old strength. He feared the Mafiosi were arming themselves with modern weapons harvested from recent battlefields. The military hardware included machine guns, trench mortars, land mines, field radios, even light field artillery, all hidden away in caves and secret stores. Worryingly, he believed that many senior Allied officers had already fallen under the influence of the Mafia:

> [Sicilians] claim there are numerous cases of our own CAOs and interpreters of Sicilian origin and ancestry, whose family connections or antecedents in the United States have led them directly into the sphere of Mafia. They maintain that higher ranking officers have succumbed to the blandishments of the landed gentry, who are in close association with Mafia . . . They affirm that our officers are being misled and blinded by corrupt or influenced interpreters and advisors, to the extent that they are in danger of becoming the unwitting tools of Mafia.

The result was that Sicilians had lost confidence in the Allies' ability to deal with the Mafia. That encouraged the Mafia to attempt ever more daring crimes, such as large-scale hijacking and looting of food and other articles from Allied-controlled warehouses. It was a vicious circle, with the crimes conducted under the very noses of the military. For many Sicilians, Scotten could see that the situation was possibly worse under the Allies than it had been under the Fascists:

> Under Fascism there was shortage and rationing of food and a black market, but the food ration was actually forthcoming and the black market was partially controlled, whereas today the ration is unobtainable much of the time and the black market in food has gotten completely out of hand . . . Under Fascism, Mafia, if not entirely suppressed, was at least held very much in check, whereas at present it is growing at an alarming rate and is even enjoying a favoured position under AMG.

In conclusion, Scotten submitted that the Mafia presented the Allies with their most pressing problem – a situation that could not be fully appreciated by anyone who did not live on the island. But how should the Allies deal with the Mafia? Scotten believed there were three possible answers: direct and prompt action to bring the Mafia under control; a negotiated truce with the Mafia leaders; or the abandonment of any attempt to control the mobsters, with the creation of protected enclaves around Allied military bases. Encouragingly, he stated:

> The first course would appear to be the only one consistent with the expressed objectives of military government. It would require the most cautious and secret preparations, strong reinforcement of the Carabinieri with allied military personnel, and concerted and simultaneous arrest, regardless of personalities and political connections, of between five and six hundred leaders, and their deportation without any semblance of trial for detainment for the duration of the war.

Cesare Mori would have been proud of the American Military Intelligence officer! Alarmingly, however, Scotten spent more space discussing the second option – a truce in which the AMG concentrated on prosecuting the war effort and left the island to the control of the Mafia, just so long as they desisted from taking food supplies intended for the local population and were tackled when they committed any common crimes.

> The third course [said Scotten], is the course of least resistance. It is the course of weakness and will so be interpreted by the enemy, by the rest of Italy, by other enemy-occupied countries who are watching the experiment of AMG, and by the home populations. It may well mean the abandonment of the island to criminal rule for a long time to come. On the other hand, its chance of success is certain.

Scotten's clear preference for the first course of action was a rallying call to the Allies to do the right thing and fight a crusade against the Mafia in Sicily. But it was never going to happen. Troops were needed to fight the war against the Germans – not the Mafia. The Allies would never commit such resources to a major campaign directed at criminals. This was not their job – their job was to win the war. Scotten may well have been disappointed by the lack of official interest in his solution, but it did demonstrate there was a strong feeling in the Allied intelligence community against the Mafia – it did not seek any accommodation with it. In this respect, Scotten mirrored Lord Rennell's own views.

An American intelligence report of 3 December 1943 drew attention to the growing political problems on the island:

> The political situation in Sicily is a threatening one. Recently, demonstrations and disturbances have been taking place in many of the island's large centers. Those disturbances have not been pro-Allied in character, but have been staged in favor of the extremist parties, communist or fascist.

These demonstrations had broken out in Palermo, Monreale, Trebia, Agrigento, Licata, Termini Imerese, Canicatti and Raffadali. They were thought to be primarily caused by a shortage of food and other necessities, but public anger could easily be turned to a political end. A break down in law and order was also considered to be another problem facing the Allied government in Sicily. One of the reasons for this, said the report, was that a lack of respect for the government was fed by the sight of members of the Mafia taking up positions of power thanks to the apparent support of the Allies.

Interestingly, this suggests that the assumption of power by the Mafia was not seen as a popular move by the local population – but a cause for concern. To counter this lack of support, the Mafia turned to their own political cause – independence for Sicilians. 'The Separatists had a recent rally in Palermo', noted the American analysis, 'but according to reports the turn out was not large, and as yet this group has not captured any large section of popular support.'

Other political parties sought to push their own view of events. The manifestos of the left-wing Labour Front and the centrist Christian Democrats both deplored an increase in violence and lawlessness. The Labour Front urged the Allied government to 'eliminate Fascists, Mafia members, and King's party men from positions of authority.' According to the left, the Mafia were viewed as part of a right-wing problem.

One aspect of the difficulties faced by Allied authorities in maintaining law and order was the lack of resources available for the local police, said the intelligence report:

> The Carabinieri are paid about 175 lira a week, or $1.75. A small loaf of bread on the black market costs 50 cents.

> Regularly distributed bread is often unobtainable. The result is that the maintainers of law and order must break the law themselves in order to live and feed their families. Naturally this leads to lack of respect for law and order, and plays in to the hands of the political parties which might wish to foster disturbances for their own ends.

Also in December 1943, a meeting of AMG officers took place in Palermo. It was called to discuss one topic – security in western Sicily. Lieutenant-Colonel R. A. Snook of the Public Safety Division (which had commissioned Scotten's memorandum) gave an introductory run down on the problems they faced:

> The main threat to security is the lack of food. This lack of food leads to general unrest and is exploited by criminal and political factions. At present the Carabinieri have the people under control. The Carabinieri are being strengthened and prepared for possible serious uprisings. It is not contemplated to call for the assistance of troops against unruly crowds unless the Carabinieri can no longer cope with the situation.

However, the Carabinieri had their own problems. They had restricted communication facilities and limited transport. It meant they could not get in force to any one spot to meet an emergency. They were also out-gunned. 'The accessibility of explosives in the form of hand grenades etc to civilians', warned Snook, 'complicates the security enforcement.'

To anticipate any upcoming problems, AMG was setting up a data-gathering network to report on crime, political movements and other factors which might tend to lead to unrest. Snook reminded everyone that basic AMG policy virtually prohibited all political activity and they must adhere to that. It was noted that the Christian Democrats were attracting the wealthy and professional classes, as well as a number of former Fascists. The party had not been officially recognised by the AMG, and civilian officials continued to be chosen on the basis of individual merit rather than on their party affiliations. But, admitted another intelligence officer at the meeting, 'This party stands in best with AMG.'

In contrast, the Independent Sicily party was criticised for being the only party not to have issued a manifesto recommending calm and support for AMG. Despite their wish not to get involved, AMG was being drawn into a political quagmire.

On 10 December 1943, Captain Scotten produced a second analysis of the political and criminal situation in Sicily. This time it came through his Security Intelligence Subsection at AMG HQ in Palermo:

> The professional politicians of the pre-Fascist era are few in number, aging and cynical . . . They are cautious, non-committal and are following a policy of waiting to see which way the wind blows. Some are flirting with the remnants of the old political Mafia. A few are already committed to the Christian-Democrats.

Scotten then described the role of major landed proprietors in the wake of the Allied invasion:

> Though they are few in number, they have at hand a powerful instrument in the form of Mafia, with which they have been of necessity allied since time immemorial. Without attempting to define what Mafia is or not, it will suffice to say that Mafia may be described as a system of political racketeering on the higher levels and criminal racketeering on the lower levels.

Scotten saw signs that the landed proprietors and their Separatist associates were preparing an alliance with the Mafia. It was at an early stage, however, as he thought the old Mafia leaders did not want to be caught on the wrong side and were negotiating with other political parties, including even the left.

This analysis was a pale echo of Scotten's concerns expressed more strongly and directly in his October memorandum – in which he urged direct action before it was too late. 'In the eyes of the Sicilians', he had said earlier, 'the AMG has allowed itself to become surrounded with separatist friends and advisors and has consistently appointed to public office either outright separatists or persons of separatist sympathy.' He gave examples of these as the prefect and the mayor of Palermo.

'According to some sources', he alleged, 'at least 80% of the appointments made by the AMG in this area have been of this class. In their opinion the AMG has not only placed itself at a disadvantage to deal with Mafia, it has even gone so far as to play into its hands.'

Two months later, however, Scotten's criticism of the Allies' relationship with the Mafia was watered down and so were his recommendations for action. Had his associates, working primarily within the Public Safety Division at AMG HQ, been silenced by the more complex politics of SCAO Lieutenant Colonel Charles Poletti and other Italian-Americans?

While the majority of those working in the Allied government in Sicily were clearly aware of the threat posed by the Mafia and sought to do something about it, there was one small Allied agency that took a more Machiavellian approach. That was the OSS.

Towards the end of the campaign, the OSS produced its own report on its activities in the island – for the eyes only of OSS operatives in Algiers. It was credited to Experimental Department G-3, a cover name for the OSS. No writer is named but it is likely that the author was Joseph Russo. A newspaper journalist from Connecticut, he became commanding officer of the OSS SI Palermo Station after fighting ended in the island and attended meetings under the title 'Exp Det G-3'.

The OSS report was written in Palermo on 13 August 1943. It recognised the presence of two political parties, one favouring complete separatism, led by Finocchiaro Aprile, and the other called Partito d'Azione, devoted to more regional representation. The OSS favoured the latter. 'It is our suspicion', said the OSS, 'that the separatist movement is being in part sponsored by the British. It is our opinion that the Partito d'Azione has a sounder platform and a better element directing its activities . . . The British have so far failed to infiltrate this group.' Again, we have here the peculiarly OSS concern expressed by Max Corvo that the British were the major problem for America in the Mediterranean. The report then turned to the Mafia:

> In connection with all Sicilian activities it must be constantly kept in mind that the Mafia plays an important role. La Mafia in turn is divided into two branches, – one, the upper branch which is composed of intellectuals and professionals, and two, the lower branch, in which are found elements willing to perform strong-arm work, (even including petty thieves and criminals). Only the Mafia is able to bring about suppression of black market practices and influence the 'contadini' who constitute a majority of the population.

The OSS then made a sensational claim – it had the Mafia in its pocket:

> We at the present time can claim the Partito d'Azione in Sicily and the Mafia. We have had conferences with their

> leaders and a bargain has been struck that they will be doing as we direct or suggest. A bargain once made here is not easily broken.

So much for Max Corvo saying that the OSS should not deal with the Mafia. The OSS report continued:

> As evidence of their good faith, they have submitted to us the names of their leaders . . . We lent a sympathetic ear to their troubles and assured them, however feeble our cooperation, that it was theirs for the asking. We have employed a number of these people as informants. Some have refused to accept any compensation. Through them, and as soon as traffic will permit, we will have an intelligence network established throughout the island. We have acted with the utmost of secrecy, and we are known only to five persons.

No doubt, it is true that the rest of AMG was ignorant of this deal. But the boast of the OSS was rather hollow for we now know that the Mafia were strongly behind the Separatist movement – not Partito d'Azione. It was also foolishly optimistic to think the Mafia could so easily be controlled by a handful of OSS agents.

The report then returned to that favourite OSS occupation – outwitting the British – and the deal with the Mafia is considered to be useful in their overall strategy:

> Because of British policy, we consider it extremely important that we continue our relations as established, not only in Sicily, but wherever we may go. It is British policy to tap every organization, political or otherwise. This we know definitely is being done and it is being done with the purpose of guiding and influencing political action in Italy . . . Furthermore, it is the American that the Sicilian loves; it is the American that he wants to see remain here and not the British. This last statement is not made with any bias on our part.

Of course not. Finally, the OSS had harsh words for the American governor of Palermo:

> Whether Lt Col Poletti is acting under orders or not, he definitely is not running the city of New York or the state of New York. He does not understand the Sicilian situation, the

> people or its internal politics. As long as he remains in office, he will continue to make mistakes and serious mistakes.

Some would say that Poletti understood the ways of the Sicilians too well.

The OSS then tried to explain its own tough words. 'We also know from personal observation the attitude taken by Col Poletti on the Sicilian situation. We do not say that he acts with malice but rather because of a misunderstanding of the situation.'

The back-stabbing between Poletti and the OSS continued long after the war. In a BBC TV interview in 1993, Joseph Russo was asked who was responsible for appointing Mafiosi to key positions throughout Sicily. Russo answered with one name: 'Poletti.' In this interview, Russo was also open about his relationship with the Mafia:

> When I got to Sicily and took over, the first thing I did I started looking for the *malavita* – the criminals – and it turned out they were mostly Mafiosi. They liked my name and the fact that my father was born in Corleone – the hot-seat of the Mafia. I got to know these people – the high Mafiosi – and they were big. They got to be real big. It didn't take them long to re-cement their solidarity – the gang. I knew every one of them . . .

Russo claimed that top Mafiosi, including Don Calogero Vizzini of Villalba, visited his office at least once a month. They wanted to talk about the political situation on the island and wondered if the Americans were going to do anything about the Communists. Russo said they were now their Allies in the war and they had nothing planned. For the Mafia bosses, it was a disappointing answer and probably pushed them to devising their own solution.

Throughout his filmed interview with the BBC, Russo was clearly holding back much more information than he was willing to divulge. Even fifty years after the events, he was still very conscious that some of his wartime Mafia contacts were still alive and he did not want to offend them. Such was the depth of the relationship between the Mafia and the OSS.

If food shortages and the activities of the black market were widely blamed for a dramatic rise in crime in Sicily then, by the end of 1943, the Allies had put a lot of effort into improving the supply situation.

Bread was handed out daily to Sicilians. The delivery of vegetables, fruit and even some meat to all market places was assured. It helped to reduce some of the tense atmosphere in the island but, despite this, the black market still flourished.

Colonel Byron R. Switzer was chief of the Joint Intelligence Collecting Agency (JICA) in Sicily and he made it his business to get a feeling for what was going on in the island. His Italian-speaking team talked to a number of leading Sicilians and, sharing an AMG tendency, these included a regional president of the Christian Democrats.

In a Weekly Stability Report for 20 December 1943, JICA praised the efforts of the Allies for getting food to the Sicilians, but it couldn't overcome their illegal entrepreneurial instincts:

> The Black Market continues to flourish with practically the entire Sicilian population either buying or selling. It has been reported that in the country most of the peasants have purchased and hidden away quantities of grain amounting to three or four quintals. This is being made into bread a little at a time and the peasants either bring this bread to the large cities themselves, or sell it to others who are travelling to the city.

In the early morning at markets and railway stations in Palermo, black marketeers stood around clutching a dozen loaves. They sold to any and everyone, including the police. Having sold the bread, they proceeded to their daily jobs. The peasants were lucky to have this extra source of income. Those working in the Sicilian sulphur industry were not so fortunate.

> In the sulphur mining regions of Sicily [said JICA], the economic situation is extremely bad. Many of the mines have not been in operation through lack of machinery and most families have been reduced to poverty and misery. Delinquency in these regions is reported to be on a larger scale than in any other sections of the island.

In the week of 10 December 1943, a major figure from the mainland Italian government visited Sicily. Secretary of the Interior, Minister Reale, had come to get first-hand information on the political situation in the island. He spent all day in his hotel talking to those Sicilians who represented the Separatist movement. Outside were representatives of other Sicilian parties. They had united to denounce the Separatists and form a Liberty Front against them. These included socialists, reformists and monarchists.

That Minister Reale considered the men of the Separatist movement more important than those politicians waiting outside was underlined by the fact that he kept them waiting all day for an interview. When these members were finally allowed in to see Reale, they accused the Separatists of being 'vulgar politicians in the pay of large land-holders, all ex-Fascists, reactionaries and protectors of the Mafia'. The Liberty Front were particularly incensed at the idea that the Prefect of Palermo, Francesco Musotto, should be proposed as High Commissioner of Sicily. They accused him of being a Separatist.

JICA reported all this, but gave Musotto the benefit of the doubt, claiming that he was not himself a Separatist, although he did have many friends who were. The institution of a Commissioner of Sicily, admitted JICA, was interpreted as a semi-official step towards Separatism encouraged by the AMG. It was a bad error. Such moves only fuelled the cause of the Separatists and the people behind them – the Mafia. JICA concluded:

> In the political field, all parties have united against the Separatists. Though few in number, the Separatists are all so wealthy that by using underhanded means they have tried to create the impression that they have a large following. It is this group of opportunists that could be most harmful since they are in position to become potential leaders of any revolutionary movement that might arise.

The Mafia were very well aware that this was the situation they found themselves in. With bluff and behind-the-scenes influence they had managed to get the Badoglio government to take them seriously. It was now time to ramp up the pressure on the Allies – and that meant more violence.

Christmas 1943 in Sicily was a reason for celebration. Mussolini's Fascist regime was gone and the island was free of war. That had passed on to the Italian mainland where the Allies had fought a savage battle at Salerno and then slowly pushed on against fierce defensive actions by the Germans. By the end of the year, the Allied advance had petered out beneath a thousand-year-old monastery called Monte Cassino.

In Palermo and other Sicilian cities, the Allies had got food into the shops. They were even planning to give a free pasta meal to all civilians once a week in the New Year. According to AMG rules, the use of wheat flour for the making of pastries was forbidden, but with Christmas approaching, sweet pastries were seen piled in the bakeries and none of the authorities seemed to mind.

American and British officers based in Sicily probably hoped for a quiet Christmas. At least, they were not on the freezing front line in Italy, but criminal forces did not take a holiday.

In the New Year, a contingent of Italian soldiers was guarding an Allied fuel dump containing petrol and diesel oil. As they chatted in the dark to relieve the tedium of guard duty, they were suddenly attacked by local gangsters hurling hand grenades. They took shelter, returned fire and the thieves disappeared. It was no surprise to hear that the stolen fuel was to be sold on the black market.

The guard details were reinforced and it didn't occur again, but it was a chilling demonstration of criminal power. The gangsters were armed with military weapons and were not afraid of a confrontation with soldiers.

It was a grim indication of what was to come in 1944.

Chapter Fourteen

The Persistent Sergeant Dickey

As the Allies advanced northwards in mainland Italy, Vito Genovese changed sides. The top New York mobster turned exile dropped his title of *commendatore* and distanced himself from his Fascist friends. As the Allies entered his realm in Nola, near Naples, in the autumn of 1943, he offered to help them as translator and guide to the region. US Major E. N. Holmgreen, Civil Affairs Officer (CAO) in Nola, was so impressed with Genovese that he wrote him a letter of recommendation on 8 November 1943:

> The bearer [of the letter], Vito Genovese is an American citizen. When the undersigned arrived at Nola District as CAO, Mr Genovese met me and acted as my interpreter for over a month. He would accept no pay; paid his own expenses; worked day and night and rendered most valuable assistance to the Allied Military Government. This statement is freely made in an effort to express my appreciation for the unselfish services of this man.

That Genovese could afford to appear unselfish is no big surprise. He knew he had just struck a new criminal gold-mine – the black market in American military goods. The FBI later quoted a US Attorney's report on his activities during this period:

> During the war he acted as translator for numerous American military government officials, and at the same time was active in black-market activities. These activities consisted of stealing United States Army trucks, driving them to supply depots,

> loading them up with flour, sugar and other supplies, which material was then driven to a place of concealment and unloaded. The trucks were then destroyed.

Genovese made a fortune. That US Army officers were not aware of this double-life – or were aware and preferred to turn a blind-eye – was demonstrated in another glowing letter of recommendation from Captain Charles I. Dunn, US Provincial Officer in Nola, written on 9 June 1944:

> This is to certify that Vito Genovese has been employed by me as my personal interpreter since the 28th of January 1944. He has been invaluable to me – is absolutely honest, exposed several cases of bribery and blackmarket operations among so-called trusted civil personnel. He has a keen mind, knows Italians as do few people and is devoted to his adopted home, the USA, and all American Army personnel.

Genovese exposed other black-market gangsters to the US authorities so he could get them shut down and take over their business.

Luke Monzelli, a lieutenant in the Carabinieri assigned to follow Genovese during his time in Italy, described Genovese's criminal network:

> Once the black market began Genovese's connections in Nola became important. Besides his power plant he controlled manpower and better than that, he had the confidence of the Camorra [Neapolitan mobsters] whose members had long since decided to collaborate with the Mafia.
>
> In Sicily there was a *capo* named Calogero Vizzini, a powerful man who operated out of Villalba. Between Nola and Villalba or, if you prefer, between Vizzini and Genovese, there began a clandestine supply line of everything you could imagine. Truckloads of food supplies were shipped from Vizzini to Genovese – all accompanied by the proper documents which had been certified by men in authority, Mafia members in the service of Vizzini and Genovese.

'He made more than a million dollars in untraceable cash in almost no time,' said Lucky Luciano. 'That connivin' louse was sellin' American goods to his own Italian people, things that'd save their lives or keep 'em from starving. He made a fortune outa penicillin, cigarettes, sugar, olive oil, flour, you name it.'

Norman Lewis was an Italian-speaking British intelligence officer posted as a member of the Field Security Service to Naples in 1944. He was attached to the American Fifth Army and saw at first hand the black market in action. 'The black market flourishes as never before', said Lewis in his diary entry of 18 April 1944. He quoted the Psychological Warfare Bureau's estimate that 65 per cent of the income of Neapolitans came from transactions in stolen American supplies, and that one-third of Allied supplies and equipment brought to Italy disappeared into the black market:

> Every single item of Allied equipment, short of guns and munitions – which are said to be sold under the counter – is openly displayed for sale in the Forcella market. It was noted that at the opening of the San Carlo opera every middle- and upper-class woman arrived dressed in a coat made from a stolen army blanket.

This was backed up by a report in the same month from Allied Civil Affairs officers to the War Cabinet in London:

> One of the large sources of supply for the black market was from imports, more particularly of military supplies, as opposed to civil affairs. No checking of supplies was possible. At one point, it is estimated that of the civil affairs supplies, 30% were being pilfered, whilst of the military supplies 45%.

Lewis believed it would be relatively easy to trace all these items back to their criminal suppliers, but he was told by his Field Security superior that the black market was none of his business. As he investigated further, he could see the whole black-market system ran on very senior patronage:

> Indeed, it is becoming generally known that it operates under the protection of high-placed Allied Military Government officials. One soon finds that however many underlings are arrested – and sent away these days for long terms of imprisonment – those who employ them are beyond the reach of the law.
>
> At the head of AMG is Colonel Charles Poletti, and working with him is Vito Genovese, once head of the American Mafia, now become his adviser. Genovese was born in a village near Naples, and has remained in close contact with its underworld, and it is clear that many of the Mafia-

> Camorra *sindacos* who have been appointed in the surrounding towns are his nominees.
>
> These facts, once State secrets, are now known to the Neapolitan man in the street. Yet nothing is done. However many damaging reports are put in about the activities to high-ranking AMG officials, they stay where they are.

How much more damning could it get?

Charles Poletti was Lieutenant Governor of New York under Thomas E. Dewey; indeed, for a brief moment – twenty-nine days – he was governor of the state before Dewey took over. He was only thirty-eight years old and was the first person of completely Italian ancestry to serve in this post. In 1943 he was appointed American Senior Civil Affairs Officer (SCAO) for Palermo. After service in Palermo, Poletti proceeded to head AMG in Italy in Rome. Later, in a 1993 interview for BBC TV, he denied any association, whatsoever, with the Mafia during his time in command. 'We had no problems at all with the Mafia', said Poletti. 'Nobody ever heard of it. While we were there, nobody heard of it. Nobody ever talked about it.'

But Poletti's two most important decisions while SCAO in Palermo involved backing Lucio Tasca as Mayor of Palermo – a leading Separatist and friend of the Mafia – and advocating Francesco Musotto as first High Commissioner of Sicily, accused of being both a Separatist and having connections with the Mafia. Poletti's response was that he had used only 'the criterion of competence to be his guide'.

Colonel Poletti revealed his own views on the situation in Sicily in an interview with a British Foreign Office minister on 7 January 1944. The minister, in fact, was future British Prime Minister Harold Macmillan, appointed British government representative to the Allies in the Mediterranean in 1942. As SCAO in Palermo, Poletti told Macmillan that he believed the transfer of control from the Allies to an Italian administration was overdue and should be achieved a soon as possible. 'Colonel Poletti said that there was considerable separatist feeling in the Island', noted Macmillan, 'but that this could be appeased by plan proposed which was that there should be a High Commissioner appointed for the Island to whom nine Prefects would work.' Macmillan concluded that 'Colonel Poletti talked with vigour and confidence. He has clearly run Sicily with enthusiasm and gusto though the shadow of . . . Tammany Hall may have been thrown lightly across the Island.' (Tammany Hall was the notoriously corrupt centre of political activity in New York City in the nineteenth century.)

A copy of Macmillan's report on Poletti was shown to Lord Rennell who made his own comments:

> Palermo province was the most heavily staffed province in Sicily at all times. He [Poletti] always tended to put in an allied officer instead of using Italians and was consequently reproved for this. Colonel Poletti likes having a lot of officers under him because it makes him feel important.

Lord Rennell went further:

> I have already expressed my views about the proposed appointment of Colonel Poletti to the Headquarters of the Allied Commission of Control as Administrative Director. I consider him, most *un*suitable for this appointment.
>
> He is a not unattractive creature who has obviously succeeded in winning Mr MacMillan [*sic*] after a short acquaintance. I know him longer. He has administrative experience but he has been by no means so responsible for running Sicily as he appears to have made out to Mr MacMillan. I suggest that Mr MacMillan and others should ask advice of certain American officers before this appointment is made.

Rennell knew that Poletti was not even very popular among his own officers. In an earlier despatch written in June 1943, Rennell noted the US reaction to Poletti in North Africa:

> He [Colonel Poletti] was very frigidly received by General George Patton's staff. It took all Brigadier General McSherry's powers to make the situation even tenable. The 1st [American] Division bluntly stated that they were quite capable of looking after Civil Affairs themselves in their sector and wanted no American or British officers under Colonel Poletti attached for the purpose.

Such forthright views had little effect on Poletti's promotion to mainland Italy. In April 1944, Poletti contributed his own report on the black market to the Allied Control Commission (ACC). At the time, he was ACC Regional Commissioner for Campania, an area including Naples:

> The most urgent problem is that of the 'black market'. A reorganisation of distribution of AMG food has taken place and we are now using our own transport to take food from the docks to district warehouses. The police have been strengthened; individually they now have a greater appreciation of their jobs. Some of the head racketeers have been pulled in and it is hoped to bring about prosecution and sentences speedily.

Obviously, this did not include Vito Genovese – who was the biggest racketeer of all in the Naples area.

'In the communes', boasted Poletti, 'citizen squads have been started with efforts to make the people feel that honesty can be achieved.'

Lucky Luciano had his own description of Poletti's usefulness in Italy:

> As it happened, the Army appointed Charlie Poletti, who was one of our good friends, as the military governor in Italy and Poletti kept that job for quite a long time . . . Vito wound up as the official Italian-American interpreter. Maybe if I had it to do again, I would've arranged for Poletti's troops to line Vito up against a wall and shoot him.

Norman Lewis tells a story about AMG corruption involving an Italian industrialist who had been sent to jail for a year for dealing in stolen Allied goods. 'His wife', said Lewis, 'went to the "Beacon", the best of the Neapolitan brothels, and asked for the loan of their most intelligent girl. She dressed her in her smartest clothing, lent her her jewels, and paid 4,000 lire for the girl to impersonate her.' The girl, pretending to be the industrialist's wife, visited the AMG official and pleaded for the release of her husband. 'The visit was a success', continued Lewis, 'and two days later the gates of Poggio Reale prison swung open for the industrialist. The average Neapolitan's comment when hearing this typically Neapolitan story is, "What a pity she didn't send a girl with the syphilis."'

Vito Genovese continued to make a fortune from his mastery of the black market in wartime Italy until August 1944. Luke Monzelli claimed that a young Italian army sergeant investigated the discovery of a mysterious freight carriage full of cereal and salt parked in a siding near Nola. He revealed the link with Vizzini, but was told to forget about it – it was a secret military matter. He was later transferred out of the region, as was Monzelli.

It would be up to a fearless and determined 24-year-old US sergeant called Orange C. Dickey to blow Genovese's cover.

Sergeant Dickey gave his account of his investigation into Vito Genovese in Italy before three law officers in the Brooklyn office of District Attorney George Beldock on 1 September 1945:

> I arrived in Italy on or about the 19th day of December 1943. My assignment was Intelligence Sergeant of a Service Squadron. I was appointed criminal investigation agent [Criminal Investigation Division] on the 2nd of February.

He first came across the name of Vito Genovese in late April 1944. 'At that time I was investigating the black-market activities in olive oil and wheat in Italy, between Foggia and Naples.' Dickey had a lucky break in that a former senior gang-member of the Camorra had married an American girl and bought his way out of the organisation. This man now pointed the finger at Vito Genovese, calling him the head of the Mafia in southern Italy.

During the first part of May, Dickey single-handedly began a complete investigation of Vito Genovese in the district of Nola, east of Naples:

> On or about the 2nd day of June, I proceeded to a vineyard located approximately seven miles from Nola proper in the Commune of San Gennaro, where I found several United States Army trucks which had been destroyed by fire.
>
> In tracing these trucks by serial numbers and other identification means we found the trucks had been stolen from docks in Naples and been driven to a quartermaster supply depot, where they were loaded principally with flour and sugar, after which they were driven to the area where they were found by myself, and the supplies unloaded onto cars and transported into nearby towns, for sale – after which the trucks were destroyed.

Shortly after this discovery, Dickey arrested two Canadian soldiers who had deserted their posts to serve as drivers of these stolen trucks. 'The important part of their statements', said Dickey, 'is the fact that they were told that when they reached the point of destination for these trucks, they were to say "Genovese sent us" . . . And the truck is parked and they are paid off and then leave the area.' Dickey continued to gather his evidence and then presented it to his superior officers. They gave him the okay to arrest Genovese.

On the day that Genovese was arrested, a copy of a report from the Allied Provincial Public Safety Officer in Viterbo, north of Rome, was sent to Poletti's office. Getting wind of the mobster's imminent arrest, Poletti wanted to clarify exactly what their relationship had been with Genovese. The Viterbo report said:

> Careful examination of the records and antecedents of the above named [Vito Genovese] has been made of all employees on the AMG Payroll of this Province, and it is definite that such a person is not employed in this Provincial organization.

That was hardly surprising as Genovese operated way to the south of Viterbo, around Naples. The report then tried to identity the mobster with another bad character:

> In the records of the Questore a subject named Vito Genovese di Giuseppe, born on 12/7/88, at Avignano, resident in America for many years, was charged on 9th July 1935, before a Military Tribunal in Naples for the offence of desertion, and was sentenced to one years' imprisonment in a Military Prison. He is known by the nickname of 'Mafrita', and it would appear that this man is identical to the subject of the enquiry.

Except that this man was not the same Genovese. He was almost a decade older and had been in prison in Italy while the gangster was running a criminal empire in the US. The same report did, however, acknowledge that Genovese was employed by Major Holmgreen and three other US officers. Now that was the real Genovese.

Whether this report was a genuine attempt to identify the mobster or a smoke-screen to distance the US administration in Italy from him, we will never know. It was dispatched on the exact day that Genovese was arrested.

On 27 August 1944, Vito Genovese arrived in the office of the mayor of Nola to request a travel permit. He was accompanied by an armed chauffeur. While the Mafioso's bodyguard parked the car, Dickey made his move:

> I approached Vito Genovese, in the company of two English soldiers, and requested that he accompany me to the Military

> Police Office in Nola, which he did . . . Immediately after the arrest of Vito Genovese, I proceeded to downtown Nola and confiscated the vehicle in which Genovese had been riding. This vehicle was an Italian civilian car, Fiat model 1500.
>
> I searched the vehicle and in the compartment in the rear of the front seat – I mean the private front seat, I found two Italian weapons, one a 9-mm Beretta and the other a 7.65 Victoria – both fully loaded.

A few hours after the arrest of Genovese, Nicola Cutuli arrived at the AMG offices in Naples. He was Questore of Rome, the most senior investigative police officer in the country. He demanded that Genovese be released into his custody and taken to Rome. The Americans refused. Later, a sheet of paper with Cutuli's name on it was found in Genovese's apartment.

While Dickey proceeded with the paperwork of his arrest, an informant in Nola gave him a copy of a book entitled *Gang Rule in New York City*, by Craig Thompson and Raymond Allen, published in 1940. In the book, he found a photograph of Genovese and it identified him as a former gangster associate of Lucky Luciano. Dickey showed his prisoner the picture. 'Sure', said Genovese, 'that's me when I was in New York City.' When he asked him about running the black market in Italy, he denied some of the charges but accepted others. Dickey now contacted the FBI and they informed him that Genovese was wanted for questioning over a murder in New York.

Coincidentally, earlier in the month, a New York newspaper report of 9 August 1944, said:

> The whereabouts of all six [wanted for the murder of Ferdinand Boccia] were said to be unknown but an interesting sidelight on Genovese was that he was reported recently to have been in Italy acting as an interpreter for the Allied Military Government there.

'The Army officials are going to bring him back', said Brooklyn DA Thomas Hughes. 'How or when he will brought back I cannot say.'

With Genovese safely under arrest, Dickey searched his apartment in Nola and found a bundle of documents:

> Among these papers there was a small paper on which was written a number, easily identified as the number of a US Army truck. Beneath this number was written, 'The Shed'. In

> a previous case I had learned that the shed was a large underground storeroom and was used as a storage place for contraband wheat.

Dickey then proceeded to Genovese's apartment in Naples where he found large quantities of PX supplies, such as soap, candy bars and cigarettes. He also found a powerful radio receiver – used for receiving information on the arrival of valuable contraband. Among the documents found in Genovese's apartments were several business cards and other papers that linked him to prominent businessmen in the area as well as judges, the mayor of Nola, the president of the Bank of Naples, and AMG officers.

There were nine official AMG travel passes, several just made out to the bearer – a sign of Genovese's influence within AMG. They even entitled the bearer to fill up with American fuel. One was made out to a leading local dealer in olive oil. Two papers signed by AMG officers entitled Genovese to receive American food supplies – in violation of Army regulations. One business card belonged to Innocenza Monterisi, a mistress of Genovese who, according to Dickey, also supplied women for Allied officers.

Nowhere was found any significant stash of money. Dickey had his suspicions about a safe deposit vault in Banco del Lavoro in Nola. Genovese denied having a vault or a key for it. Dickey knew that one of Genovese's henchmen had visited it on the day he was arrested. The bank records said the vault belonged to the gangster, but when he went before a tribunal in Naples, Dickey was refused a court order to force its opening.

Genovese was still in military custody in November 1944. Dickey was waiting for an arrest warrant to arrive for him from the US, but no one wanted to take a decision on what to do with him. There was no suggestion of putting him on trial for black-market charges in Italy. 'At this time', said Dickey, 'the Army did not seem very interested in returning this man to the States, and I was told that I was "on my own, to do anything I cared to".' It was an extraordinary situation, but clearly Genovese's associates in and outside the US Army were working their influence as best they could and stopped any fast action in the hope that Dickey might get fed up and let him go.

That this might be the tactics of very highly placed US officers was demonstrated when Dickey visited Rome to talk to Colonel Charles Poletti, then Commissioner of Allied Military Government in Italy. 'I wanted him to tell me whether I should try him by civilian authorities', said Dickey, 'whether Allied Military Government intends to try him, or whether the US Army has control, or what I should do with him.'

He arrived at Poletti's headquarters at 10.00 a.m. and was told to go straight to his office and walk in. Excited at the prospect of finally getting some advice on what to do next with Genovese, Dickey pushed open the door of Poletti's room, but he wouldn't be getting any sense out of the colonel. 'He seemed to be asleep', remembered Dickey. 'He had his arms folded on the desk and his head down on his arms.' Dickey returned twice more that day to see Poletti but did not get to speak to him:

> On both these occasions his office was jammed with people . . . I was kept waiting on both occasions for long periods, and after making several attempts to talk to him, I left . . . [Poletti was] just walking around, giving orders to the girls; but it didn't seem to be essential business, just more or less enjoying himself.

It was outrageous behaviour from Poletti who, obviously, did not want to be dragged into the Genovese affair. Then, in the hall outside Poletti's office, Dickey bumped into William O'Dwyer who was on leave from his post as District Attorney in Brooklyn to serve in Italy. He knew all about the Genovese case but underlined the policy of his boss, Poletti, to steer well clear of it. He advised Dickey to bypass his senior officers and deal directly with Brooklyn DA Thomas Hughes. O'Dwyer was later charged by a grand jury with incompetently failing to prosecute senior mobster Albert Anastasia.

Returning from Rome to Naples, Dickey reported Poletti's behaviour to his immediate superior officer. 'He took no particular notice of the information', recalled Dickey, 'said that he had heard rumors to that effect previously, and with a few casual remarks it was dismissed. So that is the last that was said about Genovese up until the time I made an all-out effort for his extradition.'

Dickey pressed on, but by now Genovese was getting desperate. The mobster offered Dickey $250,000 to forget about the whole matter and let him go. At the time, the US Sergeant was earning just $210 a month. 'Now, look, you are young', Genovese told him, 'and there are things you don't understand. This is the way it works. Take the money. You are set for the rest of your life. Nobody cares what you do. Why should you?' When Dickey refused the money, the mobster turned nasty and threatened his life and that of his family. Dickey would not be intimidated.

Finally, in January 1945, Dickey got the news he had been waiting for. With the help of the War Department, the Brooklyn DA's office had set in motion extradition proceedings. The news travelled fast. Just seven days later, Genovese's American mobster friends swung into action. The one witness to his involvement in the murder of Boccia was Peter La Tempa, but he was in jail. No problem for Genovese's friends. On 15 January 1945, La Tempa awoke in his cell with acute gallstone pains. The valuable witness was then given sedatives strong enough 'to kill eight horses'. Luciano later claimed it was Frank Costello and his associates who set up the murder.

With the only major witness against Genovese gone, the mobster no longer feared returning to the US. In fact, he was glad of the free return journey. 'Kid', he said to Dickey, 'you are doing me the biggest favor anyone has ever done to me. You are taking me home. You are taking me back to the USA.' Dickey was designated Genovese's guard on the voyage across the Atlantic. Handcuffed together they set sail on board the steamship *James Lykes* and arrived in New York on the morning of 1 June 1945.

No one met Dickey and his gangster prisoner at the port. He had to organise his own transport to arrive at the District Attorney's office of Kings County in Brooklyn that afternoon. He presented himself to the policeman on duty and DA assistant Edward A. Heffernan came down to greet them. When Heffernan recognised the mobster chained to Dickey's wrist, he whispered into the young man's ear. 'Do you mind my saying', said Heffernan, 'I am surprised. We never expected to see this boy back here.' Heffernan was later charged, alongside his boss O'Dwyer, with failing to prosecute gangster Anastasia.

When Genovese finally appeared before a US court in June 1946, all charges were dropped against him for lack of evidence. 'By devious means', said the county Judge, 'among which were the terrorizing of witnesses, kidnapping them, yes, even murdering those who could give evidence against you, you have thwarted justice time and again.' Dressed smartly in a double-breasted blue suit, white shirt and maroon tie, Genovese smiled. He was now free to continue his career as one of the top Mafiosi in America and exploit his links with the old Mafia in Sicily.

Dickey's heroic efforts had all been in vain.

Chapter Fifteen

Splitting the Allies

In the Mafia's war of independence in Sicily, their first small victory was to create a split between the Americans and the British. Irritation with their British allies was entering the thought processes of certain Americans as a group of Allied intelligence officers gathered for a meeting in Palermo on 12 January 1944. Among the agencies represented were JICA (Joint Intelligence Collection Agency) and the OSS. Joseph Russo, commanding officer of the OSS SI Palermo Station, was present at the meeting under the cover of Experimental Department G-3. The notes taken from the meeting reveal a sense of drift among the intelligence agencies. Having occupied the island, they were not quite sure what they should be doing next. The Combined Chiefs of Staff had agreed to give permission for the resumption of political activities on the island from 1 January. So where did that leave the Allied forces?

> The great problem [complained the intelligence officers] in any kind of political intelligence work in Sicily is the absence of a political policy set down by the Allies . . . Nothing is known about the kind and form of civilian government for Sicily that will be supported, or at least encouraged, by the Allies. It is impossible to counteract such rumors as 'the British favor an autonomous Sicily, while the Americans don't' without a statement of policy by the Allies.

Separatist politicians played on this sense of divergence in the Allied policy towards them. Andrea Finocchiaro Aprile was the front-runner in the Separatist movement and the favourite candidate of the Mafia and the Sicilian aristocracy. In a speech at Misilmere, he claimed that the British Foreign Secretary, Anthony Eden, had made remarks indicating his support for Separatism in Sicily. This left the Americans in a tricky situation. Did they go along with the British commitment or oppose it?

The mood of resentment was clear among US intelligence officers at the Palermo meeting. The JICA representative said that they had spoken to Finocchiaro Aprile and that he had told them he would consider a union with Italy after a period of complete independence, provided the Italian government was not a monarchy, was not Communist, and was not under the control of the Catholic Church.

Not that the Separatists were themselves a united front. Aside from Finocchiaro Aprile, US intelligence identified two other Separatist factions. One was La Giovanna Sicilia, led by Duca di Salomone, who had broken with Finocchiaro Aprile, accusing the latter of being an opportunist politician. He preferred to work more closely with the US administration. Then there was a group of small businessmen who resented paying tax to the mainland government, without any benefit to themselves in Sicily.

But the 65-year-old Finocchiaro Aprile, elegantly dressed with a goatee beard, was the main adversary for the Allies. Trained as a lawyer and an academic by profession, he was a highly skilled orator. He had entered politics in 1913 as deputy for the Corleone region – a Mafia stronghold. During the 1930s, he maintained an anti-Fascist position, even defending the legal rights of Jews being persecuted in northern Italy, but he also managed to shield himself against Mussolini's wrath by praising many of his foreign policy achievements. His links with Mussolini later discredited him in the eyes of many Americans.

In 1941, Finocchiaro Aprile became president of Sicilia e Liberta, an anti-Fascist group embraced by early Separatists. The following year, he took over existing separatist factions and told Sicilians to prepare for an Allied invasion and victory. On his assumption of leadership, he chose to incorporate a whole range of political views and was proud of the fact that supporters of Separatism ranged from conservatives and liberals to socialists and communists. Subsequently, his political promises remained vague, promising a better life for all Sicilians after independence.

Despite his frequently professed belief that the Allies backed an independent Sicily, it did not stop Finocchiaro Aprile from also being their most vociferous critic. His newspaper *L'Indipendenza Siciliana* published personal attacks on AMG officials and was shut down after its second issue by the Allies, although they preferred such matters of political censorship to be handled by regional prefects. It was also worrying for the Allies that local libraries were featuring books both about Fascism and Separatism.

JICA's Stability Report for January 1944 reported a slight reduction in black-market prices. For JICA, this seemed to be the key to the entire Sicilian situation:

> The recent imports of grain, the regularity with which rationed bread is distributed, and finally, the proposed pasta ration, have caused grain speculators to lower their prices considerably. If the black market on food could be stamped out, conditions in Sicily would be tremendously improved because the average citizen (the working class and the farm laborer), are more interested in food than in politics.

This move in the right economic direction appeared to have come too late to reverse the Separatist political climate:

> Apparently, the Separatist Movement is growing stronger [said JICA]. Led by very active men who enjoy great financial and social prestige, Separatist propaganda is being spread throughout Sicily in a strong effort to attract adherents.

As early as November 1943, the Research and Analysis Branch of OSS believed the presence of AMG itself on the island was encouraging the Separatist movement:

> There is more than plausible ground for believing that if we – the Allies – willed it, we could do almost anything in Sicily, and with excellent prospects of success. We could, if we willed it, even create a separatist and independent Sicily, and without even appearing to be responsible for such a development.

The substance of this OSS report was a criticism of Lord Rennell and his own report on Separatism, which the OSS considered vague and informal, but it also revealed a suspicion that British intentions were to allow a separatist Sicily in order to gain an independent British military base. It was a suspicion that chimed with the Separatist leaders' own conviction that they had the support of the Allies.

In the heart of Mafia country, in the town of Corleone, before an audience of 2,000, Finocchiaro Aprile gave a speech on 23 January

1944 in which he claimed that Sicilian-born Americans would demand that their government support Sicilian independence. He also repeated his assertion that British Foreign Minister Anthony Eden had declared his own government's understanding that most Sicilians wanted independence from Italy.

Even the Sicilian Christian Democrat party were thinking that this might be a bandwagon well worth climbing aboard. In a pamphlet distributed in January, they denounced the monarchy and asked that the island be granted self-determination in order to protect it from communism and dictatorship.

That the Separatists considered the Christian Democrats their main rivals for the conservative vote was revealed in a rally on 14 May held at the Bellini Theatre in Palermo. An Italian journalist was there and contributed to a JICA report on it. He noted that a Separatist speaker called Di Martino took to the rostrum first:

> Di Martino started off by an attack on the Christian Democratic Party. After having explained how the Christian Democratic Party was the direct offspring of the late 'Partito Popolare', alone responsible for the coming to power of fascism, he stated that the Christian Democratic Party was harbouring ex-Fascists among its members.

'Any ex-Fascist who is not admitted to join any other party,' said Di Martino, 'is welcome in the Christian Democratic Party.' This caused a noisy protest from Christian Democrats who had turned up to the meeting. Someone then shouted out that many Communists were ex-Fascists too, which angered the Communists in the crowd. 'This is not true', said Di Martino, who then proceeded to attack the 'Christian Democratic minister of the Interior, Salvatore Aldisio for keeping in office as director of "Public Safety" Senator Senise, who held the same office during the Fascist regime . . .'

It appeared the Separatists preferred to offer a friendly hand to the Communists rather than the Christian Democrats. In the meantime, they enjoyed the discomfort of the divided Allies.

On 11 February 1944, the Allies handed back administration of Sicily to the Italian government, but Allied administrative bodies remained in place and exerted a strong influence through the Allied Control Commission (ACC). On the Italian mainland, Naples remained an

AMG enclave until December 1945 when the Allies finally quit the country.

A native governor of Sicily was appointed by the Allies. He was Francesco Musotto. The OSS noted the process of selection. 'The selection of a native governor brought forth suggestions from all quarters', said an OSS report of 10 January 1944, 'the separatists included, with the conservatives of the Mafia (not the so-called delinquent class) winning out.' The various parties approached Poletti with their candidates. Finocchiaro Aprile favoured a prominent member of his party, but, according to the OSS, Poletti had already made up his mind:

> Meanwhile, it seems Poletti had beforehand made a choice in the person of Musotto. His close association with various top-flight, well-to-do families prominent in the upper Mafia supported the belief that Musotto was the candidate suggested by this source. Up to now Musotto is the Poletti-approved candidate, though still unappointed, with the field closed to all others and his eventual appointment taken for granted.

Francesco Musotto was a former prefect of Palermo who fell out of favour with Mussolini. During the 1920s, according to the OSS, he returned to his business as a lawyer:

> . . . his clientele being drawn from the Mafia. He was engaged as defence counsel in the Mafia prosecutions ordered in Sicily by Mussolini. His relations with the upper Mafia are good, and his connections with the lower Mafia can be taken for granted. The argument is made that the appointment was a smart one in view of his background and connections.

Such networking did little to impress local Sicilians who considered it further proof of Mafia infiltration of the AMG.

The British Royal Navy had its own intelligence-gathering section and in February 1944 it made a report on the situation in the east of the island. 'The Italians are gradually taking possession of Sicily', said Captain H. F. Waight, 'and troops are arriving to take over duties of guards etc . . .'

But Captain Waight was very concerned with the fate that awaited the Sicilians:

> The whole country is run by graft. There is no sense of honesty. Attempts are made to bribe by indirect methods.

> British Government Stores appear to be looked upon as legitimate prey and pilfering and deliberate robbery of storehouses is very prevalent which involves British personnel.

Royal Navy Lieutenant-Commander L. V. Mason was another who noted a deterioration in law and order:

> Instances of theft and pilfering are becoming increasingly frequent and recent large scale incidents in this respect are viewed with growing concern at Army Headquarters. In one such incident, an unruly mob endeavoured to break into an Army Ordnance depot and the guard had to open fire, killing one and wounding others before they could be dispersed.
>
> These incidents are believed to be the work of an organised gang, but so far it has been impossible to trace the ringleaders.

That there was a gathering wave of violent discontent with the presence of Allied troops in the island was revealed in an incident in April 1944. A unit of some 1,300 French paratroopers had arrived in the town of Xitta, near Trapani, in the westernmost tip of Sicily. Rather than sleep in tents, they set about requisitioning buildings for their use. The people of Xitta and nearby Trapani claimed that the French acted in a boorish manner. They ate at restaurants and refused to pay the bill. They took over the homes of local citizens without going through the proper requisition procedure. When they got drunk, they chased the local women. The Sicilians responded by insulting the soldiers and throwing stones at them.

On 9 April, the deteriorating situation took a turn for the worse. At 6 o'clock in the evening, some French soldiers attempted to grab a local woman. Local men intervened and moments later, the French claimed, they came under fire. The paratroopers retreated, only to come back, one and a half hours later, fully armed with pistols, rifles and machine guns. They fired wildly in the air and a young man was killed in his bedroom by a stray shot. Four paratroopers then broke into the house of Michele Schifano. He claimed to be ill at the time and his wife and family fled before the soldiers. Mrs Schifano hid in a closet, but the soldiers shot through the door and she was killed.

Fearful of armed reprisals, the French swamped the town and put it under siege. They set up road blocks at both ends of Xitta and machine guns were placed at strategic points. The local police were ordered out.

Twenty local civilians were taken into custody by the French and beaten.

Only after an American CIC detachment intervened were the prisoners released and the French ordered to leave the town. They had to be told twice before they finally went. It was suggested they sleep in tents outside the town, but after a few days the restrictions were lifted.

In this incident there were echoes of the notorious thirteenth-century Sicilian Vespers uprising in which Sicilians slaughtered their French occupiers. The Mafia frequently claimed their historical roots stretched back to this act of defiance and vengeance. In Xitta and Trapani, the brutal actions of the Allied French paratroopers compounded a local sense of injustice that only the Mafia could avenge.

As the Allies discussed what to do next about the Separatists, Finocchiaro Aprile pressed on with his campaign with speeches and rallies across Sicily. In July 1944, on the anniversary of the Allied liberation of Sicily, he ramped up the tension by making a direct appeal in a letter to Prime Minister Winston Churchill:

> I have pleasure in conveying to you on behalf of the National Committee, representing the whole of the Sicilian people, the expression of the most sincere affection and the most profound gratitude, together with the assurance that we shall never forget the valuable aid given by Great Britain to Sicily.

With the niceties out of the way, Finocchiaro Aprile quickly proceeded to business:

> As I previously pointed out to you, I repeat that Sicily can and will no longer remain united to Italy. We have suffered too many wrongs, too many acts of violence, excesses and abuses to which we have had to submit for the situation created in 1860 to persist. We have firmly decided, even at the cost of having to take up arms, to win our independence and form a sovereign State of Sicily under a republican regime.

Finocchiaro Aprile hoped that Britain would fully support this desire for independence, but there was a threat here that even without British support the Sicilians were willing to take military action. There is no copy of Churchill's reply to this letter in the British Foreign Office file.

A few days later, Finocchiaro Aprile must have been delighted to read a generally positive article about Sicily and the Separatist movement in the London *Times*. It called Finocchiaro Aprile 'an old gentleman of plausible charm' and said 'When asked what place they expect an independent Sicily to take in the Europe of the future they remark ingeniously that they would gladly accept British protection.' With such an article appearing in *The Times*, it is little wonder that some Americans and Italians thought the British actively supported Separatism

Sir Noel Charles, British High Commissioner in Rome, spoke to the Italian Under-Secretary of the Ministry for Foreign Affairs, and got an uncomfortable view of the situation. 'Marchese Visconti stated what I have already heard from different sources', said Sir Noel Charles in a telegram to the Foreign Office back in London, 'that Separationists are asserting that their movement has the support of Great Britain and the United States; they say that the Allies cannot openly come out in their favour because of the war.' Marchese Visconti told Sir Noel that, of course, the Italian government knew the Allies had nothing to do with the Separatists but ignorant people in Sicily continued to believe it. The implication was that some statement was needed to kill the rumours. To underline the seriousness of the threat, the Marchese Visconti also divulged his belief that the Separatists had linked up with the Mafia and they were terrorising the peasants into supporting the cause.

Six days later, Sir Noel submitted a more detailed report to Churchill's Foreign Secretary Anthony Eden at the Foreign Office. In it, he quoted Finocchiaro Aprile boasting to Italian newspapers about how the Allies were protecting him. 'I want to make public the fact', said Finocchiaro Aprile, 'that when [Prime Minister] Bonomi wanted to arrest me, the Allied authorities laughed. The reason I am here today is because the Allies wish it.'

The flurry of correspondence between Italy and the Foreign Office in London culminated in a lengthy memorandum, *The Sicilian Separatist Movement*, written by Harold C. Swan, Consul-General at Naples:

> The big landowners are the prime – if not the only movers of the free Sicily project . . . Led by Avvocato Finocchiaro Aprile of Palermo and Barone Delmonte of Catania, encouraged by the fact that all political parties in Sicily are in a renewed state of infancy, the Separatist Movement has every hope of rising to dominance within the island and of absorbing, by promises fair and foul, the other neo-political factions . . .

> It is my impression that the landed gentry who to prosper did not hesitate in the past to go into close and lucrative partnership with the nefarious Mafia, are encouraging the recrudescence of that terrorist organisation . . .

It was an alarming analysis for which Swan felt the Allies bore some responsibility for encouraging the Separatists. He said there seemed to be little doubt that the Separatist movement had received support from some American officers, who even let them have meetings on US bases:

> These meetings invariably had a strong pro-Ally flavour, the Stars and Stripes and Union Jack being prominently displayed on the platform; expressions of cordiality and loyalty towards the United Nations were an ever-warm feature of the speeches. All this, plus the attendance at the meetings of American officers, would seem to lend some degree of truth to the Italian Government's contention that the Allies are giving aid and comfort to the Separatist . . .

So the Americans were convinced it was the British who were encouraging the Separatists and the British blamed the Americans. For Swan, the finger pointed to Colonel Poletti, but he couldn't find any evidence. 'I was unable to obtain confirmation', said Swan, 'of one rumour that Colonel Poletti was an actual instigator of the movement . . .' If only he had seen an earlier letter written by Lucio Tasca on 31 August 1944 in which the leading Separatist and Mafioso thanked Poletti as a 'dearest friend, for the assistance and help you have always given our country, which I hope you will continue to assist for the conquest of its supreme good and that is . . . Independence!' It was an intimate communication that indicated a strong friendship between the two.

As for the role of the British, Swan believed there was little proof of their involvement and noted that some senior officers had banned Separatist meetings. With an air of Foreign Office arrogance, Swan tried to reason why the Americans should be so drawn to the Separatists:

> It is somewhat difficult to see why the Americans lend particular favour to the Movement. They can have scant commercial interest in the matter . . . It therefore seems probable that the innate snobbishness which so frequently leads the average American to seek the companionship of the

> bearers of high-sounding titles may be a not diminutive factor in the situation – and the Sicilian landowners are, of course, not infrequently the possessors of ancient and impressive titles of nobility.

Inevitably, the OSS considered any British support of Sicilian Separatism to be part of a larger strategic plan to keep Italy weak. This was made clear in an OSS report of August 1944:

> The apparent tendency of British policy as a whole is to reduce Italy to a position of complete, military, political, and economic dependence on Great Britain . . . The fundamental objective of this policy appears to be the elimination of any future Italian threat to the Mediterranean–Red Sea–Indian Ocean line of British imperial communications.

According to the OSS, Britain was pursuing this aim by allying itself with monarchist-conservative forces in Italy. Showing a complete blindness to forthcoming Cold War politics, the OSS report recommended that Britain should follow a more disinterested path such as that embraced by the American and Soviet governments, 'which are less directly interested in Italian affairs . . . It is doubtful whether Russia wishes to convert Italy into a Communist state.' Such a naive view of Soviet intentions would change considerably over the coming years, but it is striking how the OSS was blind to that threat as late as 1944, preferring to direct its suspicions towards the British.

As Finocchiaro Aprile considered his next step, law and order in Sicily and respect for the Allied authorities broke down further. The island was struck by a major crime wave. Just in the province of Palermo, the annual rate of homicide leapt from 84 in 1943 to 245 in 1944; the number of robberies from 148 to 646.

'The secret criminal organisation known as the Mafia has sprung up again in Sicily in a new and vigorous form', said an American newspaper report of 30 October 1944, 'with hold-ups and kidnappings becoming a common occurrence, according to latest reports from Palermo.' The situation was so serious, said the report, that Sicilians feared to travel on highways at night as bandits were halting cars, taking money and jewels, and even forcing victims to undress.

Palermo police headquarters was said to have identified eight major Mafia gangs who were acting independently of each other. They cited an example of a wealthy local landlord, Vittorio di Salvo, who was kidnapped while driving and held for six days until he paid a 2,500,000 lire ransom. He then assumed, as in the old days, that having paid up he would be safe from any further Mafia attacks. Not at all, said the gang, they were acting alone and couldn't guarantee protection from any other mobsters.

On 19 October, there was a serious incident in Palermo. After four days of general discontent and protest, a crowd assembled in the centre of the city and marched on the prefect's offices. The crowd consisted mainly of local government workers demanding bread and higher wages. When they reached the prefecture, they started throwing stones and broke several windows in the building. This was the signal the Italian soldiers had been waiting for. They unleashed a hail of fire on the crowd. Their weapons included machine guns and hand grenades.

Joseph Russo, commanding officer of the OSS SI Palermo Station, sent a report to Allied Forces Headquarters (AFHQ):

> Casualties on Palermo noonday massacre officially estimated at 162. Death toll 16 with figure expected to rise. Number of civilians wounded 137, Italian military 11. 50% of casualties are children. Figures do not include injuries in stampede. Most wounds in back from shrapnel. Several decapitations.

Russo then warned of an outbreak of disorder after nightfall as mobsters promised a vendetta against the soldiers considered responsible for the massacre. If the Mafiosi in Palermo were not responsible for stirring up the crowd, then they could be depended on to avenge the injustice.

That the Separatists and the Mafia considered the time was ripe for more concerted action against the Allies was revealed by a JICA intelligence report of a key Separatist meeting:

> On 26th October, Finocchiaro Aprile, Leader of the Separatist Movement in Sicily, met with other Separatist Leaders, including Varvaro, Lucio Tasca, Pameduri, Dott Gallo (from Catania) and Atty Arrigo, in Varvaro's office in Palermo. At this meeting, they are reported to have decided that the time had come to take more active measures than before in support of the Separatist principles.

They agreed to spread the word across the island and mobilise their forces. One of the reasons for taking action had been the riot in

Palermo, which had triggered left-wing support for their cause. Another reason for action was reported by Separatist Lucio Tasca who had spoken to the Questore of Palermo that morning. Tasca told his comrades that the Questore had received orders to prosecute the Separatist leaders on charges of endangering the security of the state. Finocchiaro Aprile interrupted Tasca and said 'the time has come'.

JICA warned that some sort of 'putsch' would be attempted over the next ten days. US Commodore Ellery Stone, Acting Chief Commissioner at AFHQ, considered the threat important enough to pass it on to Ivanoe Bonomi, the new Italian Prime Minister. He quoted the JICA report:

> [The Separatist leaders] are reported to have decided that, since their arrest might be imminent, it would be well to take the bull by the horns and try to establish de facto independence before the unitarian forces could bring in additional armed forces. The Separatists are also said to be banking on the fact that there are virtually no Allied troops left in Sicily, and that the Allies are reported to be in no position to send troops to Sicily at present to keep order . . .
>
> It must be kept in mind that the Separatists sometimes deliberately spread false reports of their planned actions, in order to stir up public agitation and confuse the law enforcement agencies. Whether the foregoing is merely another example of those tactics or whether they really mean business this time remains to be seen.

It was put up or shut up for the Separatists and their Mafia backers. The time for armed rebellion had come.

Chapter Sixteen

The 49th State

That the Mafia was violently involved in supporting the Separatist movement was demonstrated by an incident in Villalba, home town of Calogero Vizzini. Don Calo was the Mafioso who had supposedly proved so useful in removing Axis troops before the Allied advance towards Cammarata. He was town mayor now, appointed by the Allies from the end of July 1943. 'When Don Calo Vizzini was made mayor of the town', said an anonymous witness, 'almost the entire population was assembled in the square. Speaking in poor Italian, this American lieutenant said, "This is your master".' And that was that.

Don Calo had always ruled the town, but this made it official in the eyes of AMG and the grateful Americans. It was a process of Allied recognition that happened throughout the island. Lord Rennell later acknowledged this was a fault of Allied government:

> With the people clamouring to be rid of a Fascist *Podesta*, many of my officers fell into the trap of selecting the most forthcoming self-advertiser, or following the advice of their self-appointed interpreters who had learned some English in the course of a stay in the USA. The result was not always happy.
>
> They invariably chose a local Mafia 'boss', or his shadow, who in one or two cases had graduated in an American gangster environment. All that could be said of some of these men was that they were as definitely anti-Fascist as they were undesirable from every other point of view. The difficulty in early days of an occupation for a foreign element to weigh up

> the value or danger of local characters must be clear to anyone who has given the subject a moment's thought.

Luigi Lumia, resident of Villalba, agreed. 'During those days', he recalled, 'when there was complete disintegration of authority and no form of organised power, the Mafia appeared to the Allies as the only force capable of looking after the people.'

On 2 September 1944, Don Calo – Mayor of Villalba – played host to Finocchiaro Aprile, the Separatist leader. In the main Piazza Madrice, Finocchiaro Aprile gave a speech on the virtues of an independent island nation and the crimes wrought by previous centuries of foreign rule.

At the end of the speech, his followers gave out badges with a number forty-nine on it to show that Sicily could be the forty-ninth state of the United States. Other badges showed a green silhouette of Sicily in the middle of the Stars and Stripes.

On 16 September, another political party got a completely different reception. They were Communists and among them was Michele Pantaleone whose family lived in houses looking over the Piazza Madrice. Don Calo had allowed them to give speeches only on condition that they did not mention land reform, the large estates, or the Mafia, and that no peasants were allowed into the square to hear them. To ensure that his rules were obeyed, Don Calo stood in the middle of the square holding a stick while his gun-toting henchmen leaned against the walls of the surrounding buildings.

The star speaker was Girolamo Li Causi. Since August 1944, he had become the leader of the Communists in Sicily and, with his talent for fiery speech-making, was Finocchiaro Aprile's main political rival on the island. Although the Communists had at first aided the Separatists, under Li Causi they rejected them and instead supported autonomy. As he begun to talk in the town square, the Communist leader ignored the restrictions imposed on him and railed against the ancient burdens endured by Sicilian peasants and how the Mafia had only made the situation worse. 'Do not be fooled by those landowners', said Li Causi, 'that offer you a sliver of land for your support . . .'

Don Calo ordered his priest brother to ring the bells of the church on the piazza to drown out Li Causi, but this only attracted curious peasants and citizens who started to fill the square. Li Causi carried on addressing the audience, despite the pealing bells. It was too much for Don Calo. 'It's a lie!' shouted the Mafioso chief. This was taken as a command by his gangsters to stop the meeting – and they started shooting at the crowd and the speakers. The Communists returned fire with their pistols and hurled grenades. Fourteen people fell wounded.

'Stop, you miserable wretches!' shouted Li Causi, but he fell too, shot in the knee. Michele Pantaleone grabbed the wounded politician and hauled him on to his shoulders. As he ran out of the square, bullets tore up the plaster behind him. From behind the wall of a nearby bank, Pantaleone pulled out his own gun and fired three shots in the air. Eventually, the local Carabinieri intervened and restored order. It was a turning point for the young left-winger. He was now committed to a life-long battle against the Mafia.

This description of the Villalba massacre is told by Carlo Levi in his preface to Pantaleone's book *The Mafia and Politics*. OSS made its own report on the fight at Villalba and it exposed a different dimension to the clash:

> The two families of Farina-Vizzini and Pantaleone have been on unfriendly terms for ages. The feeling between the two families became more acute recently because both aspired to rent the ex-Micciche property, belonging to the Princess di Trabia. This property, owing to its location near the town, is very desirable. The case was decided in favor of the Vizzini-Farina family.

The decision angered the Pantaleone clan, and the two families became political rivals. Michele Pantaleone hoped to strike a blow against the Vizzini by inviting Li Causi to talk in their town. He even went so far, according to the OSS, as to get him to mention the Micciche affair. It was this reference that caused Don Calo to shout 'It's a lie!' The OSS therefore considered this a personal feud and not a demonstration of political conflict. 'It is advisable', concluded OSS, 'to give the incident as little publicity as possible.'

Pantaleone declined to do this and gave it immortality in his book. And, of course, one should not assume that the OSS was unbiased in its reporting of the incident. Their version is too sympathetic towards Vizzini and was strongly influenced by the Mafioso's personal connections with the OSS in Palermo. In fact, its acceptance of the Vizzini angle demonstrated its closeness to the Mafia and a willingness to protect them.

Pantaleone believed the Mafia's association with the Separatist movement suited their aims perfectly:

> A few months after the liberation of Sicily the Mafia decided to support the right-wing of the Separatist movement. One

> reason was the influence of the Sicilo-Americans with the Mafia chiefs, with whom they had established strong and profitable connections. Besides, the Mafia feared that a national democratic government might modify the island's social structure, whereas a Separatist victory would mark the Mafia's identification with the island's ruling class.

He claimed that the island's Mafiosi had attended the first meeting in Palermo of the Separatist movement on 9 December 1943. The twenty-eight leading members present had agreed the use of violence, if necessary, to disrupt rival political meetings.

Pantaleone attended a speech given by Finocchiaro Aprile at Bagheria in early 1944. The practised speaker opened his remarks by quoting letters he had written to 'dear Winnie' and 'dear Delano' telling the Allied leaders about Sicily's need for independence. He then made it clear where he stood in relationship to the old Mafiosi. 'If there was not a Mafia already', said Finocchiaro Aprile, 'one would have to invent one. I am a friend of the Mafia, even though personally I am against crime and violence.'

This speech, according to Pantaleone, appealed immensely to the Mafiosi of Palermo and convinced them to join the Separatist movement. Don Calo Vizzini's involvement with the Separatists also began in late 1943 when he attended a conference in Catania. He was seen as an intruder by the left-wing Separatist Antonino Varvaro, who asked him on what authority he claimed to represent the Caltanissetta region. 'You shouldn't bother too much about membership cards', said Don Calo. 'When your lordship gives me the hint, I'll have all the Camere del Lavoro [trade union headquarters] in the province burnt down.'

As a result of the Mafia's involvement in the movement, Finocchiaro Aprile was allowed to give speeches in the provinces under their control, such as Caltanissetta and Agrigento. Those opposing him could be sure of a rough welcome. When a minister in the Italian government visited Palermo in March 1944 to put the case for national unity, he was pelted with rotten fruit and vegetables. That was relatively mild. In Villalba, you could be shot.

A conversation between British Vice-Consul Manley and Sicilian High Commissioner Salvatore Aldisio in December 1944 confirmed Allied suspicion that the Mafia was closely involved with the Separatists. 'Aldisio told me', said Manley, 'that some of the brigand bands in Sicily were supported by elements of the Mafia who were also supporting the Separatists, and that the Separatists through the support given them by the Mafia had access if necessary to the bands.'

A report by JICA in January 1945 analysed further the links between the Mafia and the Separatists. It said that Finocchiaro Aprile had been visited by several key Mafiosi, including the mayor of Piana dei Greci, Don Ciccio Cuccia, the same Mafioso who had humiliated Mussolini during his visit to Sicily in 1924 and been imprisoned by Mori.

> At the present time [continued the JICA report], it can be said that the Mafia exponents represent to Separatism what the Catholic clergy represents to the Christian Democrats. In other words, the Mafia leaders of rural centers are the Separatist propaganda agents in their bailiwick. This explains why Finocchiaro Aprile frequently speaks highly of the Mafia and why he emphasized the difference between Mafia and delinquency.

JICA then criticised the attempts of the Separatists to claim the support of the Allies. JICA had heard a rumour that Britain was secretly sponsoring the Separatists because it wanted to maintain tight control over the Malta Channel, but they knew of no real evidence of such claims. Similarly, the involvement of America was suggested by the use of campaign buttons showing an American flag overprinted with a map of Sicily. The US State Department responded to this by secretly asking the Italian authorities on the island to prohibit any further use of the insignia. Said JICA:

> One of the alleged leaders of [the Separatist] movement is reported to be a certain Don Calogero Vizzini, allegedly a Mafia leader from Caltanissetta. The extent of his relations and sympathies with Finocchiaro Aprile still remains a mystery.

The extent of their relationship was revealed more clearly to the Allies in a US Naval Intelligence report, coming a little later, which said that, on 30 January 1945 several Separatist representatives arrived in Palermo and wanted to speak urgently to Finocchiaro Aprile. They were told that their leader was absent from the Separatist HQ because he was at a dinner engagement with Calogero Vizzini and other Mafiosi.

Separatism and the Mafia, it appeared, were merging.

December 1944 brought more bad news for the government of Sicily. Separatist threats of action were about to be dramatically fulfilled. Following on from earlier disturbances in Palermo, there was now a hunger for a major assault on the authorities. During 11–17 December, students at the city's university demonstrated every day. Much of the anger was aimed at the Italian government's demand for Sicilians to join the army to help the Allies fight the war.

'Sicilians, ex-service men of all ranks', said one poster, 'Do Not Register for Military Service! Do not allow the name of Mercenary to be added to those of Traitor and Vanquished . . . Sicilians, now is the time to demonstrate that you are no longer sheep.'

In Palermo, on 11 December, a mob set fire to the tax office, destroying most of the documents inside. Hand grenades were thrown at the town hall and telephone and telegraph communications were cut. Order was restored by the Carabinieri, but they reported being fired on by the crowd.

On 14 December in the town of Palma di Montechiaro, in the province of Agrigento, a crowd of a thousand paraded with rifles, automatic weapons, and hand grenades. In a well-organised uprising, they occupied outlying points of the town, cut communications and then turned on the town's administration, setting fire to municipal offices and making a point to destroy documents inside, including property registers. The mob proceeded to the law courts, where they seized stored weapons, then set fire to the tax offices, destroying further documents at the Bank of Sicily and the post office. Finally, they held up a bus from Agrigento and robbed the passengers. A truck loaded with pasta was also looted.

Police and army reinforcements arrived later in the day but they were unable to gain control, even though some of the citizens invited them into their homes to fire at criminals from their windows. Shooting went on for several hours and the town centre was not secured until the following day. Fighting went on until the 17th.

Some of the armed protestors were said to have been carrying red flags but this may well have been a ruse by the Mafia to cover their own orchestration of the events. The town had a bad reputation for law and order and was at the heart of the Mafia-held province of Agrigento.

Further north, in western Sicily, the town of Alcamo, not far from Castellammare del Golfo, was the scene of another major incident. The Allied authorities had shut down several flour mills and bakeries in the area in order to crack down on local criminal speculation on the price of grain. The result of this had been to double the price of bread on the black market. Perhaps in retaliation to this strike at Mafiosi-run mills, a Separatist agitator, a student known as Milazzo, was encouraged to give a speech to other students protesting at the Italian government's conscription plans.

Milazzo stood before the crowd in the central Piazza Ciullo. They were bearing placards saying 'Down with the Monarchy' and 'Down with the Army'. 'We will not go to war', said Milazzo, 'until we know why we are going. We are sick of war – the concentration camps of England, America and Russia and Germany are full of our prisoners of war. Therefore we will not present ourselves for military service.' Milazzo then protested at the closure of the flour mills and the crowd roared their approval, demanding bread and the re-opening of the mills. The commissioner of public safety intervened and tried to calm the crowd but Milazzo said they would all meet in the square the next day.

During the night, anticipating trouble, Carabiniere Captain Miraglia telephoned for reinforcements from Trapani. The prefect of Trapani responded the next morning by calling for the mills to be re-opened, but it was too late for the citizens of Alcamo. At 9.00 a.m. on 18 December, a crowd of 6,000 people gathered in the Piazza Ciullo. Avvocato Cassara, President of the Alcamo section of the Separatist Youth League, stood on a balcony above the square and started to stir up the crowd. He condemned local taxes and the crowd responded by shouting 'Burn down the tax offices.'

Captain Miraglia begged Cassara to calm the crowd, but the situation was out of control. An angry mob marched off to attack municipal buildings, including the town hall, tax offices and magistrates' offices. Furniture and documents were pulled out of the offices and burned. The mob then turned on the Magazini Granai del Popolo, where they looted stores of grain, chemical fertiliser and American tinned food. Finally, an assault was attempted on the inter-provincial police office but was stopped by the Carabinieri led by Captain Miraglia. The crowd fired at the police and threw hand grenades. The police returned fire. The crowd dispersed and, later in the day, reinforcements of police and Italian soldiers arrived from Trapani. Several arrests were made as the troops secured the town and sent out patrols.

A US Naval Intelligence report from Palermo gave details of the riot at Alcamo to AFHQ:

> It is impossible to exaggerate the seriousness of the present situation in Sicily. No one is prepared to make even a

> suggestion as to how the matter can be kept under control. If the calling of Sicilians to military service and the threatened ending of the flour supply occur simultaneously, no constructive steps can be taken that will reconcile the opposing Sicilian and Italian interests. Actual assumption of military control of the area by Allied Governments will be the only solution.

The Allies had no taste for relocating soldiers back to Sicily. They had their hands full with the conquest of Hitler and the Nazis in western Europe. The Mafia and the Separatists knew this full well and 1945 would bring even more violence as they attempted to win their war of independence.

In the first week of January 1945, Italian Prime Minister Ivanoe Bonomi was forced to address his fellow government ministers in Rome on the trouble in Sicily. 'The underlying causes of the disorders may be laid to the Separatist and the hidden Fascist elements in the Island', he said. 'The situation at present is seemingly quiet, but still tense. Further incidents may break out at the slightest provocation.' They did.

New words were used to describe the wave of violent incidents in Sicily in early 1945. US Naval Intelligence described rioters and law-breakers as 'insurgents' and 'rebels' – and the level of violence was growing, with casualties to match.

A naval report sent to AFHQ on 8 January 1945 described a catalogue of escalating assaults. Italian troops were needed across the island to deal with outbreaks of violence. In Ragusa, 1 officer, 1 NCO and 2 soldiers were shot dead, 15 were wounded and 9 missing. Ten insurgents were killed and 50 wounded. Only the arrival of an artillery regiment escorted by a tank and armoured car quietened the situation. At Comiso, a Captain Sabatini was kidnapped by rebels and an Italian column of machine gunners had to blast their way into the town. The promise of action by Finocchiaro Aprile and his Mafia-backed Separatists, made back on 26 October 1944, seemed to be coming true.

In that same month, General Castellana had arrived in Sicily to take charge of a reactivated *Aosta* Division. He was very frank with the OSS when he spoke with its officers in Palermo. 'It is reported that General Castellana', said the OSS, 'is convinced that the strongest political social force to be reckoned with is the Mafia. He is extremely anxious to establish cordial relations with high Mafia leaders.'

The US Psychological Warfare Board (PWB) was in no doubt about who was behind the insurgency. In a report to AFHQ on 10 January 1945, it listed among the causes for rebellion the fear that Sicilians would be called up to serve in the Far East, and the continuing rationing of bread and pasta. All these reasons were 'enflamed by Separatists, Fascists, and MAFIA [their capitals].' Despite any lingering connections between Allied intelligence agents and their Mafia helpers of eighteen months before, the Mafiosi were now being seen more as the problem than the solution. The PWB had to admit its more subtle uses of propaganda were failing and it recommended strongly that the Italians assert their authority with police round-ups of Fascist and Mafia elements. This was a call for a return to the days of Cesare Mori and his *retate*.

The PWB also wanted to clarify the Allied position on Sicilian Separatism. 'London, Washington be asked produce new statement', said its report, 'condemning mob law categorically denying Allied support for Separatism.'

As the Allies debated what to do next, there was a further dimension to the trouble erupting in western Sicily. Armed criminal bands were joining the insurgency and leading raids across the region. On 27 January 1945, a band of forty armed men held up a train running on the Licata–Agrigento line at Contrada Saladino in Camastra. They robbed the passengers and disappeared. On another train, suspected of carrying rebel arms, seventeen people were arrested. On them were found fourteen rifles, a pistol, two hand-grenades and a stock of ammunition. On 15 January, three Carabinieri patrolling Sciacca were shot at by four men. One of the Carabinieri was killed. The raiders ran away.

The authorities had little choice but to go back to Mori's tactics and on 10 February, in Agrigento, a round-up netted seventy-four Sicilians who were arrested on suspicion of using weapons and being involved in the Camastra train hold-up.

On 15 February, US Naval Intelligence said that 'Emissaries from Palermo province reported that armed bands, in full "war" equipment, with arms, ammunition, supplies, logistic and medical services, were making their way to the vicinity of the town of Corleone.'

Corleone was notorious as a main centre of the local Mafia.

Salvatore Aldisio, a Christian Democrat and High Commissioner for Sicily, summed up events in the island in a secret report to the Italian Ministry of the Interior of 21 February 1945:

> The disorders which occurred in Sicily during the month of December degenerated into armed revolts in the provinces of Agrigento and Ragusa during the month of January . . . Order was restored everywhere on 13 January. Various battles between the troops and rebels were inevitable, as a result of which 12 Carabinieri, 1 officer, 1 NCO and 2 soldiers met their death in Ragusa while 15 other troops were wounded. Among the rebels 13 dead and 50 wounded are reported . . .

The last revolt took place at Palazzo Adriano in Palermo on 25 January when 700 rebels fired machine guns at Carabinieri barracks, damaging neighbouring homes. The troops responded fiercely and stopped the rebels from occupying the barracks. Aldisio put the blame for this violence on the Separatists.

Feeling emboldened by the action, the Separatist Movement had held a convention in its Palermo headquarters on 15/16 January. This made an announcement calling for the administration of the island to be taken away from the Italian government and handed to them, or at least to the Allied authorities.

In his report, Aldisio made a veiled reference to the Mafia, calling them:

> Capitalistic interests of no slight importance . . . [They are] known to sponsor the movement for the purpose of centralising power in their own hands and remaining masters of the situation in Sicily, once the economic ties with the government is broken. This would give rise to a feudal regime with an anti-democratic system of privileges from which the sponsors alone would derive the benefits.

Food shortages and lawlessness added fuel to the fire, said Aldisio. Criminals were getting bolder and attacking long distance bus routes and trains. He feared the growth of heavily armed bands of ex-prisoners operating across the country. Finally, he named one of the prime figures he believed was responsible for the deteriorating situation. 'The band led by Giuliano', he said, 'blamed for numerous crimes committed in the Partinico area, continues to reign.'

Salvatore Giuliano – it was a name that would strike terror in everyone on the island – including the Mafia.

Chapter Seventeen

A Shift in Enemies

Salvatore Giuliano was Sicilian gangster number one during the Allied occupation and after. His bandit life began on 2 September 1943 when he was still a teenager. He stole a sack of flour that he was going to sell on the black market when he was cornered by a Carabiniere. He was ordered to give up the flour but killed the policeman instead. He embarked on a life on the run – and would be accused of having killed seventy-three Carabinieri and twenty-seven other policemen by the end of his criminal career.

Giuliano's family was not poor. His father had made his money as an emigrant to the United States where he worked in Minnesota. When he returned to Sicily, he bought some land and a house in Montelepre, a mountainous area not far from Palermo. As a bandit, Giuliano made this his realm and few passed through it without paying homage to him. He formed a gang with escaped prisoners from Monreale and proceeded to terrorise the countryside around Palermo. He extorted money and food from the landowners and gave some of it to the local peasants so they began to love and fear him – shielding him from the authorities.

Giuliano was fearless and in his first months as a bandit he showed no respect to the Mafia. One old Mafioso was found on the road to Castellammare del Golfo with his face smeared with cow dung and a note tied round his neck, saying 'This is how Giuliano treats the Mafia.'

In the old days, the Mafia had controlled banditry in their region by making links with the bandits, planning operations and sharing the profits of their crimes. They offered protection to landowners from raids in return for a fee. But their power was diminished since the Fascist regime and the countryside in the war years was overrun by bandits operating beyond the reach of the Mafia. These armed bands, mentioned in numerous Allied reports of the time, were kidnapping prominent locals, attacking buses and trains, looting government stores, fighting with the Carabinieri and Italian Army.

That said, Giuliano was too dominant a personality in an area too close to the heart of the Mafia to remain for long outside their society. Sometime in 1944, he was contacted by Concetto Gallo, commander of the Mafia's Voluntary Army for Sicilian Independence – *Esercito Volontario Indipendenza Siciliana* (EVIS). This armed force – consisting of several bandit groups – had the full backing of senior Separatist supporters and was intended to give military-style weight to their insurgency.

Gallo met with Giuliano at Bellolampo on the outskirts of Palermo and offered him the rank of colonel in EVIS. He promised that when the Separatists won independence, Giuliano could become head of the island's police force. Giuliano was not even twenty when he had this meeting and was flattered by the attention of senior Mafiosi and Separatist leaders. At a subsequent meeting, Giuliano and his 100-strong unit were formerly incorporated into EVIS. A later Sicilian police report was explicit about Giuliano's involvement with politics:

> Giuliano and the Separatist leaders met at Ponte di Sagana in the presence of a number of well-armed bandits. They discussed tactical plans to get power in Sicily and stamp out Communism. Giuliano submitted a plan for an attack in the area of Monreale, Montelepre and Partinico and asked for 10 million lire to finance it. But the duke [of Carcaci] and Baron La Motta seemed rather puzzled. Another bandit suggested that the needed funds could be raised by kidnapping and blackmailing wealthy people. This suggestion was approved . . .

With Giuliano incorporated into their ranks, EVIS ambitions grew. Its leaders even considered a march on Palermo to capture the capital of the island. However, they were never more than a few hundred strong and their activities in early 1945 remained low-level raids, with handfuls of bandits attacking Carabinieri headquarters and looting ammunition dumps. This begged the question: having started an armed rebellion, did Separatist forces really have enough support throughout the island to carry on to victory? Would they ever be more than just nuisance bandits?

Rome kept a tight control on news about the Sicilian Separatist uprising from late 1944 to early 1945. It did not enter the international press until 1 February 1945 when veteran *New York Times* reporter Herbert L. Matthews broke the story with the headline 'Sicily in throes of Civil Disorder':

> Not a word of this has gone to the outer world, because of the blackout on news that the Rome Government keeps over Sicilian disorders. Once it is over, there will be a carefully controlled statement whose accuracy will depend on political factors, but whose incomplete lack of correctness will also be due to the fact that it is impossible to get the true story of what happens.

Matthews was based in Palermo and did his best to give a summary of the major disturbances in Sicily from Palermo on 19 October 1944 to the rebellion in Ragusa and Agrigento in January 1945. 'The Communists and Socialists in Rome like to blame this and other Sicilian troubles on the Fascists', said Matthews. 'There is only one good word to describe the accusation and that is nonsense.' Instead, Matthews pointed the finger at the Separatists, led by Finocchiaro Aprile, and the Mafia:

> The Mafia is one of the unknown factors in an extraordinarily complicated situation. In its upper brackets the Mafia is naturally separatist – first, because of its traditional links with the great landowning interests and, second, because it is to its advantage to have those politicians whom it chooses or backs under its control in Palermo rather than out of control in Rome.

As for the crime wave and the widespread banditry in the country, Matthews believed it was in effect a challenge to the authority of the Mafia:

> One thing for which the Mafia will not stand in the long run is unorganised widespread crime such as is now occurring in the island. It must either absorb and control the present unruly elements or fight and destroy them. Unfortunately, what signs there are show that efforts are being made by the Mafiosi to gather in rather than to oppose the present delinquents.

It was a shrewd and accurate portrayal of the events and Matthews may have gained his information from Allied intelligence agencies based in Palermo. Indeed, the information may even have been leaked to the journalist to put some international pressure on the Italian government. A follow-up article by Matthews carried a threat to the Italian government, that unless it sorted out the situation, the Allies would intervene:

> Sicilian separatists want the Allies to come back and re-occupy Sicily, and they have it in their power to force this issue. The movement for the 'Independence of Sicily' is Italy's gravest national problem and Rome's efforts to minimize it are not going to conjure it away.

This sounded very much like a warning from the Allies to the Italian prime minister. Matthews then compared the situation to that in India with the Muslims wanting a separate Pakistan. He believed it was an Allied problem as much as an Italian one. 'Sicily was the first place we liberated in Europe and it is a good example of what disturbing forces liberation is setting free in this old world from which our own people came.' He repeated the charge that 'the Mafia, that peculiarly Sicilian institution which is almost a government to itself, is also deeply involved.'

Sicilian High Commissioner Salvatore Aldisio's idea for defeating the widespread lawlessness in his island was the formation of a special battalion of Carabinieri, but the problem was that they seemed to be out-gunned from the very beginning. That the authorities still felt extremely nervous about the forces they faced was reflected in their security measures for the anniversary of the Sicilian Vespers held in Palermo on 31 March 1945. It was over-kill: armoured cars were placed at strategic points throughout the city; public safety agents, troops, and Carabinieri were stationed at all government buildings; complete infantry and alpine companies were positioned in different parts of the city; Carabinieri stood guard on rooftops near the Separatist headquarters; road-blocks were set up on routes leading to Palermo to prevent the possible entrance of trucks carrying armed Separatist followers. All this for an event that attracted only 200 Sicilians!

Finocchiaro Aprile hosted the evening and must have been satisfied by the security panic. Another Separatist leader, Lucio Tasca, gave a rousing speech. 'I wish Allied observers would realise', said Tasca, 'that there will never be peace in the Mediterranean until Sicilian aspirations are guaranteed. Domination based on armed might will not change the desires of the people. We will defend our independence. Sicily's hour is near.'

The authorities were embarrassed by their show of nervousness. Perhaps surprised and then encouraged by the lack of trouble at the event (plus that at the Separatist Congress held the following month), anti-Separatist elements took their turn to go on the offensive. An OSS report quoted both the Christian Democrat and Communist parties as asking the Italian government to take prompt disciplinary action against the Separatist Movement. In the streets of Palermo, this culminated in an assault on the headquarters of the Separatist party. A British Field Security officer described the action:

> At 9.00hrs on 21 April [1945], a group of 200 small boys and students was observed proceeding down Via Liberta, Palermo, bearing the Italian flag, with paper pasted over the insignia of the House of Savoy. These boys, it was stated, were protesting against the cession of Trieste. On reaching the centre of the town they were joined by other groups until a crowd approaching two thousand was formed.

After milling around the streets, the crowd was escorted by Carabinieri and public safety agents towards the Separatist headquarters in Via Ruggero Settimo. They arrived about 11 o'clock. Inside the Separatist HQ were some forty young supporters. Some stood at the first-floor windows and exchanged insults with the crowd on the street. Suddenly, a shower of stones was thrown at the Separatist HQ and the protestors stormed inside. Fighting broke out inside the building while protestors hurled papers, chairs, and typewriters out of the upper windows. Separatist youths got the worst of the fighting and were carried out of the building.

> Some of the Separatists [reported the Field Security officer] were successful in rescuing the Sicilian flag, with which they beat a retreat. This flag was replaced by the Italian flag, which flew from a first-storey window of the premises for the rest of the day. By this time most of the office material was out in the street. After the defeat of the Separatists, mounted CC.RR appeared on the scene and the street was cleared. Calm was restored by 12.00 hrs. No Allied personnel were involved.

The mob may have been originally protesting about keeping Trieste Italian, but their protests were quickly diverted against the Separatists. That this could happen in broad daylight without any intervention by the authorities shook Finocchiaro Aprile. Where were his armed forces? A local newspaper took this up. 'It is not felt that this demonstration was a spontaneous outburst against Separatism by "the citizens of Palermo",' said the *Giornale di Sicilia*, 'but rather an organised effort by the Italian government to deal with the embarrassment of Separatism in its own indirect way.' 'This demonstration', said the British Field Security officer, 'caught the Separatists off their guard and there were no responsible leaders of the movement in the HQ at the time of the incident. The weekend 21/22 April found them nursing their wounds and vowing vengeance.'

On the same day, Finocchiaro Aprile wrote a stinging letter to Admiral Stone, Chief of the Allied Commission in Rome. He blamed the authorities for the attack:

> For the purpose of belittling the exceptional importance of the second congress of our Movement the Italian government organised a gang of one thousand criminals and schoolboys in a demonstration against our movement. Carabinieri and policemen destroyed our headquarters in Palermo. In the headquarters were only approximately twenty unarmed youths who were brutally assaulted and arrested. This ignominious act, contrary to Allied interest has deeply shocked the citizenry.

Finocchiaro Aprile promised a serious reaction, but what he really wanted – just when Allied troops were being withdrawn from the island – was to pitch the Allies against the Italian government. 'As for myself', he said, 'I renew the request that Sicily should be once again occupied by the Allies in order to prevent even more serious disorders.'

British Vice-Consul Manley believed the raid on their Palermo HQ plus the later closing of other offices across the island pushed the Separatists to a more sinister phase:

> The subsequent closing of all the MIS [Movimento per l'Indipendenza della Sicilia] headquarters throughout Sicily drove the MIS underground. On account of this a number of the younger members were reported to have fled to the mountains and joined the bands in order to avoid arrest. Concetto Gallo a member of the MIS committee in Catania

> was one of them. This is another possible link between the MIS and the bandits and subsequently the EVIS.

Political rivals of the Separatists could sense weakness and began circling the party. The Separatists might have their so-called EVIS army of bandits but that only operated in the countryside. In the urban battle zone they were vulnerable.

In late April, Monarchists approached Don Calogero Vizzini for support. He declined their invitation, but such manoeuvring planted seeds of doubt in the heads of the Mafia leaders behind Finocchiaro Aprile. Following the failure of their armed insurrection to inflame the whole island, and the authorities brazen assault on their Palermo HQ, the Separatists were starting to look like losers. They certainly appeared weak and the Mafia could not risk their fearful reputation by continuing to back them. Should they persist with the Separatists or dump them?

Beyond the shores of Sicily, in the rest of Europe, world war was coming to an end. Adolf Hitler shot himself in his bunker deep beneath the ruined centre of Berlin on 30 April 1945. Two days before, he had heard about the humiliating end of his Fascist comrade Benito Mussolini. The circumstances probably convinced Hitler to commit suicide rather than face capture.

On 27 April, Mussolini was being driven north from his Fascist enclave to the Swiss border in a German convoy. He hoped to escape to the country that had given him refuge as a young political activist, but Italian partisans intercepted the convoy and found Il Duce hidden beneath a blanket in the back of a truck. He was wearing a German helmet and a Luftwaffe jacket and the Germans tried to explain away his presence by saying he was a drunken comrade. The partisans were not fooled and took Mussolini to a secluded mountain cottage. His mistress, Clara Petacci, and other Fascist prisoners were taken to the town hall at nearby Dongo.

US Sergeant Dan Polier, a correspondent for *Yank* magazine, spoke to two of the partisans who guarded the 62-year-old dictator during his last night alive. Mussolini was confident of his fate, they remembered:

'I know my destiny. I shall be taken to San Donino prison in Como and then to San Vittore prison in Milan. [He had been imprisoned in both as a young left-wing agitator.] I shall be given a trial, and I will tell the world I have been betrayed nine times – the last time by Hitler.'

'Why did you tell the people Germany would win the war?' asked George Buffeli, one of the partisans.

'My dear fellow', said Mussolini, 'you must know that Hitler's Gestapo was so strong around me I could be alone only in bed.'

'Do you realise now', said Buffeli, 'that you were allied with a madman?'

'Hitler was a foolish man', said Mussolini. 'He should have known that it was impossible for one man to become master of the world. Every human force has a limit. A tree cannot grow to the sky.'

Mussolini shivered in the cold of the mountain cottage. A partisan offered him the Luftwaffe coat he had worn when he was captured.

'*Basta Tedeschi* [Down with the Germans]', growled Mussolini and pushed it away.

Later that night, Mussolini was joined by Petacci. His interpretation of his future was wrong. The next day, they were both given a brief trial by the partisans and at 4.10 p.m., without ceremony, they were shot dead. That night, the bodies were taken to Milan in a van and dumped in the Piazza Loreto – a place previously used to execute partisans. The bodies were beaten by the crowd and then strung up on an iron fence, upside down, outside a petrol station.

Hitler did not want to end up like that. Two days later, he shot himself and had his body burned. World War II ended in Europe on 8 May 1945.

On the same day, in New York, Lucky Luciano's attorney, Moses Polakoff, filed a petition for executive clemency for his client. With the war over, Luciano wasn't wasting any more time. He had delivered his side of the bargain and now he wanted out. The newspapers were pretty clear about what happened, as the *New York Times* reported:

> Because Charles (Lucky Luciano) Lucania, serving a 30-to-50-year State prison term as a 'vice king', had aided the military authorities for two years in the preliminaries leading to the Sicily invasion by the Allies, his lawyer revealed yesterday, an application has been made to Governor Dewey, who prosecuted Luciano in 1936, for executive clemency. The application now is before the state Prison Parole Board.

Luciano's lawyer at this hearing was Moses Polakoff and he declared that Luciano's services were enlisted by a Major Murray Gurfein of Military Intelligence. Polakoff then told the court that Luciano had provided this information from his cell in Great Meadow prison in

1942 and that 'many Sicilian-born Italians furnished information regarding the conditions in Sicily that was helpful in the armed forces'. A very straightforward and open account – and yet mystery and controversy remained around Luciano's contribution to his country's war effort for decades to come. This brief statement by Luciano's attorney would only be amplified by later investigations.

By the late summer of 1945, the general situation in Sicily seemed little improved. The US Army Office of Communications Censorship intercepted a letter from a citizen of Catania, Enrico Sorrentino, written in August, and distributed copies to AFHQ and the British War Office.

> Of course the price of petrol goes up [complained Sorrentino]. At present it is 150 lire and is still increasing. Things are different from Rome northwards. Our treatment is always the same, and therefore the Sicilian Separatist movement gains ground. Professor Canepa of our University, who headed the movement was killed in an incident with the public authorities and his successor has published a bellicose proclamation believing that the time for a rising is at hand. If this is so, blood will once more be shed on this tortured soil.

Sorrentino went on to paint a bleak picture of life in post-war Sicily:

> Our country is a very sorry sight today. Firearms are plentiful and killings take place on the slightest pretext. Everyone takes justice into his own hand. In a court of assize, a partisan Carabiniere who was guarding a prisoner executed his own judgement by using his arms without waiting for that of the judges. And so it goes on everywhere, robberies, rapine, threatening letters, kidnappings, etc., are daily occurrences. The police make mass arrests; the prisons are crowded and within the prison walls there are rebellion, arson and other crimes.

In contrast to Sorrentino's view of events, AFHQ felt the situation had calmed since the beginning of the year. A report from Lieutenant Colonel G. E. Monsell in the Office of the Assistant Chief of Staff, US Army, made in September, declared that the general situation in Sicily gave no indication of any revolutionary or anti-Allied activity. There was more concern about the Sicilian Communist party:

> Although no reliable information has been received about Communist activities, undoubtedly the Italian Communist party is in close contact with the Sicilian Communist Party and attempting to extend its influence as in other regions.

According to Allied intelligence figures, membership of the Sicilian Communist party numbered 48,000 and the Socialists 29,000. The Separatists had 30,000 signed-up members, while the conservative Christian Democrats had 45,000. There was a distinct fault line between right and left in Sicily and Monsell considered this the main threat to stability. Elections were to be held in Sicily in 1946 and all parties were manoeuvring towards this. 'The incidence of crime is said to be on the increase', said Monsell, 'possibly due to a combination of economic unrest and the turbulent Sicilian temperament but since June 45 no subversive activity or major incidents have been reported.'

As autumn in Sicily unfolded, the Italian authorities decided that the Separatists were sufficiently weakened by the events of previous months for them to make a final move against them. On 2 October 1945, leading Separatist politicians were arrested, including Finocchiaro Aprile, Andrea Varvaro and Francesco Restuccia. They were charged with plotting against the integrity and independence of the state and sent to the prison island of Ponza. It could have been a risky gamble by the government, provoking rioting on to the streets and armed uprising in the countryside, but the muted confrontations of previous months, from the Sicilian Vespers anniversary onwards, had suggested otherwise.

The majority of Palermo newspapers reacted positively to the news, welcoming the firm action taken by the government. The Orbis news agency said that most Sicilians received the news with calm and indifference. The Christian Democrats in their newspaper, *Sicilia del Popolo*, said they only supported the aspirations of the Separatists because they believed they had the support of the Allies. There were no riots in the streets. The government had tested the mood of the Sicilian population and got it right. The Mafia reacted to the arrests by shifting their allegiance away from Finocchiaro Aprile. They could see that he did not possess the power of the streets – there were no mass protests or strikes at his imprisonment – and now that the war was over the Allies were less interested in the Separatist cause.

As the Cold War era dawned, the Allies were more concerned about Soviet domination in Eastern Europe spreading to the Mediterranean. They wanted Sicily to be part of a strong, united and anti-Communist Italy. For the Allies, the Christian Democrats were looking the better game in town – and the majority of the Mafia were starting to agree. The Christian Democrats favoured regional autonomy and they declared their intention to concentrate on defeating Communism. To them, the Mafia and the Allies, this was the biggest enemy faced by Sicily – not the Italian government.

But there was a minority of the Mafia, led by Calogero Vizzini, who still believed in the revolutionary dimension of Separatism. Along with Lucio Tasca, they had contacts with Salvatore Giuliano and the other outlaws who formed the bandit army EVIS. They set their aims on continuing a guerrilla war against the authorities.

A Security Intelligence report for December 1945 described a major confrontation between the police and EVIS at San Mauro di Caltagirone in Catania. 'The bandits had surrounded a country house', said the report, 'and were dressed in khaki uniforms and had German vehicles. They were using arms, and casualties, including one NCO killed, had been inflicted on the CCRR.' In fact, the authorities had cornered Concetto Gallo, the commander of EVIS forces who had invited Giuliano to join him. Some 250 Carabinieri and 350 Italian soldiers fought 150 Separatist bandits for several hours. The government forces eventually broke the stalemate with a mortar barrage and captured Gallo.

EVIS might be broken in the east of the island, but Giuliano remained defiant in the west and it would take a much bigger operation – plus the involvement of the Mafia – to silence him.

Chapter Eighteen

Courteous Raiders

What was it like to be on a train raided by Salvatore Giuliano's bandits? Flight Lieutenant R. J. H. Gillingham knew – he was there. Gillingham was returning from a visit to an RAF base near Trapani to Palermo when his train came to a crashing halt outside a tunnel near Partinico on the afternoon of 23 January 1946:

> There were two loud bangs, which I imagined were caused by the train hitting some rocks on the lines. Almost immediately all the passengers dived for cover and I heard the sound of shots on the starboard side. The driver quickly brought the train to a standstill.
>
> Shots were fired over the train and it was quickly boarded by persons carrying weapons and after some talk in Italian the passengers began leaving the train. I was the last to leave it, with the exception of the women, and as I got out I stated to one of the bandits that I was English. He made me understand that I was to stay where I was and made some remark similar to 'Inglesi buono'.

The rest of the male passengers were taken 100 yards away from the train and had their money and valuables taken from them. The passengers' suitcases were then thrown from the train on to an embankment where they were looted. 'As my suitcase was still in the train', said Gillingham, 'I managed to make one of the bandits realise that it was there and he gave me to understand that I should go to the other side of the train, whereupon I was handed my luggage and told to go back to the port side.' After the luggage had been robbed, the passengers were told they could get back onto the train. But the engine was damaged and they had to wait for another locomotive to arrive to tow them to the nearest station.

When Gillingham got back to his hotel in Palermo, he was interviewed by a US Navy Intelligence officer, who wanted to know everything about the raid. Gillingham also passed the details of his experience on to the British Consulate. 'I should just like to add', he told the British consul, 'that I was spoken to courteously by the bandits, more so when they became aware that I was an Englishman, and that they, as far as was possible, went out of their way to be courteous to me.'

The reason for the bandits' courtesy is that they were part of Salvatore Giuliano's gang and, still being Separatists, held out hopes for the Allies intervening on their behalf against the Italian government.

The level of lawlessness in Sicily in early 1946 attracted the attention of several Allied intelligence organisations. Special Agents Gabriel B. Celetta and Saverio Forte worked for the US Army CIC Naples Detachment. They made a special study of the Separatist violence in Sicily and uncovered some startling connections with the Mafia. They identified two main rebel bands in operation on the island. One band was composed of about a hundred Separatists, two members of which were Duca di Carcace, a leader of EVIS, and his aide, Giuseppe Tasca, son of Lucio Tasca, the first mayor of Palermo during the Allied occupation.

> Also with this band is the Giuliano outlaw gang [said Celetta and Forte], composed of about eighty men. This latter group, headed by Salvatore Giuliano, has made common cause with the Separatists on promises from the Separatists that in the event of a victory the members of the Giuliano band would be given full amnesty and richly rewarded for their effort in the 'liberation movement'.

This first band functioned in the west of the island. A second band, originally led by Concetto Gallo and operating in the east, had been reduced in their significance ever since his capture at the end of 1945. The members of these rebel bands were said to be well equipped with modern American, British, German and Italian rifles, machine guns, hand grenades and several mortars. Radio transmitting and receiving sets were used by them to co-ordinate their movements. Despite this impressive armoury, it had come to the attention of Special Agents Celetta and Forte that many Mafiosi were no longer interested in supporting the rebel Separatists:

> They too would like to see the Italian Government allow these misdirected EVISsts to disband and returned to their homes. The undersigned Agents have been reliably informed that should this come about, the Mafia themselves would quickly liquidate both the remnants of the Niscemi band [in the east of the island] and the Giuliano outlaws. The Mafia is known to be well represented in every city, town and hamlet in Sicily.

According to Celetta and Forte, the Mafia wanted to reassert their dominance over banditry in Sicily and were willing to kill those who would not submit to them and the government. That said, the CIC agents did admit that some important members of the Mafia were still sympathetic to the Separatist cause. They mentioned Don Calogero Vizzini as being especially close to Lucio Tasca, whose son was directly involved with the rebel band. 'Vizzini has the utmost faith in Lucio Tasca', said the agents, 'thus the possible danger of a Mafia–Separatist outlaw affiliation, which would indeed be a combination hard to curb.'

Celetta and Forte interviewed General Amedeo Branca, overall commander of the Carabinieri on the island, and Colonel Armando Calabro, commander of the Palermo Carabinieri, and they admitted their weakness in weaponry in the face of the bandit gangs. The Carabinieri commanders wanted the government either to grant the outlaws an amnesty or send large reinforcements from the mainland, including 6,000 extra men, a dozen armoured cars and fifty jeeps. It wasn't helping the situation that the rebels were getting extra arms from across the sea. 'Reliable information', said the CIC agents, 'has been obtained that American arms and ammunition are being smuggled from Calabria for use by the rebels. American and British uniforms are also being worn by some members of the EVIS.'

There were even rumours of Allied agents going native and fighting alongside the Separatists. A British intelligence officer from Palermo, called Major Oliver, was said to be one of the Allied deserters to have joined them. It was an added complication – and embarrassment – that the Allied authorities would definitely want buried. The involvement of renegade Allied officers, caught up in the web of Mafia and Separatists, seemed to be a growing reality as Celetta and Forte uncovered another surprising secret alliance:

> Information has been obtained by these Agents that an Italian named Nicola Gentile, a member of the Mafia, who was deported from the United States in 1937 has returned to Palermo from a trip to Rome with a story that while in Rome he had been approached by an American Colonel who had known Gentile in the United States.
>
> The American Colonel had taken Gentile to meet Prince Umberto, Lieutenant General of the Realm, and there had been told to convey a message to the Sicilian Mafia that their united effort to back the Monarchy was desired. The American Colonel had then told Gentile that the retention of the Monarchy was also what the United States desired.

This rang alarm bells with Celetta and Forte who wanted to investigate the claim immediately and identify the American colonel. Lucky Luciano knew Nick Gentile and he knew Colonel Poletti, both of whom had been operating on different sides of the law in New York before the war. Gentile had worked for Luciano during the Castellammarese War. Had he and Poletti met up in Rome? It is an intriguing possibility. Poletti's military service in Rome came to an end in November 1945. He then joined a Manhattan law firm as a senior partner. During 1946–7, he served as an arbitrator for labour disputes in the New York coat and suit industry.

In late January 1946, while still in Palermo, Celetta and Forte picked up news that Giuliano's gang had graduated from robbing trains and buses to attacking a strategically more important target – the Bocca di Falco airfield, just a few miles from the centre of the city. It was used by both Americans and Italians, said the CIC agents:

> One of the objectives of the gang may be the destruction of several tri-motored Italian airplanes on the airfield which they may fear might be used against them, either for reconnaissance or strafing purposes. Attempts have also been made on several occasions against the motor pool and the communications equipment belonging to the Italians.

Aside from robberies, Giuliano also led raids against Carabinieri bases. On the night of 7/8 January, they attacked a Carabinieri HQ and killed three policemen and wounded fifteen more. A second attack on

Carabinieri barracks led to the capture of six more policemen. By the end of January, the alliance between the Mafia faction led by Calogero Vizzini and the rebels, feared by CIC Special Agents Celetta and Forte, seemed in danger of happening. They warned:

> Because of the threatened arrest of Vizzini, one of the Mafia leaders and a fiery Separatist, the Mafia has threatened to order active participation by the Sicilian Mafia on the side of EVIS and the outlaw bands. Because of their known power, this would mean real civil war in Sicily. Vizzini's threatened arrest is said to be caused by the alleged confession of an EVIS rebel who has stated that he was personally recruited for the EVIS by Vizzini to fight against the Carabinieri.

Aldisio, the High Commissioner of Sicily, tried to defuse the situation as he knew that Vizzini was trying to negotiate a compromise settlement with the government. Instead of being arrested, Vizzini was told to leave Palermo and go back to Caltanisetta. Celetta and Forte spoke to Aldisio in early February and he told them that the Italian government would be willing to negotiate with EVIS only from a position of strength. Proof of the government's muscle arrived in the form of nearly 1,000 troops from the Garibaldi Regiment, equipped with armoured cars. Celetta and Forte confirmed this:

> The undersigned witnessed the arrival of several companies of troops from the Garibaldi Regt as they marched through the streets of Palermo. They appeared to be seasoned troops, apparently armed with British rifles and automatic weapons, clothed in British battle dress, but with distinctive Italian Alpini headgear. There was no cheering on the part of the Palermo natives – only a deep silence – very un-Italian in character.

The CIC agents then spoke to Colonel Calabro, Carabinieri commander of the Palermo region, and he disclosed that the Carabinieri also had the assistance of an Allied military advisor – a British major. He immediately made a request for extra uniforms, weapons and vehicles for the police forces. The government meant business but it had a time limit – just twenty days – before the extra troops would have to go back to the mainland.

As troops of the Garibaldi Regiment prepared themselves for an assault on the Mafia, some of them were caught up in a dispute on the streets of Palermo involving Allied servicemen.

> At about 20:00 hours on 9 February 1946 [said Celetta and Forte], four American sailors, allegedly intoxicated, engaged in a free-for-all in the streets of Palermo, in which members of the Garibaldi Regiment . . . and civilians participated. During the fracas, several shots were fired over the heads of the combatants by Italian police. A grenade was thrown by the usual 'unknown person' and two civilians were injured.

The *Giornale di Sicilia* gave a more detailed account of the street fight in Via Roma:

> The [sailors], undoubtedly drunk, addressed the Italian soldiers with insults in Neapolitan dialect, and the latter asked for the reason of such free insults. As a reply, the sailors started to fight.
>
> It is believed that they were ready to fight because they drew out their belts and wrapped their fists with them, leaving the buckles exposed. The four soldiers were beaten and only one of them could escape, though he had a pistol, while the others tried to protect themselves from the hail of blows. A huge crowd of several hundreds of people gathered around the fighters and a few civilians tried to take away the unfortunate soldiers from the aggressor's hands, but they were also given violent blows.

Eventually, the police and a Naval shore patrol arrived to break up the fight. Celetta and Forte investigated the incident and tried to dampen down newspaper coverage of it. Threats of revenge were heard from Italian soldiers against the American sailors and it was feared this might spark further incidents and political unrest. Celetta and Forte even considered that the fight might have been a set-up by agents wanting to create ill feeling between Sicilians and Americans.

The government offensive against Giuliano and his bandits began in the second week of February. It centred on the mountainous region of Montelepre where Giuliano had his base. According to a US military intelligence report of Thursday 14 February:

> Large military forces are fanning out along the hills and the operations are beginning to yield excellent results. The 'Nembochi' Division and 'Aosta' Brigade are with the 'Folgore' Division, as well as the regiment of the 'Garibaldi' division. Today four bombers and reconnaissance aircraft went into action.

Controversially, flamethrowers were used to force the rebels from their mountain hide-outs. Over a hundred bandits were arrested and the equipment seized included horses, mules, numerous weapons, a mixture of old 1891 rifles and looted German guns, and stores of ammunition. A government spokesman later denied the use of flamethrowers.

On 21 February, it was reported that Captain Mazola, a well-known Sicilian bandit leader of EVIS, had been captured in Palermo province. Some 300 suspected bandits were taken into custody with him, plus rifles, grenades, and 200 light guns. On 27 February, an AFHQ report mentioned that army units in the Prizzi–Bivona–Licara area had arrested a further 300 suspects and captured two 47-mm guns, machine guns, and small arms. The bandits were feeling the pressure and a 200-strong unit of EVIS was noted to be on the move, led by a bandit called Avila and a Separatist Nino, alias 'Cannone'. They were planning to attack an army barracks.

By early March, however, the area south of Palermo had been secured. An Allied intelligence report recorded that a mopping-up operation in the Corleone area, conducted by detachments of the Garibaldi Regiment and Carabinieri, detained fifty outlaws and took possession of rifles, machine-guns, hand grenades and other military material.

EVIS as a military force was at an end. Giuliano and his followers remained at large, but the news of the arrest of other major EVIS leaders impacted on the prospects of the Separatists. With their guerrilla units defeated in the field, all Finocchiaro Aprile and his party colleagues could look forward to were the national elections to be held in June 1946. They were released from prison in March, but they faced an uphill struggle. In May, the Italian government outmanoeuvred them by devolving more power to the high commissioner of Sicily and establishing a regional assembly of twenty-four members representing various aspects of Sicilian life.

The gift of autonomy completely undercut the appeal of the Separatists and Finocchiaro Aprile faced final humiliation on 2 June.

Out of forty-nine deputies elected in Sicily, only four were Separatist candidates – Finocchiaro Aprile, Antonino Varvaro, Concetto Gallo, and Attilio Castrogiovanni – the latter two, EVIS commanders, were in prison at the time of the election but were released because of parliamentary immunity. The Separatist party received only 8.71 percent of the total vote or 166,609 votes, despite claiming a signed-up membership before the election of 600,000.

CIC Special Agent Gabriel Celetta returned to Sicily in June with a new partner, Frank de Santis, to investigate the political and criminal situation following the election. At first they considered the Separatists were no longer an important factor. A month later, it got worse:

> The Separatist Movement is at present undergoing a serious crisis, caused by dissatisfaction and disaffection within the organization . . . Finocchiaro Aprile is said to have been strongly criticized because of his chameleon attitude, prior, during and after the 2 June elections.

The clear winners on the island and across Italy were the Christian Democrats. It was a slap in the face for those Mafiosi who still believed in Separatism, and, if they had any doubts left, they quickly switched all their powers of patronage and intrigue to the Christian Democrats. This would be their party of the future. It was now a two-horse race for political power in Sicily – between the Christian Democrats and the Communists.

Released from their association with the Separatists, the Mafia were seeking to stake their own claim to power and influence on the island. 'The Mafia is alive again on a greater and more dangerous scale than ever before', said Celetta and Santis in their July 1946 CIC report. But they noted a new generation of more violent mobsters was contesting the power of the old gangsters:

> At present those professing to be 'Mafiosi' are under no control, each one works for himself and keeps all spoils. Old time Mafiosi who, after the fall of Fascism, had begun to operate 'legitimately', as before, are in opposition to this new Mafia and often the police find individuals who have been mysteriously killed. The present crop of Mafiosi are often ex-soldiers and well armed.

An Allied military intelligence summary of June reinforced this view. Mafia gangsters were said to be killing rival small-time criminals at a rate of four to five every night. Even the Socialist mayor of Palermo was stopped by Mafiosi and robbed, but, it was noted, a party of Monarchists passing the same place a few minutes before were unmolested. This was a reference, perhaps, to mobster Nick Gentile's dalliance with Monarchists in Rome.

Despite the successful military campaign against Separatist EVIS gangs at the start of the year, Celetta and Santis reported that banditry remained a major problem on the island:

> The most notorious of the brigand bands and one of the largest is the group headed by Giuliano operating in the vicinity of Palermo. Members of this band have penetrated the city of Palermo itself and openly kidnapped rich merchants, who are often murdered when the requested ransom is not promptly paid.
>
> Giuliano's success is partly due to the Sicilian hero-worship of bold malefactors and the fact that the 23 year old bandit operates 'à la Robin Hood', often giving money and succor to the needy by whom he is kept informed when danger of capture threatens his band.

Poor Sicilians were not the only fans of Giuliano, according to the CIC agents:

> His reputation and renown has spread even to the ranks of personnel of the American Naval Detachment in Palermo, who have been heard to openly praise Giuliano as being the best man in Sicily today and should be made its first president. According to them he is doing good by taking money from war profiteers and distributing a good part of it amongst the needy.

Having survived the flamethrowers of the Italian Army, and with the praise of some Allied personnel, Giuliano was now ready to re-position himself – no longer as a Separatist guerrilla – but as an anti-Communist hero.

On 3 January 1946, Governor Thomas E. Dewey commuted Lucky Luciano's sentence – along with the sentences of six other foreign convicts held in US prisons – in preparation for their deportation. Luciano was forty-eight years old.

> Luciano is deportable to Italy [said Dewey in a statement to the Legislature]. Upon the entry of the United States into the war, Luciano's aid was sought by the armed services in inducing others to provide information concerning possible enemy attack. It appears that he cooperated in such effort though the actual value of the information procured is not clear. His record in prison is reported as wholly satisfactory.

To the press, Moses Polakoff repeated his assertion that Luciano's help had been given over two years, was related to the invasion of Sicily, and was procured by Gurfein, who had been a special prosecutor on Dewey's staff.

The deportation process took just over a month. On 2 February, Luciano was taken from jail and placed in a cell on Ellis Island. He was visited by Frank Costello and Polakoff. 'He was locked and guarded', said Ellis Island Chief of Detention, Lloyd H. Jensen. 'Costello brought him his baggage and other personal items. His room was as plain as all the others in his wing, contained just a chair, a bed, a toilet. Costello came on one ferry and left on the next.'

However, *New York Times* journalist Meyer Berger made several surprising claims in his 9 February 1946 report of Luciano's deportation:

> Luciano was under sentence of from thirty to fifty years but was pardoned by Dewey, ostensibly for help he gave the Office of Strategic Services before the Army's Italy invasion. It is understood that Luciano provided Army Intelligence with the names of Sicilian and Neapolitan Camorra members, and a list of Italians sent back to their native country after criminal conviction in the United States; that many of these men helped defeat the enemy in Italy.

In the light of subsequent revelations, it appears that Berger got it wrong about the OSS and Army Intelligence – he should have said Naval Intelligence. But even he knew some deal had been struck between the government and the gangster. Again, little mystery here. It is interesting to note that the journalist alleged a Neapolitan mob connection. This would make a lot of sense, as Luciano, through Vito Genovese, would have had access to Neapolitan crime rings. This was never mentioned by Naval Intelligence.

On 9 February, Luciano was escorted by two agents of the US Immigration Service onto the 7,000-ton freighter *Laura Keene*. He spent the night on board, ready to sail from Bush Terminal, Brooklyn, the next morning. Journalists crowded on the dockside begging to be allowed to interview him. Luciano declined to answer any of their questions. 'I've seen the press enough', he growled. To stop any journalists breaking onto the ship, a menacing guard of longshoremen was provided by the Mafia, each of them armed with baling hooks.

Aside from a cargo of flour, it was claimed, Luciano was the only passenger on board the ship. Rumours in the press said he had a farewell dinner of spaghetti and wine held on the ship the night before his departure. Six men were said to have attended the party, including Frank Costello and Albert Anastasia. Meyer Lansky was on board for the farewell party and he remembered it more precisely than the newspaper reports:

> We had a wonderful meal aboard, all kinds of seafood fresh from the Fulton Fish Market, and spaghetti and wine and a lot of kosher delicacies. They brought it in huge hampers, along with crates of French champagne . . .
>
> Lucky also wanted us to bring some girls to take along with him on the ship to keep him company. I asked Adonis to do something about that . . . Joe found three showgirls from the Copocabana Club and there was no difficult in getting them aboard. The authorities cooperated even on that. Nobody going into exile ever had a better send-off.

According to Lansky, the guest list of mobsters on board included Bugsy Siegel, William Moretti, Frank Costello, Tommy Lucchese, Joe Adonis, Stefano Magaddino, Albert Anastasia and Joe Bonanno. As Luciano sipped champagne, they joked about old times and how they used to ship illicit liquor across the Atlantic. Bonanno, however, denied ever being at the farewell party.

'There was no indication whether Luciano would debark at Genoa, the ship's first port of call', speculated a newspaper, 'or continue to Sicily. Underworld gossip had it that within a short time the gangster would leave his homeland for a base of operations nearer the United States.'

The *New York Herald Tribune* took a more robust approach to Luciano's departure. In an article entitled 'Luciano Departs for Italy with 3,500 Tons of Flour', it quoted former New York Mayor La Guardia. 'I'm sorry Italy is getting this bum back', he said. La Guardia was also angry that Frank Costello, a known racketeer, had been allowed to visit Luciano a week before his departure while held at Ellis Island. During a radio broadcast interview, he asked the New York Police Commissioner 'What is the limit of Costello's power in the city?'

After a seventeen-day voyage, the *Laura Keene* arrived in Naples on 28 February. Straight away, Lucky Luciano visited the local police headquarters and explained to them that he would stay in Naples briefly with a relative and then travel on to Sicily to see other family members. After that, he planned to tour Italy. A journalist asked him to explain what help he had given to the US government to gain his early release. This is exactly what Luciano feared. He didn't want the whole of Italy knowing he had collaborated with the foreign invaders. 'You know I can't talk about those things', he said – and that was that.

Fifteen years later, Luciano recalled his plans for his first months of freedom:

> The last day on Ellis Island, Lansky and me had a meet, just the two of us. I told him sometin' that none of the other guys knew up to that point – that I had already made connections in Italy to get visas under my real name, Salvatore Lucania, that would be good for Cuba and Mexico and a whole lotta countries in South America . . .
>
> Of course, I had another reason for pickin' Havana. The war bein' over, people was beginnin' to flock there, what with the place bein' wide open, the gamblin' good and the broads beautiful. With a combination like that, Lansky and his friend Batista [former President of Cuba] was rakin' the dough in and I had no intention of bein' left out of that . . .

Luciano wanted to cut the 4,000 miles Dewey was putting between him and New York to just ninety miles between Miami and Havana.

In Sicily, Luciano visited his home town – Lercara Friddi – 50 miles inland from Palermo. When he arrived, the main piazza was packed with people. The mayor, wearing the red sash reserved for occasions of state, welcomed the gangster and invited him to sign the official register. Everyone cheered him. A cousin then stepped forward and introduced Luciano to other members of his family. In the evening, long tables were put out in the piazza and every woman brought a dish of food – saved over days from their meagre rations. Luciano sat down to a feast of spaghetti marinara.

Luciano was moved by his reception and distributed money and gave away some of his clothes to his family. Best of all, he paid to turn part of a house into a cinema where they watched movies for the first time in the town.

> The first picture we showed [said Luciano], *Little Caesar*, made me such a big man like you'd never believe. The people were comin' up to me and practically kissin' my hand – not only because I brought them the pictures but because they wanted to show me that I was a bigger shot than Little Caesar. They made me feel like Salvatore Maranzano.

Luciano had long resisted the traditional Sicilian Mafia style of his former boss, but in Lercara Friddi he was submerged in it. After a few days, Luciano moved back to Palermo. His presence was noted by the British consulate in July:

> The ex Sicilian gangster Luciano, who was recently deported from the United States is living at the Hotel delle Palme (the most important hotel in town). I am told, on good authority, that some of the leading members of the Mafia have called on him at the hotel on more than one occasion. Rumour has it that he is now in somebody's pay working against the communists.
>
> This bandit, or ex-bandit, is very much in the public eye. He has two luxurious American motor cars; dresses and lives expensively, and is often seen in the company of an elegant but vulgar Italo-American woman.

The reference to Luciano being funded to work against Sicilian Communists is interesting. Does it indicate that he still had links with US Naval Intelligence but in a new Cold War role? It would not be surprising as he spent much of his criminal career enjoying an ambivalent relationship with the authorities – using them to his own advantage and to defeat rivals.

After Palermo, Luciano went back to Naples and Rome. The Italian black market in American goods was as profitable as it had been under Vito Genovese. Luciano linked up with Mafiosi in Sicily and mainland Italy and, by the autumn of 1946, the mobster had replenished his coffers and felt ready to return to the world of American crime. Luciano does not mention Don Calogero Vizzini at all, but does deal with a leading Sicilian Mafioso called 'Il Barone' – Riccardo Barone.

Luciano arrived in Havana, Cuba, in October 1946 and, despite his distaste for the title, assumed the mantle of Boss of Bosses. With Meyer Lansky, he organised a meeting of the top American Mafiosi at the Hotel Nacional in December. Frank Sinatra flew in to entertain them.

Vito Genovese turned up at Luciano's palatial residence in Havana and revealed his ambition by suggesting that the Sicilian go into retirement. When he refused, Genovese demanded half of the black-market business in Italy. 'I set up that whole thing in Europe', said Genovese, 'the black market, the truck routes to Germany, everything.'

'You're nuts', snapped back Luciano. 'I ain't going back to Italy. I'm stayin' in Cuba.'

'I understand different', said Genovese. 'I heard that Washington knows you're in Havana and they're getting ready to put the screws on the jerks in Cuba to get you thrown out.'

'You greedy fuckin' pig', shouted Luciano.

'As we was yelling' at each other', remembered Luciano, 'it suddenly come back into my head what that shitheel had done during the war . . . workin' hand-in-glove in Italy with our enemies and with the Nazis . . . So I done somethin' that I never done before . . . I pushed him up against the wall and I beat the livin' daylights out of him . . . I told him he was . . . a fink American who turned on his own country like a fuckin' traitor.'

Genovese was badly beaten, but he was right. The US government put pressure on the Cuban government and Luciano was thrown out of the island, returning to Italy in April 1947. Genovese now became the dominant figure in the New York underworld.

Chapter Nineteen

Beautiful Bandit

Lucky Luciano had no love for the Communists. Near Mount Vesuvius in 1947, he gave money to assist a local priest battle against the Communist Party in his village. 'From what I could see later', he recalled, 'it helped, and I was proud that he was knockin' the shit outa the Communists up there.' His summing up of post-war politics in Sicily was that Communism posed the biggest threat to the Italian government and that the Americans were propping them up. He was not too far from the truth.

In 1947, the OSS became the Central Intelligence Agency (CIA), with responsibility for co-ordinating all US intelligence activity abroad. In its report on the situation in Italy that year, its main concern was Communism:

> It is of vital strategic importance to prevent Italy from falling under Communist control. In particular, it would greatly facilitate Communist penetration in France, Spain and North Africa. Militarily, the availability to the USSR of bases in Sicily and southern Italy would pose a direct threat to the security of communications through the Mediterranean.

Italy was struggling. The CIA considered it on the edge of economic and political collapse. It could not call upon Western Europe for help. Britain imported Italian fruit and vegetables, but could neither pay for them with money or coal. Italy remained financially dependent on the US. The dire economic situation also encouraged crime, with the Italian government failing to curb inflation or the flourishing black market. For the moment US and British forces remained in Italy but they would be withdrawn in December 1947. The CIA did not have much confidence in the Italian Army:

> The Italian armed forces are incapable of major military operations. They are considered to be generally capable of maintaining internal order, but would be hard pressed if required simultaneously to defend the frontier and to suppress internal insurrection.

In this situation, with Italian national elections due in 1948, the US felt fully justified in exerting its influence though massive injections of economic aid:

> The outcome of the April elections will depend not only on the results of interim aid, but also on the prospects for the success of the European recovery program . . . Adverse developments and the consequent disillusionment would enhance the possibility of a Communist electoral victory.

In local elections in Sicily in April 1947, Communists and Socialists won 30 percent of the vote, against 21 percent won by the Christian Democrats. It was a surprising set-back for conservative forces on the island and reflected the fact that the economic situation did not seem to be getting any better for the average Sicilian. The Separatists did little better than they had the year before and it marked the end of their political presence. The next year, following more election failures, Finocchiaro Aprile resigned as leader of the party. For him, the beautiful dream of Sicilian independence was over. Lucio Tasca and some of his associates soldiered on, but only a few people remained dedicated to the idea.

Christian Democrat regional autonomy had outflanked the Separatists and the Mafia were happy with that. But with the rise of the left at the ballot box, it looked as though the Christian Democrats were in danger. The Mafia swung into action and their most potent weapon was the bandit leader Salvatore Giuliano. Since the demise of EVIS, Giuliano had shifted the focus of his political campaigning to the anti-Communist cause and was a willing executioner for the Mafia.

On 1 May 1947, left-wing peasants living in three villages outside Palermo gathered on hills near Portella delle Ginestre to celebrate May Day. They spread out picnics of bread, cheese and broad beans and waited for politicians from Palermo to give speeches. But none arrived, so after hours sitting in the baking sun, a Socialist shoemaker stood on a rock to give a speech. When he did so, the crowd heard sharp cracks around him. Some thought they were fire-crackers and did nothing. In fact, they were bullets coming from the slopes of Monte Pizzuta. People and animals fell to the ground, bleeding. After three minutes of firing, eleven people were dead and fifty-six wounded. The shots had come from Salvatore Giuliano and his bandit soldiers. It was his declaration of war against the left in Sicily.

A campaign of terror followed in which Giuliano and his army of bandits – several hundred strong – raided peasant unions and left-wing party headquarters in the provinces of Palermo and Trapani. Armed with machine guns, hand grenades and petrol bombs, they killed several Communists. He made several attempts to assassinate Girolamo Li Causi, the leader of the Communist Party in Sicily, and the man Don Calogero Vizzini had tried to shoot in the piazza at Villalba.

For Giuliano it was a crusade and, on 24 June 1947, he made his intentions clear in an announcement to the press:

> Sicilians! The decisive hour has sounded. Those who do not wish to be an easy prey of those Red gangsters who, after having betrayed, fooled and covered us with mud in international circles, are now attempting to destroy what is left us and what we will defend at all costs – the honour of our families – must make a decision. Those men who want, by hook or crook, to throw us into the lap of that terrible Russia where liberty is a chimera and democracy a legend must be fought.

It was the elaborate language of the Mafiosi, calling upon all Sicilians to defend the thing they held most dear – their honour.

Giuliano's actions soon caught the attention of the world's press. It certainly helped that he was a remarkably handsome young man. A photo of him widely published at the time showed a jet-haired strong-jawed bandit who looked more like a movie star. A London Foreign Office official was struck by a photo sent to him. 'I have always wondered whether the photographs and interviews were genuine', he mused. 'I suspect that there are a number of young Sicilians who would be very glad to pose as Giuliano for any journalist or photographer.' The Foreign Office appeared to have started a fan club for him. 'Here,' said the same official, 'we put our money on Giuliano . . . '

In Sicily, according to a British Embassy report from Rome, Giuliano passed through his realm like a medieval monarch:

> He apparently does not even hesitate to inform householders that he proposes to borrow their beds on such and such future nights. When Giuliano announces where he proposes to pass the night, his host stocks up his larder and removes himself, his family and dependents elsewhere, knowing that he will find the house in order and an envelope on the chimney piece containing 10,000 lire.

Stories about Giuliano's exploits grew in the telling.

> We need only tell how, not long ago [said the same Embassy report] the chief of a country-town police station, who was hastening to Palermo in response to a radio despatch in cipher, was ambushed en route and lost five of his men killed. It was later discovered that Palermo headquarters had sent no such message, since Giuliano's band had ciphered and despatched it themselves . . .

On another occasion, Giuliano banned a bus company from running routes through his territory until it paid him a tribute. His high-profile kidnappings included a prince, an ex-mayor, a rich businessman and two prominent landowners. He extorted from them ransoms varying from 20 to 50 million lire, doubling that of a local aristocrat when he was caught emerging from a brothel and wanted to keep it quiet.

The Italian government responded to Giuliano's threats by posting a 3 million lire reward for his capture, but left-wing parties in Sicily were deeply unimpressed and wanted more action. Li Causi condemned the weakness of a government that had encouraged lawlessness. Another leading Communist wanted Giuliano's victims avenged or else threatened that the workers' anger would be hard to control. Labour unions called for a general strike.

Eventually the interior minister sent the head of the Carabinieri to Sicily with orders to capture Giuliano. Hundreds of troops swarmed across the island's mountains, but the bandit eluded them all.

In November 1947, a wave of left-wing riots spread across Italy. In southern Italy, at Cerignola, armed gangs of Communists attacked Carabinieri barracks with automatic weapons and hand grenades. The chief of police was fatally wounded. In Rome, a general strike saw Carabinieri armed with rifles riding beside bus drivers. In Palermo, riots erupted under the newspaper headline 'People of Palermo destroy the Lairs of the Enemies of Democracy'. For many Italians, it was all too reminiscent of the political clashes of the early 1920s, before

Mussolini crushed the left and took over. In Sicily, the chaos only encouraged the supporters of Giuliano's murderous campaign against left-wingers.

The proof of his success came in the elections of 1948, deemed critical by the CIA. In the region where Giuliano's bandits had terrorised the left, votes for the Christian Democrats more than doubled. Sicily was firmly in their control and the left had been soundly defeated. The Mafia – through Giuliano – were triumphant. Having delivered this electoral victory, Giuliano now expected a prize – a pardon and a political position perhaps. When this failed to arrive, he turned on some of his backers. Senior Christian Democrat politicians were gunned down. In July 1949, Giuliano became more brazen. Near his mountain hide-out in Montelepre, his men ambushed a police patrol and killed five officers. A report in the *New York Times* described an even more ambitious attack:

> Sicilian bandits carried out under cover of darkness early this morning a surprise attack with hand grenades and machine guns against two Carabinieri barracks in the small town of Partinico, probably in an effort to replenish their supplies of weapons and ammunition. The attack failed as the Carabinieri kept the bandits at bay while reinforcements arrived in trucks from nearby points.

The tactics deployed by the police against the bandits reprised those of Cesare Mori. One newspaper report spoke of a mass round-up in which more than a thousand heavily armed police in armoured cars arrested 200 suspected members of Giuliano's gang in the Montelepre area. The mass operations made the police vulnerable and, in August, Giuliano's men launched an ambush on a police column at Bellolampo, not far from Palermo. They used anti-tank mines and hand grenades and killed seven Carabinieri and wounded many more. It sent a shudder through Italy.

Such acts of defiance embarrassed the government and turned many Sicilian conservatives against the bandit. Enough was enough. Even for the Mafia.

Newly elected Christian Democrat Prime Minister Alcide de Gasperi had to break his vacation in the mountain retreat of Sella di Borgo to give his comments on Salvatore Giuliano:

> Nobody can deny that banditry in Sicily has developed in conjunction with special situations both political and social, and it is obvious that the government does not think that it can resolve such problems only with repressive measures. But today attacks are being carried out, there is shooting, there is killing. The first duty of the Ministry of the Interior is to blunt the offensive, to safeguard the security of the person, to impose on all people the power and dominion of the law.

The minster of the interior responded by creating a new 1,500-strong elite force of Carabinieri commanded by veterans of the fight against bandits. It was called the Armed Command for the Suppression of Banditry – CFRB – and was led by Colonel Ugo Luca. He too used Mori methods and indiscriminately swept up anyone with the least suspicion of being involved with Giuliano. An Englishman wandering around Montelepre was arrested and held in army barracks for several days.

This force hounded Giuliano, reducing his activities dramatically. Going beyond road patrols, which could be easily ambushed, Colonel Luca sent his men in groups of ten across the countryside, sweeping areas, and keeping in contact with field radios. In October 1949, Colonel Luca gave an interview to *Messaggero* about his pursuit of Giuliano:

> In the past, owing to the troubled situation in Italy and especially in Sicily, Giuliano had some political contacts; some of Giuliano's relations at times were seated in the distinguished persons stands at 'separatist' public ceremonies . . . [but] now he is isolated on every side. He now hates all parties; he is in a sanguinary psychological period . . . The hills about Palermo are a very difficult operating ground owing to the many natural grottoes and the artificial hiding places very ably prepared in past years by the bandits themselves . . .
>
> Giuliano has two powerful allies, money and fear. It is difficult to say where fear ends and the conscious 'omerta' of the population begins. It is certain that Giuliano is much feared. One man said in public in the Piazza at Montelepre: 'When will this affair end? What are they waiting for to arrest him?' He was found murdered a few hours later in one of the village streets.

Luca was optimistic and believed his Carabinieri were becoming friendly with the local population who had so far sustained Giuliano and his bandits. The *Messaggero* journalist was not so sure. He quoted a priest asked to bless Luca's Carabinieri. In an open air mass, the priest turned towards his congregation of policemen and delivered a chilling speech:

> Dear boys, you are here in Sicily, on these barren hills in touch with danger and ambush. You are here for the good of this island . . . and in respect of the law, you are risking your lives. Well, in order that your task may be made easier, I must at once tell you an unpleasant truth . . . you are hated.

There was shocked silence among the congregation as the priest continued:

> The people in the villages do not consider you as protectors, but as pitiless executors of laws which do not originate in the island. Your arrival in the towns will not be greeted as a liberation but as a cause for mourning: wherever you may go hundreds of people will be detained, arrested, searched, sent to jail. And should you arrest 10 persons in one town, you may be sure that you have struck the whole town. We are all *compari* [close associates] and to be a *compare* is something more than being a cousin or blood relative.

It was an astonishing expression of *omerta* – from a very unexpected source. But the priest knew he had to step back on to the right side of the law and encouraged the Carabinieri to act in a friendly way towards his *compari*:

> You must prove by your action, that you are friends and not enemies of the people, you must make them forget your grey-green uniform, in order that the country people should feel you are their equals, mothers' sons, and should show their trust in you. Only by this means will you succeed in overcoming the net of silence which will certainly surround your work.

It was good advice, but Luca already realised he was engaged in a guerrilla war he could only win if the people turned against the bandit leader. Most importantly, if Giuliano was ultimately protected by *omerta* then he could also fall to it. Sir Victor Mallet at the British Embassy in

Rome underlined this connection in a letter to the Prime Minister Clement Attlee:

> His Majesty's Consul says that there are few Sicilian landlords who do not pay tribute to the Mafia or brigands' agents and it would seem that many of the prominent families of Sicily are anxious lest the suppression of brigandage may also cut at the roots of the Mafia, from which so many of them benefit.

The situation had gone too far for that. Giuliano was an international embarrassment to Italy's leaders. The failure of the minister of the interior to arrest his fellow Sicilian was an easy target for the government's opponents. Such continued humiliation pushed the Italian government towards considering the re-introduction of the methods that had formerly proved successful but unpopular under the Fascists.

That Giuliano and his gang were feeling the heat and thinking of escaping abroad is revealed by a curious story from London's Soho district. Harry Arduino was a small time crook, born in Malta, who worked as a kitchen porter in several Soho restaurants. He served in the Royal Air Force in India during World War II and when he came back he was restless. He got into trading forged passports and in December 1949 he believed he was on to something big.

'Harry said to me one evening that he wished to tell me something', said his girlfriend, Anne Braithwaite Young, in a police statement. 'I told him not to tell me anything he might regret. He said, "Well, I will tell you. Do you know Giuliano?"'

'I said "Who?" and he replied, "The Sicilian bandit. I have an appointment to see him this time." I warned him to be careful and advised him to cut out whatever game he was up to, but he just laughed.' Arduino began to prepare for his trip to Sicily. 'Harry said he had to buy some heavy boots and a tunic for the trip as they had to go up in the mountains. I gave him the money to do this.'

On 8 December 1949, Anne Young accompanied Harry and his associate Edward Franette to Victoria Station where they caught the boat train. 'That is the last time I saw or heard from him,' she said.

In fact, the next time she would see him was in a police photograph of his half-naked corpse propped up outside a shed in Sicily with a massive black bullet hole in his neck. Franette was accused of killing Arduino and was to be extradited to Italy but a legal technicality saw him freed in London without facing charges.

A childhood friend of Arduino, Ernest Zahra, later gave a statement to the Maltese police on what Arduino was doing in Sicily:

> Some time about 1949, Harry Arduino divulged to me that he was trafficking in illegal sale of passports and that he had acquired a number of British passports from Maltese in London and was proceeding to Sicily to sell them to Sicilians in the 'Giuliano' bandit gang. Later I learnt from him that he had been in fact to Sicily and sold the passports and was going there a second time for the same purpose. The next I heard of this man was that he was killed in Sicily.

Arduino's deal had gone bad, but did Giuliano and his gang have the passports? Under Carabinieri pressure it certainly seems they were looking for a way out.

Eight months later, Colonel Luca's cunning and patience finally paid off. He was given a tip-off that Giuliano was in Castelvetrano, a small town in south-west Sicily, far away from his stronghold in the north of the island. It was thought that he might be trying to flee the country. Colonel Luca led the operation and his elite Carabinieri unit approached Castelvetrano in an army truck disguised as a loud-hailer vehicle. The bandit leader was tracked to a brothel where they allowed him to stay until 3.00 a.m. on 5 July 1950. When he left the brothel and moved on to the home of a friend, the Carabinieri followed him until he entered the courtyard of the house. The police then moved in, reported the London *Times*:

> He at once opened fire on them, but fell, riddled by bullets from police tommy-guns. Beside his body was found a submachine-gun, a German revolver, and a telescope. On one of his fingers was a large diamond ring and his belt was fastened with a gold clasp.

The bandit was surrounded as he stepped into a courtyard before dawn, said a *New York Herald Tribune* reporter, who had spoken to Colonel Luca by telephone. The police claimed Giuliano fired wildly, forcing them to reply with a fusillade of bullets that struck him in the chest and head. After official examination to guarantee identification, the bandit was buried at noon.

At the age of just twenty-seven, Giuliano was dead. His criminal reign had lasted seven years, making him the most famous bandit of the period. His rise to power paralleled that of the Separatist movement and when he died, it was the last nail in the coffin of this Mafia-backed project.

'Sicilian romanticism was Giuliano's major asset in his long evasion of justice', said the *New York Herald Tribune*, quoting Colonel Luca:

> Many Sicilians considered the youth a sort of Robin Hood . . . On [one] occasion, the bandit offered to settle his grievances by duelling with the top ten officials of the government. He specified that his only condition was that foreign observers be present in order to guarantee that he receive fair treatment.

'The bandit king will take his place', said an editorial comment, 'in the puppet shows around which the children tirelessly gather; his painted image will stand on Sicilian donkey carts.'

Michele Pantaleone and others tell a story in which Giuliano was shot in the head in his bed in Castelvetrano by one of his own bandits on the orders of Benedetto Minasola, Mafioso of Monreale. That it might have been the Mafia themselves that fingered Giuliano is suggested in a later newspaper story covering the death of two of his gang-members:

> Salvatore Passatempo, the last member of Giuliano's notorious gang, was found dead on Friday night at a deserted spot about forty miles south-west of Palermo. Near him lay the body of Emanuele De Maria, a man with a minor criminal record, and both had been shot in the back by tommy-gun fire.

Who killed the men was a mystery, but the news was received with relief by the surrounding landowners and farmers. 'Some of them, it is conjectured', said the report, 'finding his impositions intolerable, may have employed members of the Mafia to get rid of the bandit and his accomplice. It is believed that the men were killed elsewhere and the corpses taken to the spot where they were found.' It was a classic Mafia execution intended to send a message to the local population. Having for years been intimidated by Giuliano and his bandit army, functioning in its shadow, the Mafia were now back in direct control of crime in their region.

In 1955, a high-ranking Italian judge, Giuseppe Guido Lo Schiavo, declared that the police and the Mafia were working hand in hand. 'People say the Mafia does not respect the police and judiciary', said the judge. 'It's untrue. The Mafia has always respected the judiciary and justice . . . In the prosecution of bandits and outlaws . . . it has actually joined together with the police.'

It was a chilling prospect for the country.

Exactly thirty-three years after he was chased away by the Fascists, Joseph Bonanno was back in Sicily. In the autumn of 1957, he savoured the view from a fancy restaurant on the Piazza Politeama in old Palermo.

It had been a long time since he had walked these streets and many things had changed. Mussolini, Mori and the Black Shirts were long gone. A world war had been fought – his island invaded – tanks rumbling along its roads. Some gangster friends had died. But Bonanno survived and prospered. He was now the head of a Mafia family in New York and had ambitions to take his franchise around the world. Sicily was a key base in this global market.

At first, as he tells the story, Bonanno did not want to go back. He was going to take his wife to Italy the following year, but a friend, a publisher, persuaded him to join him on a trip in October 1957 to open an orphanage.

When Bonanno landed at Rome's Fiumicino airport, he was greeted by an old friend from Castellammare – Bernardo Mattarella. He was now minister of foreign trade for the ruling Christian Democrat party.

In Palermo, Bonanno was welcomed by his former deputy Frank Garofalo, who had seemingly retired there, alongside another family member, John Bonventre. One day, some Sicilian Men of Honour took him for a tour of the city and he visited some of the historical sites he remembered. For lunch, they took him to a restaurant in the Piazza Politeama. The restaurant owner greeted the Mafiosi profusely, kissing their hands and asking for their blessing.

For a moment, Bonanno was left by himself at a table and asked the waiter for a jug of water – but without ice. The waiter returned with a pitcher full of ice. Bonanno complained and the waiter mumbled under his breath in the local dialect, thinking the American could not understand him. How wrong he was! Bonanno grabbed the jug of water and smashed it on the waiter's head – blood and glass everywhere. As the waiter cowered on the floor, Bonanno berated him in the local tongue. The rest of the Mafiosi returned and the waiter, shaking on the floor, begged for his life. Bonanno was in no mood for any further violence and assured the restaurant owner it was no big problem. He even gave the waiter a generous tip at the end of the meal.

That was Bonanno's most vivid anecdote of his return to Sicily, but he also visited his home town of Castellammare, viewed the Greek Temple at Segesta he so loved and placed flowers on his parents' tomb. After a few weeks, he got ill and returned to his new home in America. He was glad to be back.

In truth, however, the trip to Sicily was not a happy accident. It was, in fact, part of a major Mafia strategy to put Bonanno and his associates at the very centre of an international crime network. The real purpose of Bonanno's trip was to organise the Mafiosi of Palermo and western Sicily into an efficient arm of the Mafia in America. He wanted to see them form a Commission, just as the Mafia had in the US, in which leading crime families came together to co-ordinate their criminal enterprises.

Bonanno and his deputy, Garofalo, who was not in retirement, but highly active making connections with Sicilian Mafiosi, brought them together at the Grand Hotel Et Des Palmes in Via Roma, central Palermo. The Sicilian contingent was led by Don Giuseppe Genco Russo – the man Don Calogero Vizzini had supposedly called on to help him assist the Allies at Monte Cammarata.

Together, in the gilt and mirrored *belle époque* splendour of the Sala Wagner (the composer had stayed there to work on his opera *Parsifal*), the American and Sicilian Mafiosi discussed how Sicily would become the major transit point for heroin out of Europe to America. The little coastal resorts of north-western Sicily, such as Castellammare del Golfo, with their food export companies, would provide perfect cover for exporting drugs to the US.

If Bonanno had played a very minor role in World War II – compared to Lucky Luciano, Meyer Lansky and Vito Genovese – he had positioned himself perfectly to benefit enormously from the regime they helped establish in post-war Sicily. The island was ruled by the Christian Democrats who had accommodated the Mafia in order to defeat the Communists. All this, with the blessing of the United States government, who faced bigger enemies in the Cold War.

For Bonanno, the view from that restaurant in Palermo could not have been better. He returned to his island as the conquering hero with the Mafia in a stronger position – both in Sicily and America – than they had been in the three previous decades.

Everything was looking very good, but the next month it all went very wrong.

Bonanno returned to the US when he did, not because he was ill or tired, but because he was expected to report on his Sicilian deal-making to other Mafiosi at a major gathering of crime family heads at Apalachin, a small country town in upstate New York in November 1957. The prime mover of this crime conference was Vito Genovese who had just eliminated Albert Anastasia. He now saw himself as Boss of Bosses, but Lucky Luciano, sidelined in Italy from the main Mafia business in the US, had one final blow to deliver against his rival.

Luciano, along with Frank Costello and Meyer Lansky, appears to have been part of a conspiracy that informed the police about the meeting at Apalachin and it was raided, with top Mafiosi farcically forced to flee into the woods to escape the law. The long list of Mafiosi recorded at Apalachin, including Bonanno, was a revelation for the national press and confirmed their view of the Mafia as the leading force of organised crime in the US.

Luciano, sitting back in his villa in Naples, could afford to laugh at Genovese's embarrassment at Apalachin. Within a few months, he set up the mobster in a narcotics deal that sent him to jail for the rest of his life.

Apalachin also shook the world of Joseph Bonanno. 'We were falling, falling, falling part', he wrote. Apalachin forced him out of the shadows and US government investigations dogged him ever after. The end of Genovese and Luciano as rulers of the New York underworld tempted him into his own empire-building, but within five years, his crime family was split by deadly rivalry – dubbed the Banana War – and he was forced into retirement.

When Bonanno published his memoirs in 1983, the US government wanted to use the book as proof of a Mafia conspiracy. When Bonanno refused to answer questions before a grand jury, he was jailed. He died in 2002 at the age of ninety-seven.

Lucky Luciano died from a heart attack at Naples airport in 1962.

Meyer Lansky retired to Israel in 1970 after making a fortune out of his casinos in Cuba and Las Vegas. His presence embarrassed the Israelis and he was forced back to the States where he was prosecuted for income tax evasion. The case failed and Lansky carried on making money during his retirement in Florida. Like most Jewish gangsters, and unlike most Italian-American mobsters, he kept his wife and children well away from his business and it died with him – there would be no criminal heir.

One of Lansky's proudest moments was when his second son, Paul, graduated as a captain from West Point, the US Military Academy. He was among the first American military advisors sent to Vietnam in 1962. 'He believed very firmly in the American role in Vietnam', said Lansky. 'And now that we're no longer involved, people are beginning to see the true situation. Paul was right. I always shared his views about our role in Vietnam.'

One of Paul Lansky's roommates at West Point was the son of a Colonel Freeman, a close colleague of General Eisenhower. When Ike became president, Meyer Lansky received a surprise invitation to the inauguration. Lansky presumed it was a mistake and the colonel didn't know his gangster reputation. He politely refused:

> But I got a reply from Colonel Freeman saying something like 'Don't forget to come to the ceremony. Don't you know that in our clubs we play the same slot machines that you've got in your casinos, and that we used to drink your bootleg whisky?'
>
> That certainly made me smile. But I sent thanks and regrets again. Big public things just aren't my style.

Lansky died in 1983. The era of Lucky Luciano and his gangsters was finally over.

Chapter Twenty

Ending the Myth

Did the Allies strike a deal with the Mafia to win the war in Sicily? It is a seductive idea that suits many supporters of conspiracy theories – especially those who have long objected to America's foreign policy. It is just another piece of evidence for them of American skulduggery. But, having investigated the allegation, it appears to be untrue. Far from it, in fact.

The American, British and Canadian armies won the battle for Sicily through impressive logistical organisation and sheer hard fighting. The thousands of casualties suffered by all Allied forces is testament to this. It was no walk-over victory. The nature of the Sicilian campaign, with a relatively smooth conquest in the west of the island, but a hard-fought series of combats in the east, was not determined by any intervention by the Mafia on behalf of the Allies, but due to Axis decisions. The Italians declined to fight and the Germans chose to remove as many of their troops and vehicles as possible across the sea to mainland Italy by conducting a fighting withdrawal along the eastern coast.

Yes, it is true that one department of one US defence intelligence agency – US Naval Intelligence – did strike an alliance with Lucky Luciano and his Mafia henchmen. The primary concern of this was to ensure the security of America's East Coast against enemy sabotage. At the time, Allied shipping was suffering badly from Axis submarine attacks and there were incidents of Nazi saboteurs on American territory. There was also significant support in New York among immigrant communities for Fascism and Nazism. All this is proven and explains US Navy concerns.

This collaboration between the US government and the underworld was then expanded to include preparations for the invasion of Sicily, requiring mobsters to provide any information available that was thought to be useful. But when it came to its deployment in the war zone, there were only four US Naval Intelligence agents present on the beaches during the first days of the invasion – just four. Their contribution, though useful, was tiny and cannot be said to have had any major impact on the rest of the campaign.

The hundreds of pages of subsequent witness interviews provided by the Herlands investigation have swollen this minor contribution out of all proportion to any other intelligence aspect of the campaign. The reality is that by far the largest intelligence contribution to the campaign was provided by the US Army Counter-Intelligence Corps, who had 80 agents on the ground throughout the fighting. There is no evidence whatsoever of them entering into any kind of alliance with the Mafia in Sicily – before or during the campaign. Similarly, the OSS went out of its way not to employ Mafia contacts either before or during the campaign. That OSS agents in Palermo then linked up with local Mafiosi after the campaign is a different matter, although crucial to later interpretations of American relations with the Mafia. The same is true of the British. They won no significant advantages in their fighting through contacts with local Mafiosi.

The most famous reported encounter between Allied troops and the Mafia – the so-called Mafia-delivered victory at Cammarata/Villalba – is largely the invention of the author Michele Pantaleone. Although a fearless opponent of the Mafia, his view of events is biased and not backed up by any American military field records. In fact, at the time of the supposed intervention by Don Calogero Vizzini, American troops were already miles ahead of both Villalba and Cammarata, having secured the road to Palermo against minimal Axis opposition.

Yes, there are at least two pieces of evidence of the British and the Americans recommending that contacts be made with the Sicilian Mafia to help in any projected invasion of the island – and the American suggestion of arming the Mafia as guerrillas was approved at a very senior level – but neither of these pre-campaign suggestions appears to have been acted on. There was no need. Events moved far more rapidly and in different ways than any intelligence report could have predicted.

What about the second great accusation? That it was thanks to the Allies that the Mafia were returned to power in Sicily. This is far more complicated and reveals a problem faced by any force occupying another country. The same problem has been a challenge in more recent years to Coalition forces in the Middle East – how to dismantle a corrupt regime and yet still impose law and order.

It is very difficult to assess the success of Mussolini's and Mori's campaign against the Mafia in Sicily in the 1920s. On the one hand, many Mafiosi were rounded-up and imprisoned or fled abroad. On the other, senior members of the Mafia avoided arrest and continued to thrive by carrying out their activities 'underground' or seeking an accommodation with the Fascist authorities. That the word 'Mafia' appeared rarely in Sicilian press coverage of crime in the 1930s did not reflect a true triumph of the Fascists, but merely underlined the illusory nature of what perhaps was always only ever intended to be a propaganda victory. In truth, it seems, the Mafia survived the purges and the Fascists covered up their resurgence by merely avoiding any mention of them.

By the time the Allies arrived in Sicily in 1943, there was a determined Mafia network throughout the island. By dismantling the Fascist hold on local rule, the Allies created a power vacuum that was easily filled by local Mafiosi. This was neither the fault nor the intention of the Allies. It was certainly not a pre-planned conspiracy among the Americans or British to resurrect the Mafia. It needed no such outside help. In fact, it is clear in numerous reports from Lord Rennell downwards that the view of the Allied occupying forces was that the Mafia were a criminal nuisance – a virus Lord Rennell called them – that should be crushed. The Allies were aware of the part played by the Mafia in local crime and worked very hard to reduce the food shortages and black-market exploitation that made the mobsters rich in the immediate post-conflict period.

In many ways, Lord Rennell was very successful in handling the Allied administration of Sicily. He took a tough stance on law and order. He was quickly aware of the problems he faced, who was responsible for them, and sought to strengthen his administration by making maximum use of the local police force. He put much effort into re-building the confidence of the Carabinieri and reinstating their authority on the island. It was a clever move.

Although Lord Rennell and his administrators did their best to halt low-level crime and break the black market – arresting many minor

Mafiosi in the process – it appears that not all Allied Civil Affairs Officers were on the same side. Some exploited the situation to make money for themselves. Mafiosi worked with these Allied officers to divert large amounts of Allied supplies on to the black market. The most notorious of these black market gangsters was Vito Genovese and he appears to have enjoyed the high level support of numerous US officers – among them Colonel Poletti. Over and over again, Poletti is criticised by other Allied officers – principal among them being Lord Rennell – for his poor administration of Palermo and his closeness to local Mafiosi. But the most damning evidence against him was his eccentric lack of interest in helping the heroic Orange C. Dickey deal with Vito Genovese.

The early success of Lord Rennell's imposition of law and order on the island encouraged senior Mafiosi to pursue their grab for power through politics instead. Initially, they backed the Separatist movement as it promised them an independent realm far removed from the state intrusion of mainland Italy. The Mafia and the Separatists made much of their supposed support from the Allies, but this was mischief making and denied frequently by the Allied authorities. The British or Americans seem never to have seriously pursued a policy of encouraging an independent Sicily, as part of a strategy to establish an Allied military base in the Mediterranean. The OSS alone appears to be the most strongly convinced agency of such a conspiracy, but this reflected an anti-British bias that pervaded much of its work in Sicily throughout World War II. Curiously, in this period, the OSS feared the British Empire much more than the Soviet Union.

As Sicilian gratitude for Allied liberation quickly passed, a traditional malaise infected the island, favouring the Mafia and Separatists. Life might have been bad under the Fascists, went the popular feeling, but at least there was a strong sense of order. Once Allied troops moved on to other battlefields in early 1944, it was left to the Italians to maintain law on the island and they found themselves overstretched and outgunned. Heavily armed with captured Axis and Allied weapons, criminal gangs took a grip of the country. The remaining Allied administrators could only stand back and witness the decline in security. They certainly did not encourage it.

At this stage, the 1944–7 period, the Allies wanted to see an end to Mafia-backed chaos and the restoration of a strong Italian state. Mafia-backed Separatism simply weakened the central state and so they did not support it. The activities of EVIS and other bandits alarmed them.

Major left-wing local election victories in 1947 brought a significant change in Allied attitudes to the Mafia – or more truly American attitudes. The year before, the Separatists had been big losers in the election and ceased to be a power in the island. As a result, the Mafia dumped their link with them and embraced the only other conservative political force – the Christian Democrats. This shift in political allegiances changed the attitudes of the Allies. Up until this point, the Mafia in Sicily were a lawless nuisance. After this, they became an integral part of the Western strategy against Communism. It may well be that close ties established between a handful of OSS agents in Palermo with local Mafiosi helped this process.

The OSS mutated into the CIA in 1947 and became major interpreters of Cold War threats for the US government. The CIA now portrayed the Mafia as effective enforcers for the Christian Democrats who were the favoured conservative alternative to left-wingers in government in Italy.

Giuseppe Alessi, one of the founders of the Christian Democratic Party in Sicily, quoted a colleague on the need of his party for armed support. 'The Communists use similar kinds of violence against us, preventing us from carrying out public rallies. We need the protection of strong men to stop the violence of the Communists', he said. Alessi did not like it, but could not see any alternative. With Stalin funding the Communist Party in post-war Italy, the Christian Democrats had to win the struggle with the Communists and they had the most powerful backers in the world – Cold War America. 'I was in the minority', recalled Alessi, 'and the "group" [the Mafia] entered en masse and took over the party.'

The US backed the Christian Democrats with aid and influence and the Mafia were allowed to help deliver them election victory in Sicily in 1948. This established a near fifty-year alliance between the Mafia and the Christian Democrats that suited American anti-Communists just fine. It is from this, largely, that the myth derives that America engineered the resurrection of the Mafia in World War II. That is not true, but the end result was.

For an Italian view of these events, it is worth turning to two leading historians of the Mafia, Salvatore Lupo of the University of Catania, and Professor Francesco Renda. Both are sceptical of the idea of a wartime Allied plot to put the Mafia back in power.

> It has often been assumed [says Lupo] that the Mafia owes its rebirth and subsequent success to an agreement made with the Allies when they disembarked in Sicily in 1943. The available sources do not confirm this view, but indicate that the relationships which developed between the Allied administration, the Mafia, local business leaders, the church and the political class were always in flux.

The myth is difficult to shift, partly, explains Lupo, because:

> . . . the most pressing reason for the long survival of the myth of the American conspiracy, is that for Italians the 'alien conspiracy' theory nicely removes their own responsibility for what occurred in Sicily as a consequence of voting for fifty years for a party like the Christian Democrats or for supporting opposition parties that were completely incapable of upsetting the prevailing system of power.

What is true is that the renewed relations between American and Sicilian Mafiosi after the war, thanks to mobsters like Lucky Luciano, Vito Genovese and Joseph Bonanno, contributed to a new lease of life for the Mafia as an international crime organisation.

> Americans who are accustomed to think of the Mafia as something that was imported from Sicily [says Lupo] may be shocked to learn that in the period after the Second World War many Italians considered the Mafia to be an import from the United States where it had acquired the attributes of gangsterism that made it different from and more dangerous than the older, indigenous Mafia.

In his definitive *Storia della Sicilia* Professor Renda also denies any intentional conspiracy on behalf of the Allies:

> The way in which the Mafia and the Allied military forces infiltrated Sicily's administration is particularly significant since it appeared to be entirely spontaneous . . . There is no proof or evidence to support any predetermined or intentional conspiracy despite that fact that the occupying forces, from the very top to the very bottom, effectively handed over power in Sicily to the hands of the Mafia.

This happened because the Allies never had any intention of hanging round longer than a few months. They did not want to rule

Sicily any longer than they needed to achieve their war aims. The Mafia took over because they were more effective at dominating their local administration than any political party, especially the Communists. By using violence – often supplied by the bandit Salvatore Giuliano – at the most crucial electoral times they out-fought and out-threatened a Communist movement that infiltrated many other European countries in this period. Whether this was good or bad in the long term for the people of Sicily is a point for debate.

Was it morally right for one department of one US intelligence agency to strike a deal with a criminal mastermind such as Lucky Luciano? This is a curiously early twenty-first-century view of warfare. At the time, the US Naval intelligence agents involved had no such problem in justifying their action – you do what you do to win.

On a philosophical level, surely a government is morally obliged to conduct a war in the most effective way possible to protect its citizens? That fundamental moral obligation should override any other moral concerns about the methods used to achieve that end. British and Americans have formed alliances with all sorts of morally dubious characters in order to win wars around the world over the last sixty years. The Western alliance with Josef Stalin in World War II is just the most obvious example of this – a more murderous gangster cannot be found anywhere in our recent history. Overall, however, the worst moral result is to lose.

In the event, the so-called devil's pact with Luciano is a minor footnote in the history of World War II – and not a major scandal. The Allies did not get and did not need the help of the Mafia to win their campaign in Sicily. Far bigger powers of industrial organisation, economic competence and military expertise eventually defeated the Axis forces in Europe – and the Mafia played no part in that.

As always, it was thanks to the sacrifice of honest soldiers that the Allies won the war.

Notes on Sources

Abbreviations

NA – British National Archives at Kew.

NARA – US National Archives and Records Administration at College Park, Maryland.

Chapters 1–3

Mori quotes are from Cesare Mori's *The Last Struggle with the Mafia*. This is a translation by Orlo Williams of his memoirs, *Con la mafia ai ferri corti*, published in Italy in 1932. It is the principal source for Mori's campaign against the Mafia. For other accounts of Mori's victory at Gangi see Petacco, *Il prefetto di ferro*, pp. 85–99; Spano, *Faccia a faccia con la mafia*.

Most Mussolini quotes are from his *My Autobiography*. The foreword was written by former US Ambassador Richard Washburn Child, who claims to have encouraged Mussolini to write it. It has been suggested, however, that it was Mussolini's brother, Arnaldo, who wrote the autobiography for him; see Ridley, *Mussolini*, pp. 188–9.

Mussolini's police record is quoted in de Begnac, *Vita de Benito Mussolini*, Vol. ii, pp. 291–4. His Agrigento speech is in *Opera Omnia de Benito Mussolini*, edited by E. & D. Susmel, Vol. XX, p. 264; translated by Lisa Donafee. The Orlando speech is recorded in the Sicilian newspaper *L'Ora*, 29 July 1925 and is quoted in Duggan, *Fascism and the Mafia*, p. 117. Professor Duggan's book is the best English-language account of the Mafia–Fascist struggle in the 1920s; see also Blok, *The Mafia of a Sicilian Village 1860–1960*. Cucco account comes from Cucco, A., *Il Mio Rogo* (unpublished autobiography), Chap. 2, pp. 2–3, quoted in Duggan.

The Don Ciccio Cuccia story comes from Pantaleone, *The Mafia and Politics*, pp. 47–8; Norman Lewis repeats it in *The Honoured Society*, pp. 59–60. Pantaleone's *Mafia and Politics* is a translation of his *Mafia e Politica*, published in Turin in 1962. It is the source for many of the best Mafia stories told by Lewis in *The Honoured*

Society. Denis Mack Smith, in his preface to Pantaleone's English edition, says 'This is therefore a fundamental document, authentic and original. Mr Norman Lewis, for example, though he does not say so, drew very substantially on Pantaleone for his book.' Pantaleone's accusations of Fascist torture in *Mafia and Politics*, p. 49, are repeated in *The Honoured Society*, p. 62, and have been repeated in many other Mafia books since. Lewis's book first appeared as a series of articles for *The New Yorker*.

It is worth noting that there were very few recorded deaths associated with Mori's crusade. If this had been Nazi Germany, surely more Mafiosi would have been shot before they even reached the courtroom? Professor Duggan says: 'The aim of the operation, certainly in Mori's mind (and he was an old-fashioned Nationalist), was to show that the state was both stronger and morally superior to the mafia. Use of violence by the state had tended to backfire badly in Sicily. Second, once police testimony had been accepted as decisive in trials they didn't need much in the way of confession evidence. And the key charge was "criminal association", not specific crimes.' (Correspondence with author)

All Bonanno quotes come from Bonanno & Lalli, *A Man of Honour*. In regards to Bonanno's protest at wearing a black shirt as a student in Palermo, the importance of this garb is corroborated by Salvatore Cabasino who graduated in 1937. 'I had to have a black shirt made', he recalled, 'so I could get my university degree. I also had a friend who was a member of the Fascist party and he provided me with a Fascist membership card for my graduation. I've still got it.' (Author interview)

All Charlotte Gower quotes are from Gower Chapman, *Milocca: A Sicilian Village*. See also King & Patterson, *A Sicilian Village in the Fascist Era: Milocca Revisited*. Poems praising Mussolini and Mori are quoted in Gower Chapman, pp. 248–50.

International newspaper quotes are from: 'Mussolini and the Mafia', London *Times*, 20 January, 1928, p. 14; 'Sicilian Woman, 62, Led Band of Mafisti [*sic*]', *New York Times*, 16 January 1928, p. 5; 'Mori's War on the Mafia', *New York Times*, 17 January 1928, p. 28; Cortesi, A., 'The Mafia Is Dead, a New Sicily is Born', *New York Times*, 4 March 1928, p. 87; 'Italy Rounds Up 400 in Drive on Mafia', *New York Times*, 23 June 1934, p. 30. A good account of Petrosino's career is in Radin, E. D., 'Detective in a Derby Hat', *New York Times*, 12 March 1944, p. 17.

Chapter 4

This account of Fascist activity in New York in the 1920s is based mainly on contemporary newspaper reports. Newspaper quotes are from: '27 Hurt as NY Fascisti Invade Socialist Hall', *New York Herald Tribune*, 17 August 1925, p. 4; 'Six Men Stabbed in a Fascist riot', *New York Times*, 17 August 1925, p. 32; 'Mussolini Debate Turns into Clash', *New York Times*, 12 March 1928, p. 2; 'Mussolini Doubts Democracy Here', *New York Times*, 11 January 1926, p. 4; 'Green Warns Labor of Fascist Menace', *New York Times*, 23 December 1925, p. 1; Tucker, M, 'Carlo Tresca', *The Greenwich Villager*, 22 April 1922, pp. 1–3; 'Deplores Fascismo Here', *New York Times*, 26 March 1923, p. 3; 'Mussolini Snubs Cotillo', *The World*, 30 October 1923, p. 10; 'Garfield Rebukes East on Italians', *New York Times*, 4 August 1925, p. 23;

'Police Prevent Italian Battle at Garibaldi House', *New York Herald Tribune*, 5 July 1925, p. 6; 'Fascisti and Reds in Two Riots here over Garibaldi Fete', *New York Times*, 5 July 1925, pp. 1 & 3; 'Two Fascisti Die in Bronx', *New York Times*, 31 May 1927, pp. 1 & 7; 'Mussolini Foes Kill 2 in Bronx Fascist Feud', *New York Herald Tribune*, 31 May 1927, pp. 1 & 4; 'Kill Two Fascisti in Bronx Street', *The World*, 31 May 1927, pp. 1 & 3. Witness criticism of Count Ignazio Thaon di Revel quoted from Cannistraro, *Blackshirts in Little Italy*, p. 86, an excellent short account of this period.

Bonanno quotes are from Bonanno & Lalli, *A Man of Honour*, pp. 62, 64, 70, 104–5 & 127. Luciano quotes are from Gosch & Hammer, *The Last Testament of Lucky Luciano*, pp. 94–6. Valachi quote is from Maas, *The Valachi Papers*, p. 96. Newspaper quotes are from: 'Racket Chief Slain by Gangster gunfire', *New York Times*, 16 April 1931, pp. 1 & 15; 'Says 12 Witnessed Gangster Killing', *New York Times*, 26 September 1931, p. 4. Aside from cited first-hand accounts, good overviews of the Castellammarese War and the rise of Luciano appear in Sifakis, *The Mafia File*, and Short, *Crime Inc.*

Chapter 5

Lansky quotes are from Eisenberg, Dan & Landau, *Meyer Lansky: Mogul of the Mob*, pp. 181, 184–5. See also Lacey, *Little Man: Meyer Lansky and the Gangster Life*. Luciano quotes are from Gosch & Hammer, *The Last Testament of Lucky Luciano*, pp. 31 & 265. Dewey quotes are from Hughes, *Thomas E. Dewey: Attorney for the People*, p. 86, and 'Lucania Convicted with 8 in Vice Ring on 62 Counts Each', *New York Times*, 8 June 1936, p. 8.

Hitler's Ford quote cited in Lacey, *Ford: The Men and the Machine*, p. 218. See also Wallace, *The American Axis*. Other Hitler quote is from Trevor-Roper, *Hitler's Table-Talk*, p. 618. On Nazis in America see Hoke, *It's a Secret*, p. 299; Heym, *Nazis in the USA*, p. 8; Stein, A., 'More Fond Memories of Menahan Street', *Times Newsweekly*, Ridgewood NY, 29 July, 2004; 'Veterans Fight City's Nazis on Hitler Birthday', *New York Herald Tribune,* 21 April 1938, pp. 1 & 7; 'Seven are Injured at Nazi Rally', *New York Times*, 21 April 1938; 'Germany Protests "Insult" by Mayor', *New York Times*, 5 March 1937. See also Lawrence, *The Coming American Fascism*, Higham, *American Swastika*, and Arad, *America, its Jews, and the Rise of Nazism.*

Max Hinkes's story of fighting Bund Nazis in Newark comes from Rockaway, *But He Was Good to His Mother*, pp. 231–2. Rockaway is Professor of Jewish history at Tel Aviv University. Was there a difference in the response of Italian and Jewish gangsters to the patriotic demands of World War II? 'You have to remember that Italy was allied with Germany during World War Two', explains Rockaway. 'When Mussolini came to power in the 1920s and throughout the 1930s, many Italian Americans were very proud and supportive of him. Mussolini gave them a sense of pride because he made Italy seem to be a world power. Once the war began many Italian-Americans expressed ambivalence about him. Nevertheless, Italian-Americans served in the armed forces and behaved admirably. As for Jews, they had no such ambivalence about Hitler and Germany. They hated him and wanted to see him and his regime destroyed. Everyone knew about Germany's violent anti-Semitic policies toward the Jews as soon as Hitler came to power. Jewish gangsters had acted against German Bundists in the US and Jews went willingly into the army and other branches of service to fight against Hitler.' (Correspondence with author)

The account of Thomsen's efforts to restrain Nazi activity in America is based on his telegrams sent to the German Foreign Ministry on 27 March 1940, 21 May 1940, 12 June 1940, 13 June 1940, all published in *Documents on German Foreign Policy*. The account of the Duquesne spy ring is based on the report in the US Department of Justice, Federal Bureau of Investigation, IC 65-8946. Edited highlights of the FBI surveillance film were screened as a motion picture short in 1942 entitled *The FBI Front*. See also 'Japanese Is Linked to Nazi Spies In Pre-Pearl Harbor Plots Here', *New York Times*, 21 September 1942, p. 17, and 'Columbus Day Crowd Boos Mayor and Shouts "Vivas" for Mussolini', *New York Times*, 13 October 1938, p. 1. Haffenden quote comes from Eisenberg *et al*, *Meyer Lansky*, p. 181.

Chapters 6–7

The principal source for the deal between Lucky Luciano and US Naval Intelligence is the Herlands Report of 1954. The original copy of this is part of the Thomas E. Dewey archive in the University of Rochester Library, State of New York. It was, at the time, a secret report and it has never been published. New York State Commissioner of Investigation William B. Herlands conducted the inquiry. It was undertaken at the request of Dewey in order to investigate the rumours of duplicity following the premature release of Luciano. Some 57 major witnesses were interviewed and gave sworn accounts of their involvement, producing a total of 2,883 pages of evidence, which was boiled down to 101-page report with appendices.

This account is based on that report and most quotes from the principal figures involved are from affidavits, wire taps and other evidence given to the Herlands investigators. These include Haffenden, MacFall, Espe, Marsloe, Cincotta, Wharton, Kelly, Titolo, Alfieri, Murphy, Hogan, Gurfein, Lyons, McCook, Polakoff, Lanza, Lansky and Luciano. Lansky's recollection of conversations with Haffenden come from Herlands investigation interview with Lansky on 13 April 1954, pp. 3–23; for his assessment of the 'Luciano project' see p. 29. For Marsloe's claim that discussions about the US Navy's use of the underworld dated from before the burning of the *Normandie*, from December 1941, see Herlands investigation interview with him, 3 June 1954, pp. 8–9; Marsloe's doubts about working with Mafia p. 18.

See also Campbell, *The Luciano Project*, based closely on the Herlands Report (Campbell was the editor of Dewey's memoirs); as is Block, 'A Modern Marriage of Convenience: A Collaboration Between Organized Crime and US Intelligence'.

The independent commentary of Luciano and Lansky on these events gives a different point of view. Their quotes come from Gosch & Hammer, *The Last Testament of Lucky Luciano*, and Eisenberg *et al*, *Meyer Lansky: Mogul of the Mob*. The Gosch & Hammer book is based on interviews with the aging gangster in Italy in

1961, the year before he died. The interviews were not recorded on tape and the book is based on written notes. In this process, and no doubt in Luciano's memory of the events, there are some inconsistencies with other reports of the same events. Some historians are very critical of the end result, see Lacey, *Little Man*, p. 451. New York journalist Tony Scaduto considered it a fraud and devoted an 11-page critique to it, see Scaduto, *Lucky Luciano*, pp. 197–208. But other notable recent Mafia historians are happy to quote from it, including Claire Sterling, Robert Rockaway, and Salvatore Lupo.

Meyer Lansky: Mogul of the Mob is based on interviews with Lansky in Israel and elsewhere in the 1970s; they first appeared in Dan Uri's three-part series 'Meyer Lansky Breaks His Silence', *Ma'ariv*, July 1971. It tallies more closely with the events recorded in the Herlands Report, though again adding some interesting extra information. The interviews were not taped, but the conversations were conducted by one of the authors and then transcribed. These books are as close as we will ever get to the authentic words of two top gangsters of the period.

Descriptions of the burning of the *Normandie* come from: '12-Hour Fight Vain', *New York Times*, 10 February 1942, pp. 1 & 7; 'Giant Vessel Afire at Pier, Is Kept Afloat', *New York Herald Tribune*, 10 February 1942, pp. 1–2. For further witness descriptions and photographs of the damage done to the *Normandie*, see Braynard, *A Picture History of the Normandie*, p. 90–101. See also Maxtorne-Grahame, *The Only Way to Cross*, and Harvey, *Normandie: Liner of Legend*. For Luciano's claim that Anastasia set light to the *Normandie*, see Gosch & Hammer, p. 261. For Lansky's corroboration of this see Eisenberg *et al*, pp. 189–90.

Lahousen, Canaris and Hitler quotes on Operation Pastorius come from Lahousen's secret war diary quoted in Wighton & Pies, *They Spied on England*, pp. 195–237. Lansky's claim to know about Operation Pastorius comes from Eisenberg *et al*, p. 197–8.

Vizzini's account of the Luciano deal comes from Vizzini, Fraley, & Smith, *Vizzini*, pp. 76–7. Newspaper report of Luciano's legal plea comes from 'Lucania's Aid in War Cited in Legal Plea', *New York Times*, 9 February 1943, p. 17.

Chapter 8

Luciano's suggestion of putting a contract on Hitler comes from Gosch & Hammer, p. 270. The Siegel hit on Goering and Goebbels story is in Jennings, *We Only Kill Each Other*, p. 74–7; the source is the Countess di Frasso talking to Hollywood mogul Jack Warner. See also Carpozi, *Bugsy: The Godfather of Las Vegas*, pp. 76–7, & Freid, *Rise and Fall of the Jewish Gangster*, p. 246. Berman quote is from Rockaway, *But He Was Good to His Mother*, p. 189.

Reference to Luciano and Jack Diamond setting up a drug deal in Weimar Germany comes from an FBI memorandum, 28 August 1935, FBI File: 39-2141 Section 1. Monzelli quote comes from Hanna, *Vito Genovese*, p. 64. For Genovese in Italy see also Orange C. Dickey's testimony quoted in Reid, *Mafia*, pp. 185–6. Luciano's story (Gosch & Hammer, pp. 271–2) about Genovese supplying drugs to

Ciano is not backed up by any other sources and Ciano's relations with Genovese or drugs are not even mentioned in the latest and most thorough study of Ciano; see Moseley, *Mussolini's Shadow*. Moseley says: 'I have read just about everything ever written about Ciano, and talked to a number of people who knew him, and this is the first time I have heard this story. I believe Luciano must have been talking nonsense. Certainly Ciano's enemies would have referred to this in their memoirs or elsewhere if it had been true.' (Correspondence with author)

For Tresca's murder see 'Assassin slays Tresca, radical, in Fifth Avenue', *New York Times*, 12 January 1943 pp. 1 & 14; 'Carlo Tresca Assassinated on Fifth Avenue', *New York Herald Tribune*, 12 January 1943, pp. 1 & 3; 'Death of Carlo Tresca', *New York Times*, 13 January 1943 p. 22; 'Tresca Slaying still a Mystery', *New York Times*, 13 January 1943 pp. 1 & 12; '5,000 Pay Tribute to Carlo Tresca', *New York Times*, 17 January 1943 p. 40; 'Galante case adjourned', *New York Times*, 6 February 1943 p. 28. See also Gallagher, *All the Right Enemies*, and Pernicone, *Carlo Tresca*. For Charles Siragusa's claim that Lucky Luciano knew the identities of Tresca's murderers and was willing to trade this information, see Herlands investigation interview with Marsloe, 20 July 1954, pp. 3–4.

Bonanno wartime quotes are from Bonanno & Lalli, *A Man of Honour*, pp. 299–300. Valachi quotes are from Maas, *The Valachi Papers*, pp. 169–74. Luciano ration stamp quote is from Gosch & Hammer, pp. 266–7. See also Grutzner, C., Jr., 'Black Markets in "Gas" and Fuel Oil Foiled Here by Scientific Methods', *New York Times*, 21 August 1945, p. 25.

Chapter 9

Churchill's quotes on Sicily are from his own history *The Second World War*, the abridged version published London, 1959, p. 645. For discussion of the Casablanca conference and its strategic implications see Weinberg, *A World at Arms*, pp. 437–41, and Stoler, *Allies and Adversaries*, pp. 103–13. Wedemeyer quote is from Stoler, p. 103.

This account of Haffenden's 'F' Section and his gathering of information about Sicily is based on the Herlands Report, including quotes from Haffenden, MacFall, Wharton, Marsloe, Polakoff and Lansky. Rear Admiral Pye's speech is in the Herlands Report, Appendix V. Judge Wallace's comments on Lanza come from '"Socks" Lanza gets 7 to 15 Year Term', *New York Times*, 30 January 1943, p. 17. For Marsloe's assertion that any methods were valid in defence of his country, including working with the underworld, see Herlands investigation interview with him, 3 June 1954, pp. 29–30; for his own involvement in research for Sicily, see pp. 19–20; for his account of mission to North Africa, see pp. 22–3. Lansky's recollections about Sicily research come from Herlands investigation interview, 13 April 1954, pp. 24–8.

Luciano's denial of involvement in Sicily is in Gosch & Hammer, p. 267; but see also p. 259. Lansky's story about Luciano wanting to parachute into Sicily is in Eisenberg *et al*, pp. 208–9. Kefauver and Del Grazio quotes are from Kefauver, *Crime in America*, p. 37, based on testimony taken during the Kefauver Senate Committee enquiry into organised crime in 1951. For Wharton's claim that Luciano was prepared to go to Sicily to help war effort, see Herlands investigation written statement by Captain Wallace S. Wharton, 23 June 1954, p. 5. For Lansky's denial of involvement of White and De Grazio in Luciano deal, see Herlands investigation interview with Lansky on 13 April 1954, p. 29.

Evidence of British interest in contacting Mafiosi on Sicily comes from IS (O) *Handbook on Politics and Intelligence Services*, 1943, pp. 7–12 & 40 (NA: WO 220/403). Evidence of wider US military interest in arming Sicilian Mafia and supporting them as a guerrilla force comes from *Special Military Plan for Psychological Warfare in Sicily*, a report prepared by the Joint Staff Planners for the US Joint Chiefs of Staff, 9 April 1943, pp. 48–62 (NA: WO 204/3701).

Chapter 10

Sicilian reports of violent clashes with Germans come from Rodd, G. G. R., 'British Interrogation Report of Sicilian PsW', 28 May 1943, p. 3 (NA: WO 208/4542). Intercepted German order from Kesselring, instructing German soldiers to go round Sicily in parties with side arms, from 5 June 1943 (NA: HW 1/1717).

Foreign Office report of Sicilian resistance is contained in letters from three anonymous Poles living in Italy, sent 12 December 1941 (NA: FO 371/29931). See also Foreign Office telegram, 22 October 1941, about tearing up ration cards, and 'Internal Situation in Italy', Foreign Office report, 5 October 1941, both in NA: FO 371/29930.

US Joint Intelligence Committee (JIC) report, Washington DC, saying British landing might be welcome, sent to the War Cabinet Offices in London on 28 October 1941 (NA: FO 371/29931). 'Sforza says Italy is Ready to Rebel', *New York Times*, 3 June 1942, p. 6. 'Sicilians in the United States', report by Vanni Buscemi-Montana, 15 July 1942, passed on to OSS, talking about Mafia resistance (NARA: RG 226, Entry 142, Box 2). Passages about separatist feeling in Sicily in *Memorandum on conditions and politics in Sicily* prepared by the British Political Warfare Executive in August 1942 (NA: FO 871/35220). 'Mussolini Neglected the Sicilians' London *Observer*, 11 July 1943, press clipping in War Office file (NA: WO 208/4542). FBI interview with Bavarian lawyer contained in US JIC report, 20 October 1941 (NA: FO 371/29931).

American proposal regarding US character of military administration of Sicily attached to a telegram sent by Anthony Eden from the Foreign Office to Lord Halifax, Ambassador in Washington, 22 May 1943. Telegram from Halifax about Italian-American interest in Sicily sent 2 June 1943. Telegram from Roosevelt to Churchill about US character of military administration sent 14 April 1943, and Churchill's response 15 April 1943. Macmillan's comments on British interests in the Mediterranean sent 28 February 1943 and Churchill's rebuke sent 4 March 1943. All these documents contained in NA: PREM 3/229.

All quotes from Max Corvo and his son, William Corvo, about the OSS come from Corvo, *OSS Italy 1942–1945*, pp. xvi, 22, 61, & 65. Donovan's views on the Mafia are quoted in Dunlop, *Donovan: America's Master Spy*, p. 398; for other comments on OSS and Mafia, see also d'Este, *Bitter Victory*, p. 627–9. US State Department memorandum on not using American-Italian units quoted in 'Narrative for Official History of Civil Affairs in Italy (the Sicily campaign)' by D. S. Duff, 1946, Chap. I, Part II, p. 13 (NA: CAB 44/171).

CIC Major Ray's view on the OSS is quoted in 'The CIC in the Sicilian Campaign', *History of the Counter Intelligence Corps*, Vol. xi, p. 106. This is part of a 30-volume history produced by CIC staff in 1953–5 and is reproduced in its entirety in Mendelsohn, *Covert Warfare*. In his introduction, Mendelsohn says: 'In the European Theater of Operations there was a good deal of competition between the Office of Strategic Services (OSS) and the CIC. In fact, the OSS had assumed the counter-espionage mission in Europe and the CIC did largely field security work.'

Chapter 11

Gerald Wellesley's account of Operation Husky comes from his unpublished letter and diary, 10 July–12 August 1943 (NA: WO 220/295). Herbert White's account is from 'Capture of Licata cost US 4 Lives', *New York Times*, 13 July 1943, p. 3. Accounts of US Naval Intelligence activities come from Herlands Report interviews with Marsloe, 3 June 1954, pp. 25–6, with Paul A. Alfieri, 8 June 1954, pp. 19–20, and Joachim Titolo, 8 June 1954, p. 7. Lansky's story about Alfieri is from Eisenberg *et al*, pp. 211–13.

Allied intelligence reports of surrendering Italians, the ETOUSA summary, Alexander's letter to Churchill, all are contained in a file of progress reports on operations in the Allied invasion of Sicily, July–August 1943 (NA: CAB 121/589). See also: 'Italians Surrender in Hundreds', London *Times*, 21 July 1943, p. 4. 'Report of Panzer Division *Hermann Goering* on the Sicilian Campaign', translated as Appendix C in Report No. 14, Historical Section, Army Headquarters, 'The Sicilian Campaign – information from German Sources' (NA: CAB 44/285). Fascist Italian radio broadcast quoted in 'Allied Rule in Sicily', London *Times*, 19 July 1943, p. 4. Description of desperate German resistance from 'Notes on Recent Operations, 6th Battalion, The Durham Light Infantry', by Lt-Col W. I. Watson, 24 August 1943 (NA: WO 231/14).

US Sergeant Jack Foisie's story published in 'Tales from the Sicilian Front', *Yank, The Army Weekly*, New York, 15 August 1943, pp. 4–5.

The Don Calo Vizzini/Luciano 'L' handkerchief story originates with Pantaleone, *The Mafia and Politics*, pp. 54–9; Lewis repeats it in *The Honoured Society*, pp. 12–15; see also Lewis, N., 'Mafia wins Sicily for the US Army' *Sunday Times Magazine*, 28 May 1972, pp. 18–22. On the veracity of Pantaleone's story see Schneider & Schneider, *Reversible Destiny*, p. 49: 'There is now substantial scholarship questioning the accuracy of this story, while at the same time pointing to a more nuanced relationship between American interests and the Mafia as the Cold War took shape.' The anonymous Sicilian witness at Villalba was recorded for a BBC TV documentary *Allied to the Mafia*, broadcast on 13 January 1993.

CIC quotes from 'The CIC in the Sicilian Campaign', *History of the Counter Intelligence Corps*, volume XI, pp. 82, 86, & 91. Information on the 3rd and 45th Divisions near Villalba comes from the official British narrative of the Allied invasion of Sicily, Section 4, Chapter D, 'The Advance to the Etna Line', 14 July–21 July 1943, by Major F. Jones (NA: CAB 44/125). Thanks to Richard L. Baker of the US Army Military History Institute, Carlisle PA, for his help in uncovering the precise reference to the 45th Cavalry Reconnaissance Troop being in the area of Villalba on 19–20 July; references are: Fisher, *The Story of the 180th Infantry Regiment*; Garland, *Sicily and the Surrender of Italy*.

Thanks to Eric van Slander of Modern Military Records, NARA, College Park, Maryland, for his help in uncovering: 'The Daily Journal' of the 45th Cavalry Reconnaissance Troop; the Operations Report of the 3d Cavalry Reconnaissance Troop; and the narrative of the Operations of the 3d Cavalry Reconnaissance Troop Mechanized. In the 5 July 1944 report on the 'History of the 45th Cavalry Reconnaissance Troop May to 9 Sep 1943' (NARA: RG 407, entry 4327, box 11000), no reference whatsoever is made to working with local sources of information such as the Mafia.

Luigi Lumia's memory of Don Calo interrogated by US troops at Villalba appears in Lumia, *Villalba, storia e memoria*, Vol. II, pp. 428–30, translated here for the first time into English; also quoted in Lupo, 'The Allies and the Mafia', p. 25, but not given its full weight.

Accounts of British Field Security experiences come from 'Security work by the Highland Division FS Section during the Sicilian Campaign' by Captain H. Edwards, 13 FS section, 1 October 1943; 'A Day in the Life of a FSO', 29 October 1943 (both in NA: WO 204/824A).

Max Corvo's account of arrival in Sicily comes from Corvo, *OSS Italy*, p. 73. Other story about OSS comes from 'Report on Sicilian Separatism and the Movimento per l'Indipenenza della Sicilia' by Vice-Consul Manley, British Embassy, Rome, 17 April 1946, p. 3 (NA: FO 371/67786); for Max Corvo's version of this story see Corvo, pp. 70–1.

Allied and Axis casualty figures in Sicily from d'Este, *Bitter Victory*. Hitler's comment about Italy always being on the winning side comes from Trevor-Roper, *Hitler's Table-Talk*, entry for 26 August 1942.

Chapter 12

Wellesley's description of his time in Sicily comes from his unpublished letter and diary, 10 July–12 August 1943 (NA: WO 220/295). Many of the details of his posting in Sicily were confirmed in correspondence with the present Duke of Wellington. 'My father died in 1972 at the age of 86', he wrote. 'He was chosen [for AMGOT] because he was a fluent Italian speaker and in fact served in our Embassy in Rome during the 1st World War (where incidentally I was born at that time).' Wellesley's comments on the situation in Catania and on Christian Democrats in

Caltanissetta come from 'Minutes of Meeting of SCAOs and AMGOT headquarters staff held at HQ AMGOT, Palermo' 20–21 August 1943 (NA: FO 371/37327).

Most secret cipher telegram, 1 May 1943, draft directive of Allied administration in Sicily, pp. 2 & 5 (NA: WO 220/272). Lord Rennell set out the rules of Allied government in *Sicily Gazette*, No. 3, 20 October 1943. See also Alexander's proclamation, as Military Governor of Sicily, quoted in full in 'Allied Rule in Sicily', London *Times*, 19 July 1943, p. 4. Colonel Poletti's report on CAOs of 15 July 1943 quoted in 'Narrative for Official History of Civil Affairs in Italy (the Sicily campaign)' by Duff, Chap. 2, Part II, p. 7 (NA: CAB 44/171); see also report by British CAO in Corleone quoted in D. S. Duff, Chap. 2, Part II, pp. 18–21. Colonel Poletti's 14-page report of 31 July 1943 is his 'Memorandum to Fifteenth Army Group – AMG – Siracusa', held in Poletti Papers collection in Herbert H. Lehman Suite and Papers, Columbia University Rare Book and Manuscript Library, New York (AMG file, S3).

Lord Rennell's first detailed report on Allied government in Sicily on 3 August 1943 in a confidential letter to Colonel French; second secret report by Rennell, 20 August 1943, copy sent to War Office, Whitehall; both documents in NA: WO 220/312. Rennell notes 'Reply to Points Made in House of Commons Debate', 3 August 1943, in NA: FO 371/37327. More concerns about Mafia expressed by Rennell in 'Monthly report for August 1943 on the Administration of Sicily', issued 27 October 1943, pp. 5–6, 8, & 17 (NA: CAB 122/442). For details of Rennell's life see obituary in *The Times*, 16 March 1978, p. 20.

Allegation of close relationship between Allied officials and leading Separatists in 'Report on Sicilian Separatism and the Movimento per l'Indipenenza della Sicilia', by Vice-Consul Manley, p. 4 (NA: FO 371/67786). 'Two enemies to be faced in Sicily' quote comes from Duff, *op. cit.*, Chap. 2, Part 1, p.12,; see also Chap. 3, pp. 49–50. NA: CAB 44/171.

London *Times* report on wartime situation in Palermo comes from 'Amgot Facing its Task', 21 September 1943, p. 5. The Allied assault on the 'Mafia fortress' at Castel d'Accia is reported in 'Mafia Chiefs caught by Allies in Sicily', *New York Times*, 10 September 1943, p. 4, & 'Allies Smash Mafia Society, Bane of Sicily', *New York Herald Tribune*, 10 September 1943, p. 4; see also 'Mafia in Sicily', *New York Times*, 11 September 1943, p. 12. Report linking black market with Mafia, see Section II 'Report by Mission to AFHQ for Information of CSO's for Civil Affairs Headquarters COSSAC', 1 November 1943, p. 5 (NA: WO 204/2823).

For comments on Metropolitan Police in Sicily, see Harris, *Allied Military Administration of Italy 1943–1945*, pp. 43 and 52–3. See also Howgrave-Graham, *The Metropolitan Police at War*, p. 59 (NA: MEPO 2/7030); the brief entry on the police in AMGOT concludes 'The story of their adventures and achievements ought to be told, but it is rather outside the scope of this record.' There are no other references in the MEPO files in the NA. William Capp was interviewed by the author on 6 March 2006. Thanks to Martin Gerrard for his memories of his grandfather Bertram Hefford MBE.

Chapter 13

Six-page memorandum by Captain W. E. Scotten, 'The Problem of Mafia in Sicily', 29 October 1943 (NA: FO 371/37327). Captain Scotten's second analysis of Mafia and politics in Sicily is in 'Questions relating to political, social, and economic forces in Sicily and South Italy' prepared for Security Intelligence Subsection of AMG HQ Palermo, 10 December 1943 (NA: FO 371/43918).

Minutes of Meeting of Provincial Civil Affairs Police Officers, concerning Mafia, held at HQ AMGOT, Palermo, 8 September 1943 & 6 October 1943 (NA: FO 371/37327). American EFOOO intelligence 2-page report, referring to poor conditions of Carabinieri, 3 December 1943 (NA: WO 204/12615). Notes on meeting held in Headquarters Island Base Section on 3 December 1943, involving Lt Col Snook, to discuss security in the western part of Sicily (NA: WO 204/827).

OSS Activities, 7-page report by Exp Det G-3, Palermo, admitting to close relationship between OSS and Mafia, 13 August 1943 (NARA: RG 226, Entry 99, Box 39). Russo interview was recorded for a BBC TV documentary *Allied to the Mafia*.

'Italy, Government, Political Parties in Sicily, Mafia and Separatist Movement', US Naval Intelligence report, 10 December 1943 (NARA: RG38/C-10-f/9632-H). JICA Weekly Stability Report for period 10/17 December 1943, on continuing problems in Sicily and relationship between Mafia and Separatists, 20 December 1943 (NA: WO 204/12615).

Chapter 14

FBI account of Genovese's black-market activities in Italy comes from FBI File No: 58-7146. US Army letters of recommendation for Genovese from Dunn and Holmgreen, plus Monzelli's account of Genovese and Vizzini connection, are quoted in Hanna, *Vito Genovese*, pp. 69–74. See also Reid, *Mafia*, pp. 169–70. Luciano quote on Genovese making a million dollars in Gosch & Hammer, p. 273. Level of black-market theft of Allied supplies comes from replies by American Civil Affairs Officers to questions asked at War Cabinet Offices, 19 April 1944 (NA: MAF 83/1338).

Lewis stories about black market, Poletti and Genovese in Naples come from Lewis, *Naples '44*, pp. 119–21. Poletti comment comes from BBC TV documentary *Allied to the Mafia*. Macmillan's interview with Poletti contained in telegram from 'Resident Minister, Algiers, to Foreign Office', 16 January 1944; see also Rennell's comments on Macmillan's telegram, both in NA: FO 371/43918. Rennell despatch about Poletti in North Africa quoted in Duff, *op. cit.*, Chap. I, Part III, p. 29 (NA: CAB 44/171). Poletti on black market in 'Extract from Report of Headquarters Allied Control Commission', 14 April 1944 (NA: MAF 83/1338). Luciano's comments on Poletti in Gosch & Hammer, p. 272. The 27 August 1944 report from Captain J. Kane, Allied Provincial Public Safety Officer in Viterbo, trying to identify Vito Genovese with another bad character comes from the collection of Poletti's papers and letters lodged in Columbia University Library (AMG file, S9).

Dickey's testimony about his investigation of Genovese in Italy is printed almost in full as an appendix in Reid, *Mafia*, pp. 163–84; see also pp. 85–95. Newspaper reports on Genovese are: 'Prisoner's Story "Breaks" 4 Murders by Brooklyn Ring', *New York Times*, 9 August 1944, p. 1; 'AMG Aide in Italy Held in Murder Here', *New York Times*, 25 November 1944, p. 5. List of documents found in Genovese's apartments come from a second interview with Dickey at Beldock's office on 6 September 1945, quoted in full in Reid, *Mafia*, pp. 184–9. Money offered to Dickey quote by Genovese, and 'taking me home' quote, both from Maas, *The Valachi Papers*, p. 179.

Chapter 15

Notes from meeting of Allied intelligence officers in Palermo, about Separatists, 12 January 1944, including JICA and OSS (NA: WO 204/827). JICA Stability Report on black market, 22–28 January 1944 (NA: WO 204/12615). 'Sicilian Separatism with particular reference to the report of Lord Rennell of Rodd' OSS Report, Research and Analysis Branch, 19 November 1943, p. 15 (NARA: RG59, R&A Report 1521). JICA report on Separatist meeting in Palermo, 18 May 1944 (NA: WO204/12618). The best English-language study of Sicilian Separatism in this period is Finkelstein, *Separatism, the Allies, and the Mafia.*

'Selection of a Native Governor' OSS report, reference to Mafia winning out in Palermo selection of first governor, 10 January 1944 (NARA: RG 226/55277). Royal Navy secret reports on Sicilian graft by Captain Waight and Lt-Cdr Mason sent to the Vice-Admiral, Malta, 11 February 1944 (NA: FO 371/43918).

JICA Military Intelligence Division Report on French incident at Xitta, 15 April 1944; CIC Agent Paul De Mare led the investigation (NA: WO 204/ 12660).

Three letters discussing Separatist threat from Radford and Munro in the US Psychological Warfare Branch, Allied Force Headquarters in Algiers, dated 28 June, 3 July, 8 July 1944 (NA: WO 204/6250).

Finocchiaro Aprile's letter to Churchill, 6 July 1944, and his joint letter to various foreign ministers, 20 July 1944, both in NA: FO 371/43918. 'War Recedes From Sicily . . . for and against separatism' London *Times*, 15 July 1944, p. 5. Telegrams from Finocchiaro Aprile sent to Italian government September 1944, intercepted by OSS (NA: WO 204/2168).

Sir Noel Charles's conversation with Marchese Visconti, about Mafia links with Separatists, reported to the Foreign Office on 6 October 1944; see also Charles to Eden, 12 October 1944; both in NA: FO 371/43918. 'Sicilian Separatist Movement', memorandum by Harold C. Swan, British Consul-General at Naples, 23 October 1944 (NA: FO 371/43918). Letter from Lucio Tasca on 31 August 1944 in which the leading Separatist and Mafioso thanked Poletti for his help with the Separatist movement is held in the collection of Poletti's papers in Columbia University Library (AMG file, S9). 'British Policy in Italy' OSS report, usual OSS suspicions of British, Research and Analysis Branch, 15 August 1944, pp iv–v & 23 (NARA: RG59 R&A Report 2318).

Crime increase figures in Palermo are from Blok, *The Mafia of a Sicilian Village*, p. 190. 'New Hydra-Headed Mafia Called Rampant in Sicily', *New York Times*, 31 October 1944, p. 8. Russo report on Palermo riot sent to AFHQ, 19 October 1944 (NA: WO 204/4458). JICA report on meeting of 26 October and Separatist plans for action, 2 November 1944; Letter of warning from Commodore Ellery W. Stone to Ivanoe Bonomi, 3 November 1944; both in NA: WO 204/2168.

Chapter 16

Rennell admits to failings of AMGOT in appointing Mafia mayors in Harris, *Allied Military Administration of Italy*, p. 63. See also similar comments in his first report quoted in Chapter 12. The anonymous Sicilian witness at Villalba of appointment of Don Calo as mayor was recorded for a BBC TV documentary *Allied to the Mafia*. Luigi Lumia quote from Lumia, *Villalba, storia e memoria*, Vol. II, p. 432.

The Pantaleone view of the 'Villalba massacre' is told by Carlo Levi in his preface to Pantaleone, *The Mafia and Politics*, pp. 12–13. An alternative view is given in 'Family Feud Officially Blamed in Communist-Separatist Clash at Villalba' OSS report, Palermo, 2 October 1944 (NARA: RG226/100643). See also Finkelstein, *Separatism, the Allies, and the Mafia*, pp. 95–7. Pantaleone's descriptions of Mafia links with Separatism in *The Mafia and Politics* pp. 66, 73, & 75.

'Report on Sicilian Separatism and the Movimento per L'Indipendenza della Sicilia' by Vice-Consul Manley mentions Mafia links with Separatists, p. 5 (NA: FO 371/67786); see also JICA's 'Comprehensive Outline of the Sicilian Separatist Movement', 17 January 1945, pp. 3-4 (NA: WO 204/12618). Vizzini dining with Finocchiaro Aprile reference comes from US Naval Intelligence Report for 15 February 1945, Palermo (NA: WO 204/12618).

Report by US Intelligence Division Office of Chief of Naval Operations on rioting in Palermo and Palma di Montechiaro, 10 January 1945; US Naval Intelligence report of riot at Alcamo, 30 December 1944; Prime Minister Bonomi speech about trouble in Sicily from JICA report, January 1945; all three documents in NA: WO 204/12660.

US Naval Intelligence report from Palermo to AFHQ on Ragusa insurgency, 8 January 1945 (NA: WO 204/4459). 'General Castellana Seeking Mafia Accord', OSS report, 13 October 1944. (NARA: RG226/103050). US Psychological Warfare Board report on Sicily insurgency, 10 January 1945 (NA: WO 204/4459).

Train robbery reported by Allied Commission (Public Safety Division), 16 February 1945 (NA: WO 204/12660). Armed bands approaching Corleone in US Naval Intelligence Report for 15 February 1945, Palermo (NA: WO 204/12618). Report by Salvatore Aldisio, High Commissioner for Sicily, on events in Sicily, to the Italian Ministry of the Interior, 21 February 1945 (NA: WO 204/1261).

Chapter 17

Police report of 7 March 1946 about Salvatore Giuliano meeting Separatists is quoted in Pantaleone, *The Mafia and Politics,* pp. 134–5. For short biography of

Giuliano see 'Giuliano and Sicilian Banditry', a memorandum prepared in the British Embassy in Rome under the direction of Sir Victor Mallet, 7 October 1949 (NA: FO 371/79312).

Two articles by Matthews, H. L., both in *New York Times*, 'Sicily in Throes of Civil Disorder', 1 February 1945, p. 8, & 'Separatist Crisis in Sicily is Acute', 4 February 1945, p. 16. 'Separatists Celebrate Anniversary of Sicilian Vespers', OSS Report, Palermo, 14 April 1945; 'Communist and Christian-Democratic Parties Demand Government Action against the Separatist Movement', OSS Report, Palermo, 1 May 1945; Assault on Separatist HQ reported by 51 Field Security Section, Palermo, 22 April 1945 (the last report from the FSS as it was withdrawn from Sicily by the end of April); all three documents in NA: WO 204/12618.

Separatists going underground mentioned in 'Report on Sicilian Separatism and the Movimento per l'Indipendenza della Sicilia' by Vice-Consul Manley, p. 6 (NA: FO 371/67786). 'Monarchy Seeks Support of Separatist Movement', OSS report, Palermo, 3 May 1945 (NA: WO 204/12618).

Account of Mussolini's last night alive comes from *The GI Story of the War* by the staff of *Yank*, pp. 232–5. 'Luciano plea cites his aid to US Army', *New York Times*, 23 May 1945, p. 7.

'Situation in Sicily Reported Improved', *New York Times*, 27 May 1945, p. 14. 'Landowners ask Permission to form their own Police Force', OSS Report, Palermo, 15 May 1945; 'Broadcast alleging future control of Italian territories', JICA Report, 19 May 1945; both documents in NA: WO 204/12618. Letter from Enrico Sorrentino intercepted by US Army Office of Communications Censorship and distributed to AFHQ and the War Office, 18 October 1945; Report from Lt Col G. E. Monsell, AFHQ, Office of the Assistant Chief of Staff, US Army, 26 September 1945; both documents in NA: WO 204/12615. 'Reaction to the arrest of Sicilian Separatist leaders', G-2 Report, 30 October 1945; 'Separatism in Sicily', Security Intelligence Summary, month of December, 1945; both documents in NA: WO 204/12619.

Chapter 18

Flt Lt R. J. H. Gillingham's letter about Giuliano train raid sent to British Consulate in Palermo, 24 January 1946 (NA: FO 371/60655).

Four-page memorandum on 'Sicilian Separatist Disturbances' by Special Agents Gabriel B. Celetta and Saverio Forte for US Army CIC Naples Detachment, 29 January 1946. This includes references to Nick Gentile and American colonel, as well as mentioning British officer fighting with Separatists (NA: WO 204/12619). Luciano reference to Gentile in Gosch & Hammer, pp. 93 & 95. For details of Poletti's life see obituary in *New York Times*, 10 August 2002.

CIC memorandum on 'Political situation in Sicily', 31 January 1946; Drop in Carabinieri morale, 'Security Intelligence Summary: Month of January' 7 February 1946; Vizzini arrest threat, CIC memorandum on 'Sicilian Political Situation', 4 February 1946; street fight in Palermo between US sailors and Italian soldiers reported in CIC memorandum on 'Sicilian Political Situation', 11 February 1946; all four documents in NA: WO 204/12619.

Reports of army offensive against Giuliano in February 1946 are in: 'Daily Digest of World Broadcasts and Radio Telegraph Services', 14 February 1946; AFHQ report, 27 February 1947; AFHQ report 9 March 1946; 'Daily Digest of World Broadcasts and Radio Telegraph Services', 9 March 1946; Security Intelligence Summary 16 March 1946. All contained in NA: WO 204/12619.

'Present Political Situation in Sicily', CIC memorandum, 15 July 1946; CIC report of 26 August 1946; 'Public Security', Land Forces Intelligence Summary, 27 June 1946; both documents in NA: WO 204/12617.

Dewey's statement on Luciano's deportation, Herlands Report, p. 2; see also 'Dewey commutes Luciano sentence', *New York Times*, 4 January 1946, p. 25. Berger, M., 'Deportation set for Luciano today', *New York Times*, 9 February 1946, p. 15, 'Luciano taken on ship', *New York Times*, 10 February 1946, p. 12, 'Luciano Departs for Italy with 3,500 Tons of Flour', *New York Herald Tribune*, 11 February 1946, p. 17, 'Pardoned Luciano on his way to Italy', *New York Times*, 11 February 1946, p. 26. Lansky's description of Luciano farewell party is in Eisenberg *et al*, p. 223–4; Bonanno's denial of being there in Bonanno & Lalli, p. 165.

'Luciano reaches Naples', *New York Times*, 1 March 1946, p. 1. Luciano's comments on Havana, Sicily and Genovese come from Gosch & Hammer, pp. 284, 299, 318–20. Reference to Luciano in Palermo is in note by A. E. Watkins in British Consulate, Palermo, 5 July 1947 (NA: FO 371/67786); the note also says that Luciano's presence coincided with Salvatore Giuliano's announcement of his war against Communists in Sicily and wondered whether the two were connected.

Chapter 19

Luciano's views on Communism, see Gosch & Hammer, pp. 327–8 & 295. CIA Cold War strategy comments come from *The Current Situation in Italy*, Central Intelligence Agency, 10 October 1947, pp. 1–4.

For Giuliano's anti-Communist press announcement see 'Sicilian Gangster opens war on Reds', *New York Times*, 24 June 1947, p. 14. Foreign Office note about Giuliano photograph dated 4 November 1949 (NA: FO 371/79312). Stories about Giuliano's exploits are repeated in 'Giuliano and Sicilian Banditry', memo from British Embassy in Rome, 7 October 1949, p. 4 (NA: FO 371/79312). 'Sicilian outlaws anger the Italians', *New York Times,* 6 July 1949, p. 13. '200 in Sicily Seized in Round-up', *New York Times,* 8 May 1949, p. 5.

Italian Prime Minister's views on Giuliano given to the Italian News Agency, ANSA, 27 August 1949, and reported by the British Embassy in Rome (NA: FO 371/79312). Luca's interview and the priest's sermon in *Messaggero*, 28 October 1949; the article was translated for Foreign Office use and sent with a letter from the British Embassy in Rome, 5 November 1949 (NA: FO 371/79312). Letter from Sir Victor Mallet, British Embassy in Rome, to Prime Minister Attlee, 13 October 1949 (NA: FO 371/79312).

Arduino case covered in Metropolitan Police statement by Ann Braithwaite Young, 8 June 1951, Metropolitan Police Criminal Investigation Department report, 14 February 1964, and Maltese police statement by Ernest Zahra, 11 April 1964; this file opened under Freedom of Information Act (NA: MEPO 2/9107).

Death of Giuliano reported in 'Sicilian Bandit Shot Dead' London *Times*, 6 July 1950, 'Bandit Giuliano is Slain in Sicily', *New York Times*, 6 July 1950, & 'Police Kill Sicily's Bandit King', *New York Herald Tribune*, 6 July 1950, pp. 1, 10 & 22. Pantaleone's story about Mafia killing Giuliano is in *The Mafia and Politics*, pp. 149–50 and p. 156; see also Schneider & Schneider p. 54. Pantaleone gets the date of Giuliano's death wrong, citing 14 July. Pantaleone claims that Colonel Luca worked with the Mafia to curtail Giuliano's activities (p. 154). The slaying of Giuliano's last gang members was reported in 'Two Sicilian Bandits Found Shot' London *Times*, 11 August 1952. Judge Giuseppe Guido Lo Schiavo quoted in Stille, *Excellent Cadavers*, p. 20.

Bonanno's description of his visit to Sicily comes from Bonanno, pp. 196–201. Good description of Bonanno's Palermo Mafia conference is in Sterling, *Octopus*, pp. 82–6. Sicilian Mafioso Tommaso Buscetta later claimed to have had dinner with both Lucky Luciano and Joe Bonanno at Spano's seafood restaurant in Palermo in October 1957 to discuss Mafia matters, see Sterling p. 84–5; see also Arlacchi, *Addio Cosa Nostra: La vita di Tommaso Buscetta.*

Lansky talking about his son comes from Eisenberg *et al*, pp. 230–1. See also Rockaway, pp. 202–3.

Chapter 20

Giuseppe Alessi's quote on Mafia infiltration of Christian Democrats comes from Stille, *Excellent Cadavers*, p. 19, a fine English-language guide to the history of the Mafia after World War II; see also Dickie, *Cosa Nostra*, a good overall history of the Mafia in Sicily.

Lupo quotes are from Lupo, 'The Allies and the Mafia', pp. 21, 29, & 30. Renda quote from Renda, *Storia della Sicilia dal 1860 al 1970*, Vol. III, p. 95, the definitive history of Sicily for this period in Italian; translated by Lisa Donafee.

Bibliography

UNPUBLISHED SOURCES

For precise archival references see Notes on Sources

London

National Archives (NA), Kew
WO – Records of War Office & Armed Forces
FO – Records of the Foreign Office
CAB – Records of the Cabinet Office
PREM – Records of the Prime Minister's Office
HW – Records of Government Communications Headquarters (GCHQ)
MEPO – Records of the Metropolitan Police Office
MAF – Records of the Agriculture, Fisheries & Food Departments

Washington DC

US Department of Justice, Federal Bureau of Investigation, Pennsylvania Avenue
FBI files on Lucky Luciano, Vito Genovese, Meyer Lansky

National Archives & Records Administration (NARA), College Park, Maryland
RG 38 – Records of Office of Chief of Naval Operations
RG 59 – Records of the Department of State
RG 165 – Records of the War Department
RG 226 – Records of the Office of Strategic Services

New York

Thomas E. Dewey Archive in the University of Rochester Library, NY
Herlands Report of 1954

Herbert H. Lehman Suite and Papers, Columbia University Rare Book and Manuscript Library, New York, NY; Poletti papers and letters from WW2

PUBLISHED SOURCES

Arad, G. N., *America, its Jews, and the Rise of Nazism*, Bloomington, 2000.

Arlacchi, P., *Addio Cosa Nostra: La vita di Tommaso Buscetta*, Milan, 1994.

Begnac, I. de, *Vita di Benito Mussolini*, Milan, 1936–40.

Block, A. A., 'A Modern Marriage of Convenience: A Collaboration Between Organized Crime and US Intelligence', *Organized Crime: A Global Perspective*, edited by R. J. Kelly, New Jersey, 1986.

Blok, A., *The Mafia of a Sicilian Village 1860–1960*, New York, 1974.

Bonanno, J., with Lalli, S., *A Man of Honour*, London, 1984.

Braynard, F. O., *A Picture History of the Normandie*, New York, 1987.

Campbell, R., *The Luciano Project*, New York, 1977.

Cannistraro, P. V., *Blackshirts in Little Italy*, West Lafayette, 1999.

Carpozi, G., Jr., *Bugsy: The Godfather of Las Vegas*, New York, 1973.

Caruso, A., *Arrivano i nostri*, Milan, 2004.

Chandler, D. L., *The Criminal Brotherhoods*, London, 1976.

Chapman, C. G., *Milocca: A Sicilian Village*, London, 1973.

Central Intelligence Agency, *The Current Situation in Italy*, Washington, 1947.

Corvo, M., *OSS Italy 1942–1945*, New York, 2005.

Dickie, J., *Cosa Nostra*, London, 2004.

Documents on German Foreign Policy, Series D, Volume IX, London, 1956.

Duggan, C., *Fascism and the Mafia*, New Haven & London, 1989.

Dunlop, R., *Donovan: America's Master Spy*, Chicago, 1982.

Eisenberg, D., Dan, U., & Landau, E., *Meyer Lansky: Mogul of the Mob*, New York & London, 1979.

d'Este, C., *Bitter Victory: The Battle for Sicily*, London, 1988.

Faenza, R., & Fini, M., *Gli americani in Italia*, Milan, 1976.

Feder, S., & Joesten, J., *The Luciano Story*, New York, 1956.

Finkelstein, M. S., *Separatism, the Allies, and the Mafia: The Struggle for Sicilian Independence, 1943–1948*, Bethlehem & London, 1998.

Fisher, G. A., *The Story of the 180th Infantry Regiment*, Texas, 1947.

Follain, J., *Mussolini's Island*, London, 2005.

Frasca, D., *King of Crime: The Story of Vito Genovese, Mafia Czar*, New York, 1959.

Freid, A., *Rise and Fall of the Jewish Gangster*, New York, 1994.

Gallagher, D., *All the Right Enemies: the Life & Murder of Carlo Tresca*, New Jersey, 1988.

Garland A. N., *Sicily and the Surrender of Italy*, Washington DC, 1965.

Gosch, M. & Hammer, R., *The Last Testament of Lucky Luciano*, London, 1976.

Grennan, S., & others, *Gangs*, New Jersey, 2000.

Guercio, F. M., *Sicily*, London, 1938.

Hammer, R., *Playboy's Illustrated History of Organized Crime*, Chicago, 1974.

Hanna, D., *Vito Genovese*, New York, 1974.

Harris, C. R. S., *Allied Military Administration in Italy 1943–1945*, London, 1957.

Harvey, C., *Normandie: Liner of Legend*, Stroud, 2001.

Heym, S., *Nazis in the USA*, New York (American Committee for Anti-Nazi Literature), 1938.

Higham, C., *American Swastika*, New York, 1985.

Hoke, Henry, *It's a Secret*, New York, 1946.

Howgrave-Graham, H. M., *The Metropolitan Police at War*, London, 1947.

Hughes, R., *Thomas E. Dewey: Attorney for the People*, London, 1940.

Jennings, D., *We Only Kill Each Other*, New York, 1968.

Kefauver, E., *Crime in America*, London, 1952.

King, R., & Patterson, G., *A Sicilian Village in the Fascist Era: Milocca Revisited*, Dublin, 1990.

Lacey, R., *Little Man: Meyer Lansky and the Gangster Life*, London, 1991.

———, *Ford: The Men and the Machine*, London, 1986.

Lawrence, D., *The Coming American Fascism*, New York, 1936.

Lewis, N., *The Honoured Society*, London, 1964.

———, *Naples '44*, London, 1978.

Lumia, L. *Villalba, storia e memoria*, Caltanissetta, 1990.

Lupo, S., *Storia della mafia siciliana*, Rome, 1993.

———, 'The Allies and the Mafia', *Journal of Modern Italian Studies* Vol. 2, No. 1 Spring 1997.

Lyttelton, A., *The Seizure of Power: Fascism in Italy 1919–1929*, London, 1973.

Maas, P., *The Valachi Papers*, New York, 1968 & London, 1969.

Mangiameli, R., 'La regione in Guerra (1943–50)', *La Sicilia, Le Regioni dall'Unita a oggi*, Turin, 1987, pp. 485–600.

Maxtorne-Grahame, J., *The Only Way to Cross*, New York, 1972.

Maxwell, G., *God Save Me from my Friends*, London, 1956.

Mendelsohn, J. (ed.), *Covert Warfare*, New York, 1989.

Mori, C., *The Last Struggle With the Mafia*, London & New York, 1933.

Moseley, R., *Mussolini's Shadow: the Double Life of Count Galeazzo Ciano*, New Haven and London, 1999.

———, *The Last Days of Mussolini*, Stroud, 2006.

Mussolini, B., *My Autobiography*, London, revised edition, 1939.

Nicolosi, S., *Il bandito Giuliano*, Milan, 1977.

Pantaleone, M., *The Mafia and Politics*, London, 1966.

Pernicone, N., *Carlo Tresca: Portrait of a Rebel*, New York, 2005.

Petacco, A., *Il prefetto di ferro: Cesare Mori e la Mafia*, Milan, 1978.

Porch, D., *The Path of Victory: The Mediterranean Theater in World War II*, New York, 2004.

Reid, E., *Mafia*, New York, 1964.

Renda, F., *Storia della Sicilia dal 1860 al 1970*, Vol. III, Palermo, 1987.

Ridley, J., *Mussolini*, London, 1997.

Rockaway, R. A., *But He Was Good to his Mother: The Lives and Crimes of Jewish Gangsters*, Jerusalem, 2000.

Santino, U., *Storia del movimento antimafia; dalla lotta di classes all'impegno*, Rome, 2000.

Sayer, I., & Botting, D., *America's Secret Army: Untold Story of the CIC*, London, 1989.

Scaduto, T., *Lucky Luciano*, London, 1975.

Schneider, J. C., & Schneider, P. T., *Reversible Destiny: Mafia, Antimafia, and the Struggle for Palermo*, Berkeley, 2003.

Short, M., *Crime Inc*, London, 1984.

Sifakis, C., *The Mafia File*, New York, 1987.

Spano, A., *Faccia a faccia con la mafia*, Milan, 1978.

Sterling, C., *Octopus: The Long Reach of the International Sicilian Mafia*, New York & London, 1990.

Stille, A., *Excellent Cadavers*, London, 1995.

Stoler, M. A., *Allies and Adversaries: The Joint Chiefs of Staff, the Grand Alliance, and US Strategy in World War II*, Chapel Hill & London, 2000.

Susmel, E. & D. (ed.), *Opera Omnia de Benito Mussolini*, Florence, 35 volumes, 1951–62.

Talese, G., *Honor Thy Father*, London, 1972.

Trevor-Roper, H. R., (ed), *Hitler's Table-Talk*, Oxford, 1988.

Vizzini S, Fraley, O., & Smith, M., *Vizzini: The Secret Lives of America's Most Successful Undercover Agent*, London, 1974.

Wallace, M., *The American Axis: Henry Ford, Charles Lindbergh, and the Rise of the Third Reich*, New York, 2003.

Weinberg, G. L., *A World at Arms*, Cambridge, 1994.

Wighton, C., & Pies, G., *They Spied on England*, London, 1958.

Wolf, G., with DiMona, J., *Frank Costello: Prime Minister of the Underworld*, New York, 1974.

Yank staff writers, *The GI Story of the War*, New York, 1947.

For all newspaper articles consulted see *Notes on Sources*

Index